FADING EAGLE

POLITICS AND DECLINE OF BRITAIN'S POST-WAR AIRFORCE

IAN WATSON

FONTHILL

Fonthill Media Limited
Fonthill Media LLC
www.fonthillmedia.com
office@fonthillmedia.com

First published in the United Kingdom 2013

British Library Cataloguing in Publication Data:
A catalogue record for this book is available from the British Library

ISBN 978-1-78155-117-2

Typeset in 10pt on 13pt Sabon
Printed and bound in England

Contents

Tornado diamond sixteen flypast over Abingdon, 15 September 1990. (*Author's collection*)

Preface

When I set out to write this book, the United Kingdom had, following a general election, been left with no clear majority in Parliament. Given the parlous state of the economy, this was disappointing for all parties. The result, however unpopular, inevitably gave the country a Conservative-led coalition at time of press. It could be argued that the poor result for the Conservatives, coupled with the economic situation, meant they were particularly conscious of their weaker policies in the eyes of the electorate and equally concerned that their traditional strengths – defence, maintenance of good order, etc – would be the undoing of them.

The country was engaged in two simultaneous wars and, like many other countries, was in the middle of a recession brought on by a number of factors. Among these factors was the implosion of many high street banks, for which the previous government's response was to attempt to rescue all from their own excessive folly by rectifying the situation with government funds. One suggestion was to let one or two banks fold and see how the rest, quite confident of defending ridiculous bonuses and salaries, would concentrate their efforts to avoid the same fate. With unemployment continuing to fall, public expenditure was increased rather substantially. For better or worse, those ministries traditionally given greatest priority by the left were, unsurprisingly, the beneficiaries: the NHS, education, social security and other similar bodies, all the chief recipients of Labour's largess and all considered to be popular with the electorate.

The same could not be said of the government's first area of responsibility: national defence. Throughout the post-Cold War period, successive British governments have contributed to various military operations overseas, the intensity of which has not been seen with such regularity since Britain's troublesome extrication from the Empire. But truth be known, the same governments have refused to accept the need to address these commitments with an increase in capability, but instead have sought to lose assets from one area in order to maintain the minimum level of resources for those engaged on operations. While all three of the armed forces have continued to lose existing assets and personnel, the increased demand on them all has continued through to the Strategic Defence and Security Review (SDSR). In the lead-up to this most controversial of Defence Reviews, the situation with Britain's finances, blinkered predictions over future conflicts, and short-term views led commentators from various quarters to call for the abolition of one of the three armed services. The prime candidate for this overly dramatic proposition is the Royal Air Force.

How we have arrived at this situation and how the RAF's roles and responsibilities have been met and supported over the years since its formation and, more specifically, through the years since the end of the Second World War, is what I have attempted to accomplish. I have concentrated particularly on events which have in some way or other played a significant part in altering the defence policy with any significance or controversy. Most have particularly impacted on the front line of the RAF. I trust that those who may feel that certain elements are not given equal coverage will find that this does not lessen or detract from the comprehensive picture.

Further to the above, I would like to acknowledge the contribution of various images used in this book. A significant number came from the Air Historical Branch, The National Archives, the Imperial War Museum and the Warwickshire County Records Office. I would especially like to thank the following photographers: John Wharam, John Fisher, Tony McGhee, Keith Butcher, Peter R. March, Trevor Thornton, Lloyd Horgan, Jeremy Hughes, Mark Kwiatkowski and Michael Brazier. All of these people have made sterling contributions with images, often at short notice, which would have been difficult, time-consuming and costly to obtain otherwise.

Finally, I would like to suggest a small selection of books for those who wish to explore the subject further:

Davies, Norman, *Europe at War 1939 to 1945*, Pan Books
Delve, Ken, *The Source Book of the RAF*, Airlife
Ellis, John, *The World War II Data Book*, Aurum Press
Hamilton-Patterson, James, *Empire of the Clouds*, Faber and Faber
Probert, Air Commodore Henry, *High Commanders of the Royal Air Force*, HMSO Publishings
Wood, Derek, *Project Cancelled*, Merrill Books

Introduction

In 1945, Britain, like many other protagonist countries of the Second World War, had seen its armed forces swell to a Brobdingnagian level. At the start of the year, the process of scaling down had begun and the disbandment of units commenced while fighting continued, justified by the firm belief that the Axis powers were on the verge of an almighty and decisive defeat.

Also of overriding importance to the British government was the clear understanding that the country was facing economic misery and possible bankruptcy following such a heavy contribution towards the war. The UK did not share the wartime economic circumstances of the United States. The latter was able to develop arms production without being hindered by air raids, the imminent threat of invasion, and attempts to choke off the supply of goods via the sea lanes. Further, the US had the UK on its order books. All this conspired to ensure that the two countries came out at the other end of the war as economic polar opposites.

The US also benefited from a growth of consumerism and mass commercial production driven by ruthless advertising. Other belligerents faced a long bleak road ahead. However, the UK in particular faced the worst combination of factors as Europe began to clear away the rubble and learned to live with a political outcome that had yet to be fully defined. The new superpower stand-off between East and West stretched across the next fifty years and division into spheres of influence.

For the defeated Axis powers, Germany and Japan's most senior government and military leaders faced war crimes trials together with the subjugation of their now occupied countries. For Germany in particular, this was going to stretch on to include operatives much further down the order of rank and responsibility. Britain's own chief executioner, Albert Pierrepoint, was flown to the British sector of occupied Germany in order to carry out the executions of Josef Kramer (the 'Beast of Belsen') and his camp staff, which included a female SS guard of only nineteen years of age. This ignominy aside, and the basing of a large Allied military presence on their soil to the present day, the Axis countries nevertheless could look forward to a generous aid package courtesy of Uncle Sam in the form of the Marshall Plan.

Great Britain on the other hand had two things to cling to: the proud position of being a principal victor; and the knowledge, as was observed by the late American historian Stephen Ambrose, of being regarded as perhaps holding claim to the moral high ground.

The UK had stood alone against Germany and faced the most unlikely chance of victory. In the immediate post-war period, it had the uphill struggle of coping with an exhausted economy and the ruined and bombed-out cities that were to be rebuilt. There was also the small matter of a debt to honour with our great ally, the United States of America. With no Marshall Plan to benefit from, less charitable conspiracy theorists could argue that the UK was pushed aside from the international centre stage by the emergent superpower, the US.

The US had rapidly expanded in to the role of primary military bulwark against the Axis powers in Europe and the Pacific. That said, it would not do to overlook the British military effort. While under siege from Germany and 2,000 miles away from any substantial economic assistance, Britain's own reputable but small military forces expanded with remarkable speed. Of the three armed services, one was making its debut appearance as a truly substantial strategic fighting force. Since the First World War, the RAF had operated in anger across the British Empire, but always against primitive Afghan tribes, Marsh Arabs and poorly equipped Bedouin armies. They were now the first line of defence against a more technically advanced, heavily armed and numerically superior force. Much of what was achieved by the armed forces would not have been possible without the funds and material assets provided through the Lend-Lease agreement. The loan, to be repaid after the war, funded thousands of tanks, aircraft, infantry weapons and artillery pieces, not to mention additional funds to produce armaments in our own factories.

The final Lend-Lease payment was made at the end of 2006 to both the US and Canada. Currency devaluation and other financial problems had caused the British government to defer payments on no fewer than six occasions. The further cost to Britain in countering Nazi Germany was the end of the Empire. This was largely brought about by a surge in the desire for independence and the increasing cost of maintaining peace across the various troubled outposts. The golden age of the Empire was now a costly burden which this cash-strapped post-war imperial state could well do without. In place would be an American-Soviet dominated new world order split into two opposed ideological hemispheres. The eventual collapse of the Soviet Union, however, has not brought about a safer world as was imagined early on. Instead, fresh concerns emerged or loomed on the horizon: from trouble in the Balkans through to Iraq, Afghanistan and the Arab Spring. Not so eagerly reported in the newspapers, and perhaps more ominous, is the return of an increasingly belligerent and rearming Russia, and beyond this, the threat of Chinese hegemony.

Elsewhere, there are states with which good relations are beyond retrieval and which endeavour to develop their own nuclear arsenals. For Britain, in particular, there is the return of Argentinian claims over the Falkland Islands and the topic of exploration for oil in the Antarctic. It has to be remembered that oil, for all its political controversy, is arguably the most vital means of ensuring that lights do not go out and we do not starve. For this reason alone, oil and other vital resources are likely to be at the centre of future conflicts. From the fall of Rome to the Thin Red Line, wars were fought over religious ideology. In the nineteenth century, the cause was imperialist expansion, and in the twentieth century, zealous political ideology. In the twenty-first century, we return to religious ideology, while the future threatens a return to war over natural resources. While the other matters continue, the main cause of countries bullying others and falling out will increasingly revolve around drilling and mining rights, regardless of how many wind turbines and solar panels are erected and fitted.

Great Britain stood at the centre of the world stage once, but the wars of the first half of the twentieth century have placed this position firmly in the past. Both in 1918 and 1945, Britain's power and influence was weakened. In 1939, Britain's imperial reach could have continued beyond the foreseeable future. By 1945, Britain's future prosperity depended on how soon we could abandon our imperial legacy. Truth be known, British imperial influence had been gradually eroding since before the First World War. However, there is no doubt that the First World War damaged Britain's standing on the world stage and the Second World War brought about the end of British imperial rule. While the UK still maintained a series of colonies and outposts of Empire in the early post-war years, their days were numbered and Britain's dwindling armed forces would spend the second half of the twentieth century struggling to extricate themselves from the responsibility of administering and defending them. While trying to maintain both a prominent position on the world stage and a commitment to countering the post-war Soviet threat through an independent nuclear deterrent has ensured the UK's permanent position on the United Nation's Security Council, this would not have been possible without securing a prominent position as America's best friend, otherwise known as the 'Special Relationship'. That special status was earned through the expenditure of blood and gold in the Second World War.

This then is where we come to examine the decline of Britain's military-backed influence and its decreasing ability to project that influence across the globe, specifically the RAF, the service that people do not instantly think of when military matters are discussed. Yet it carries the greatest destructive force, nuclear deterrent notwithstanding, and can be deployed anywhere in the world within hours rather than weeks. This is despite public perceptions still having a whiff of the Victorian era and soldiers with rifles and bayonets as being all that stands between them and enslavement.

In writing this book, I have not set out to complain that our country no longer has an air force or other military capabilities – an argument some sincerely advance – but to try and put together the chronology of events, decisions and mindset which have brought the RAF to where it is now: no longer an air force that can be relied upon to maintain two small detachments of aircraft on an extended period of operations without pulling the chord tight on resources. There is no doubt that the RAF has shouldered a greater burden of defence cuts than the other two services, the Army in particular. The last fifteen years has seen the greatest impact of cuts to the front-line strength of the RAF. Elsewhere across Europe, there have been reductions. But while the common perception is that European countries place less reliance on their armed forces, defence cuts among other NATO member countries have been less radical. It would be too simple to expect every penny saved from the defence budget to be handed back to the taxpayer, but a good question since 1991 is: What happened to the promised post-Cold War peace dividend? The situation since has seen more demands placed upon the armed forces of many NATO countries, not least those of the UK, than was demanded of them for much of the Cold War period, but every new operational commitment finds the military people facing the next challenge with fewer resources, fewer people and the same expectations of them. The RAF has been asset-stripped over the last fifteen years to fund various operations overseas that have placed a much greater strain on land forces. One reason for doing this would almost certainly be the political desire to protect other spending programmes. But, as we are coming to understand, both the second Gulf conflict and current deployment in Afghanistan were quite avoidable. What is more, they are both heading towards a harsh judgement in the history books.

Today, Britain's air force, which for much of the post-war era has been second only to the US, is now a much smaller outfit. Just how far down the scale the RAF has slid from the superlative air arm it once was is very much a subjective question with so many benchmarks. But what is absolutely certain is that its relative capability has not slipped; it has plummeted towards a point where we hear more and more often calls for its very existence to be reviewed, its relevance explained and its responsibilities subsumed to the Army and Navy. This is despite the fact that British defence spending is higher than the European average and that successive British governments have always striven to have this country accepted as the first lieutenant of the US. Since I started to write this book, we have had the outcome of the coalition government's Strategic Defence and Security Review. The then Defence Secretary, Dr Liam Fox, is on record as stating that this review would break away from the thinking of the Cold War once and for all. However, he insisted on retaining and eventually upgrading the Trident strategic nuclear missile force. The cost of this is quite staggering. When speaking of the SDSR, Fox said, 'This needs to be the Defence Review that puts the Cold War to bed.' One assumes this means a departure from a reliance on what are often described as Cold War weapons, but there is no greater iconic symbol of the Cold War today in Britain's defence policy than Trident.

Trident and its predecessor, Polaris, were relied on to replace the RAF's V-force, which by the end of the 1950s stood little chance of penetrating the overwhelming air defences of the USSR. And now that Chancellor George Osborne wants the nuclear deterrent funded directly from the defence budget, the future of the RAF, with the repeated calls for it to be disbanded, has never looked bleaker since its formation in 1918.

CHAPTER 1

Junior Service

British military aviation has its formal origins with the foundation of the Royal Flying Corps (RFC) in 1912. The Royal Engineers were the Army's chosen regiment to introduce manned flight with a military purpose from which the RFC derived. The RFC's formation came about following studies made into the use of aircraft for military purposes, a task assigned at the time to the Committee for Imperial Defence. However, the amount of money spent on the wider research of aviation by the government was well and truly eclipsed by that of Germany. In both cases, no one had expected air power to become a major military factor: neither side contemplated such ideas as arming aircraft for any conceivable purpose. At the start of the First World War, both sides were using machines to carry out reconnaissance flights and artillery spotting, the first military purpose for which aeroplanes were gainfully employed.

By the time of the signing of the armistice on 11 November 1918, just fifteen years after the Wright Brothers' first flight in a heavier-than-air powered flying machine, the Royal Air Force was established as the world's first independent air arm on 1 April 1918, numbering 22,000 aircraft. Of this figure, 3,300 were front-line combat aircraft, split between 188 squadrons and with a personnel strength of 291,000. Less than a year later, the RAF fielded no more than twelve squadrons in total, and in a few months, the RAF, now the third independent military force, had been reduced by 84 per cent. Those who felt air power to be a one-off unique dimension to modern warfare brought about by the most extreme of circumstances sought to have things put back to the way they were in 1914, perhaps abandoning the aeroplane as a military tool once and for all as no longer relevant, or at best, supposing air power to still have a future, moved to absorb air power into one or both of the other two much longer-established arms. This was what was being lobbied for in 1919.

The previous year, the founding head of the new independent RAF, Major-General Sir Hugh Trenchard, had held the appointment from 1 April until halfway through the month when he resigned to be replaced by Major-General Sir Frederick Sykes. His resignation had been tendered in the days prior to 1 April, but was not accepted until the new independent air arm had been formally established. Trenchard's resignation was effective from 13 April and was shortly followed by the resignation of Lord Rothermere, the new Secretary of State for Air, whom Trenchard felt he could not work with. He had his doubts from early on when appointments were first made. He further disagreed with the level to which the Secretary of State would be able to influence service matters. Lord Rothermere resigned and was replaced on 26 April by Lord William Douglas Weir. Trenchard was found another appointment worthy of his talents and experience as the Commander of the Inter-Allied Independent Air Force in France.

So, all in all, not a good start at board level for the RAF. Indeed, by early 1919, Lord Weir had resigned as Secretary of State for Air, being replaced by Winston Churchill, and Sir Frederick Sykes was replaced by his predecessor, Sir Hugh Trenchard, holding the rank now indentified as the RAF two-star equivalent for the other two services: Air Vice-Marshal. The appointments of First Sea Lord and Chief of the Imperial General Staff, the professional heads of the Navy and Army, all held five-star ranking at this time, which put the new post of Chief of the Air Staff on a very much probationary level for the time being. Trenchard's reappointment was political and was requested by Lord Weir's successor as War and Air Secretary, Winston Spencer Churchill. Now that the war to end all war's was over, there was a growing desire in influential circles to disband the RAF or at least split its functions and roles into arms of the other two principal military services. There was certainly a good argument by any standard to consider devolving air power back to the Navy and the Army for their own particular requirements.

In addition to this, and in an echo of modern-day sentiments, the UK did not have an apparent enemy to threaten its airspace any longer. The only likely candidate of the period was Germany; however, Germany did not sport an air force of any description. The French were our awkward allies, and the Belgians, Dutch and Scandinavians boasted little in the way of air power so the idea of them harbouring designs against our sceptred isle was as ludicrous then as it is now. The only practical argument for further aviation military use would be supporting the Army in operations and campaigns across the Empire or providing air defence of the fleet, as well as other functions such as communications and attack against an enemy surface threat.

Trenchard had his work cut out in order to justify the existence of an independent air arm. One avenue was to engage the general public with a similar kind of pageantry as had become so identifiable with the Navy and Army. Therefore, the RAF on 3 July 1920 held the world's first military air show at RAF Hendon in Middlesex. The Hendon Air Pageant was the RAF's equivalent of the Army's Royal Tournament and the Royal Navy's Spithead Review. As Trenchard said, when advancing the case for the second Hendon pageant in 1921, the grounds for approval for the 1920 event were based on the fact that this display was entirely analogous to naval and military assaults at arms, regattas, regimental sports and the like, and was a necessary and important part of the training of the RAF. Apart from training being of the utmost importance, a subsidiary consideration in favour of holding the pageant was that the RAF was precluded from taking any but a very minor part in the Royal Tournament owing to the total unsuitability of Olympia (the traditional venue for the tournament) for an air force display.

In addition, Trenchard put in place the RAF College. While the Army had Sandhurst and the Navy, Dartmouth, the RAF now had Cranwell. The graduates of RAF College Cranwell received the affectionate nickname of Trenchard Brats. There were also further institutions of learning such as the Central Flying School, established in 1912, which turned out turned out the service's flying instructors, and the Halton Technical Apprentice School, which would produce the skilled aircraft propulsion and airframe technicians. Furthermore, there was the staff college at Andover, the equivalent of the Army's war staff college at Camberley. Not surprisingly, the RAF's chief adversaries scrutinising its very existence were not politicians but the Army and Navy, not least because of the ever ongoing battle for resources.

A series of government reviews and reports throughout the early 1920s continually placed the RAF in the spotlight. First was the Balfour Report of 1921. The report came down in favour of the air force remaining an independent service. It was nonetheless the first of several such reviews between 1921 and 1924. During this period, Trenchard was able to bring about a staggering increase in strength of twenty-five squadrons and personnel which had been as low as 31,500. To increase numbers under any circumstances without any pressing military concerns to justify it and in such a short period is remarkable, even given the comparative simplicity of aircraft design and technology for the time. That said, in 1920, total central government expenditure came to £1.7 billion. Of this figure, £700 million was spent on military defence. On the other hand, there was no spending on healthcare, pensions or education, all of which were wholly dependent on private funding, charities and philanthropy.

This was the pattern throughout the 1920s and 1930s, and the RAF was occupied with developing bombing skills on live targets over Mesopotamia and other such parts of the Middle and Far East. The live targets were legitimately targeted as part of various campaigns similar to today. Otherwise, the RAF was attracting further criticism from its sister services at home as the world's most expensive flying club. This latter label arose from the impression gained by stories of cocky young men on a very long leash, flying around the country and occasionally dropping in to see friends at various flying clubs and air pageants at Hendon. But again, the impression

The fledgling RAF Bristol FB2s practice formation flying in 1921. (*Air Historical Branch*)

was entirely subjective as the wider public image was far more favourable. Trenchard was promoted to Marshal of the Royal Air Force in 1927, giving the appointment of Chief of the Air Staff equivalence in rank to the other two services, and he relinquished the appointment in March 1930, handing over to Air Chief Marshal Sir John Salmond. The RAF continued throughout this period to police the Empire and remained heavily committed in the Middle and Far East.

There were no significant advances in aircraft design except for a move from radial to inline engines and aluminium-stressed skin constructions in place of fabric-covered wooden frames. The bulk of RAF operations during its first twenty years were tactical bombing in support of ground troops; in other words, close air support. Air defence, often viewed as the core responsibility and justification for an independent air force, was then seen as secondary.

Since the end of the Cold War, British defence policymakers, much like those of other NATO countries, have faced some difficulty in making the case for the same kind of air defence arrangement that was deemed necessary to counter the Soviet air threat. However, in 1927, the RAF was not too pressed on this issue in order to prove its reason for being. There was plenty to do such as bombing and strafing

Marsh Arabs during uprisings in Mesopotamia (or Iraq as it became in 1921). By April 1932, the RAF had grown to sixty-nine squadrons not counting detachments and flying training schools. Of these, eleven were based in the Middle East, operating a variety of mostly forgotten types, in the main, tactical bomber and light attack aircraft including Vickers Victorias, Fairey Gordons and Foxes, Armstrong Whitworth Atlases and Westland Wapitis. Eleven squadrons were assigned to the air defence of Great Britain and were equipped mostly with Hawker Furies and Bristol Bulldogs, one squadron being equipped with Atlases. Curiously, one squadron, No. 24, sported Avro Tutors, an aircraft more commonly associated with training. Twenty-four bomber squadrons were assigned to home-based groups (the command structure as it would later be understood did not exist) and the remainder allocated to India and the Mediterranean, with one squadron, No. 8, equipped with Foxes based in Khormaksar in Aden.

Sir John Salmond's appointment as Chief of the Air Staff (CAS) ended with some sadness, as he was reappointed to the office after his older brother, Sir Geoffrey, who had succeeded him in the post on 1 April 1933, died following a sudden illness. He was eventually succeeded on 22 May by Sir Edward Ellington, who was four years older than Sir John and would have retired but for this quirk of fate.

During Sir John Salmond's tenure there was much to contend with. The country was in the mire of the Great Depression and an international mood of disarmament meant that he had a struggle on his hands to maintain public and political understanding of the RAF's viability, especially when the service continued to be defined primarily as a strike force for offensive bombing operations. Save for the RAF winning the Schneider Trophy in 1931, there was not much to give Sir John any reason for good cheer. There were indeed many parallels between this era and the circumstances of 2009 to 2010. The Army and Navy still refused to understand the need for air power to be quite so extensive or even justifiably operated and administered under an independent command structure. The Disarmament Conference of 1932 was used by them as a means of pressing the argument against offensive bombing and therefore perhaps of prompting a further review that they may have hoped would lead to the breaking up of the RAF and air power being divided between the two services. Despite this, the RAF continued to be engaged in operations throughout this period, notably in the theatres of the North-West Frontier, Burma, northern Kurdistan and Mohmand.

When Sir Edward Ellington's tenure began, unlike his predecessors, he had never commanded an operational squadron. Ellington had previously moved around various staff and headquarters appointments since being commissioned into the Royal Artillery in 1897. However, he was involved with military aviation from its embryo stage before the First World War. At the outbreak of war, he was Deputy Adjutant and Quartermaster-General at the British Expeditionary Headquarters.

Aerobatics with smoke over Hendon (possibly Bristol Bulldog), *c.* 1932. (*Air Historical Branch*)

This typified the trend of his career – he did not partake in operational flying, but had been awarded his pilot's wings in December 1913 at Upavon. By the time he was appointed CAS, he had headed four commands since 1922: Middle East, India, Iraq and Air Defence of Great Britain. What was to be his final appointment before becoming CAS (which would not have happened were it not for the illness that took Sir Geoffrey Salmond) was Air Member for Personnel. This he held from 26 September 1931. It was during Sir Edward's tenure that the rearmament programme got under way in earnest.

The RAF in May 1933 stood at a personnel strength of 30,000 and its latest and most advanced fighter was the Hawker Fury. Disarmament talks were still very much seen as the way forward for resolving international conflicts of interest. But while the Geneva conference worked towards an international airspace pact, whose signatories would be bound to agree not to launch aggressive aerial warfare on one another, Adolf Hitler was overseeing a vast rearmament programme in Germany. As part of Britain's early preparations for what might come, a decision was taken to restart, or expedite, a plan from 1923 to arm Fighter Command with a total of fifty-two

Three Siskins display aerobatics over Hendon, *c.* 1933. (*Air Historical Branch*)

fighter squadrons. This came together with an expansion programme for the RAF announced in July 1934. However, Sir Edward Ellington retained doubts about the expansion programmes, his principal concerns being about bringing different aspects of a rapidly expanding modern air force together at an even pace. For example, producing and delivering new aircraft was one thing, but to build sufficient airfields with the required infrastructure and turning out the required numbers of air and ground crew might not come together as evenly as was expected.

It would certainly be costly, but scepticism still remained among many, not least Sir Edward, that Germany's ability to launch and sustain the kind of military operation which others feared would not be anywhere near ready until at least 1942. Indeed, to rush towards military expansion on the British side could perceptibly be politically damaging for the government of Stanley Baldwin. There was not much of an appetite for facing another war with the First World War trenches still fresh in the memory, and a rush towards expansion would only generate concern that war was inevitable. By 1936, the growth of Germany's military ambitions was less easy to deny and British expansion continued with less caution. It was expected that by March

Flightline Hendon Air Pageant, *c.* 1932. (*Air Historical Branch*)

1939, 124 squadrons would be deployed within the UK and thirty-seven squadrons overseas. Furthermore, the Fleet Air Arm would operate twenty-six squadrons.

Much of the preparation for increasing the air force in readiness for war was due to a reliance upon air and sea power to take the fight to the enemy. Churchill in particular had no real confidence that the British people would accept the tremendous losses of the kind seen two decades earlier. The RAF would be relied upon in a way that was inverse to the way in which the German effort was concentrated. Hitler presided over the growth of a superlative army, often referred to as the *Wehrmacht* (the name actually referred to the armed forces in total). The Germany Army specifically was the *Deutsche Heer Korps*, Hitler's other and perhaps better known fighting force, the *Waffen-SS*, having been developed from the Führer's elite bodyguard. To give a general comparison, at the peak strength of the *Wehrmacht* and *Waffen-SS*, their numbers were in the region of 10 million. The peak strength of Britain's armed forces stood at around 4.6 million. Of these, a far greater proportion of British service personnel served in the RAF, whereas for Germany the army increasingly through the war years placed emphasis in its ability to wage war with an overwhelming land force. This had necessitated a shift away from the cohesive blitzkrieg format of a combined land and air battlefield force. As times would become increasingly desperate for Germany in the latter war years, the Luftwaffe would concentrate nearly all its efforts on the air defence of the Reich as RAF and USAAF air raids increased in tempo, with bombers with a capacity to deliver not just high-explosive bombs but also phosphorus, Amatol, Petroleum and Magnesium sticks and containers. Otherwise, the Luftwaffe was to become the beneficiary of many of Hitler's various *wunderwaffen* (wonder weapons) which would amount to little or nothing as their arrival in theatre would prove ineffective.

In 1935, the US government passed the first of the Neutrality Acts. This was not because it failed to perceive the military expansions in Europe but was in direct response to what was happening. War was still not inevitable, certainly not another world war on anything like the scale that would come to pass. The expectation was that conflict may arise, but few at the time had the insight to grasp the severity of the threat from Germany. Many people in British politics likewise were unprepared for what was to come. It has been said that if Hitler had died from an assassin's bullet in 1936, he would have gone down in history as one of history's great leaders. It could be argued that until 1941, the conflict on the Continent was an unfortunate breakdown in relations between civilised industrialised nations which should have known better, and this was largely the sentiment and logic behind the American Neutrality Acts of 1935 to 1939.

Few people can look back on the First World War, a largely intra-European conflict, and explain just what the principal aims of the chief belligerents were, save to contain and reverse the expansion of the German martial state. It is farcical that the two principal protagonists of the First World War became the UK and Germany when the original dispute was between Austria-Hungary and Serbia. The spark came from the assassination of Archduke Ferdinand of the Austro-Hungarian Empire by the Black Hand Gang, a renegade mob of Serbs whose collective goal was a Greater Serbia. They were, in all probability, the first recognisable terrorist organisation. The evoking of treaties in each direction from these two states – ending with Russia coming to Serbia's aid, Germany to Austria-Hungary's, France to Russia's, and Belgium in turn threatened by Germany looking to invade France in order to weaken Russia's hand – thereby breached the Treaty of London. Not that Belgium was a signatory, but this treaty signed by all aforementioned in 1839 guaranteed Belgian independence and neutrality, so reasoned the British government.

It is this which led to the carnage of the First World War, with millions of British, French and German men being slaughtered at Verdun, Ypres, Cambrai, the Somme and other infamously celebrated battlefields across Europe. Indeed, there was less justification for the Great War than for the campaigns fought during the years since 2001 against the Taliban. The campaign in Afghanistan has had many official explanations along the way: eliminating Al-Qaeda; routing the Taliban; reconstruction; emancipation of Afghan women; and now that all coalition forces are to dash for the exits, training the Afghan native police and army to take over once they have gone.

What is certain is that in both the First and Second World Wars there was no fixed date for completing hostilities. It happened when one side was clearly defeated, and no more comprehensively so than at the end of the Second World War. But the experiences of the First World War had determined many not to repeat this particular mistake of the past. America at the end of the First World War was in as good a position to assert itself and use its influence as an emergent superpower on the world stage as it was at the end of the Second World War, but chose the path of isolationism instead.

Before Sir Edward's retirement as the professional head of the RAF, he had seen the first direct display of National Socialist German aggression, and with it a demonstration of what the RAF would be up against in later years. This was when the Luftwaffe was first deployed in anger, when Hitler came to the aid of General Franco during the Spanish Civil War to test the Luftwaffe's latest cutting-edge fighters and bombers. Early Heinkel 111s, Junkers 87s and Messerschmitt Bf 109s were used to devastating effect against anti-Franco rebels in 1936. At the time the Spanish Civil War was being fought to the point of victory for the German-supported Franco government, the RAF was undergoing a change of operational structure. Up until then, all operational command and control of air force units based in the UK had been collectively titled Air Defence of Great Britain, much as the present-day RAF has since come full circle to be brought under a single command identity, Air Command. The overseas elements, however, were separate command and control structures from the outset. The new structure was a series of new commands within the home-based RAF: Bomber, Fighter, Coastal and Training.

Change was afoot for the now obsolete equipment as well; many of the open-cockpit biplane designs that had entered service at the end of the last decade and beginning of the 1930s were rapidly replaced. The Heyfords, Hinds and Harts – many of the latter still served well in the Middle East where one Arthur Harris was developing new bombing techniques – were replaced with Hampdens, Whitleys and Wellingtons. The Hawker Fury with some of the new biplane Gladiators were still the backbone of the defence fighter force, but the radical new designs from Supermarine and Hawker were at the prototype stage.

Sir Edward's appointment as CAS had almost coincided with Hitler's electoral victory in Germany. The pursuit of parity with Germany was prompted in the coming months by the increasingly clear move towards military expansion in the Third Reich. For the RAF, there was no fixed ceiling of aircraft numbers and it was given high priority in terms of Britain's responsive rearmament plans. Shortly after Sir Edward handed over his office to Air Chief Marshal Sir Cyril Newall on 1 September 1937, the first Hawker Hurricanes were delivered to Fighter Command and operationally deployed.

Bombing of a fort during mock battle at Hendon Air Pageant in 1932. (*Air Historical Branch*)

Hendon new park, 1932, the forerunner of Farnborough in many respects. Many new types appeared for the first time here. (*Air Historical Branch*)

Like all his predecessors so far, Newall had started his military career as an army officer. Compared to Ellington, Newall was relatively young. Born in 1886, he was taking over the reins of the now fast expanding air force at the age of fifty-one. Newall learned to fly in 1911 while home on leave from serving with the 2nd Gurkha Rifles in India. He became an instructor at the Central Flying School in India after gaining his pilot's wings with the Central Flying School of the Royal Flying Corps in 1913.

At the start of the First World War, Newall was posted as one of the first flight commanders on No. 1 Squadron. At the time, the squadron was operating a mix of Henri Farman F20s, Boxkites and Longhorns. These machines were airborne observation posts and could best be described as 'flying machines' rather than aeroplanes. By the end of the war, he had been given the temporary rank of Brigadier and Command of the 8th Brigade that later became the Independent Air Force in France, commanded by Major-General Trenchard, to whom he became deputy. With the end of the war and rationalisation of the armed forces, Newall received a permanent commission at the rank of Wing Commander in the RAF. In the post-war years, he was Deputy Commandant at the No. 1 School of Technical Training overseeing the training of apprentices who would become aircraft maintenance fitters and mechanics, and in later years was Director of Operations and Intelligence, Deputy Chief of the Air Staff, AOC-in-C Middle East and Air Member for Supply and Organisation. Newall's first move on becoming CAS was to propose an update to the expansion process known as Scheme J, which was designed to catch up and reach parity with German air expansion by 1941.

The RAF at the time was, despite earlier moves towards development of equipment and increased strength, still in a largely unfit state. In 1938, it became clear that the pace of Scheme J was not sufficient within the timescale forecast. This resulted in a proposal for Scheme L from the Air Ministry, entailing increased expenditure, but this was opposed by the Chancellor of the Exchequer and the Minister for the Co-ordination of Defence, Lord Thomas Inskip. Newall, however, was convinced that the RAF would need to field the ability to deliver a decisive strike against Germany. The current expansion schemes were designed to build up the air capability over a period of years, but as Newall now saw it, time was in short supply and it was vital to prepare for a war footing. Schemes K and L both proceeded, the latter thanks to Newall.

When he was appointed in 1936, Lord Inskip had had his work cut out resolving disputes between the Admiralty and Air Ministry. This time, the RAF had to be persuaded to accept the resurgence of the Fleet Air Arm. But now, Newall was being opposed by Inskip and the Chancellor over the question of likely German plans to bombard the country into submission. Newall eventually had to respond to the continued political concerns, albeit laudable ones, about the financial implications and whether the various long-term expansion schemes were indeed necessary. At one point, speaking in defence of Scheme L – the planned production of 12,000 aircraft over two years from 1938 – he told the vacillators, '... the time for mincing words is past ... the issue is that of survival of British civilisation'. However, Inskip did believe that the expansion effort, as far as the RAF was concerned, should emphasise the development and production of fighters in order to counter a decisive air strike by Germany. To this end he had proposed a new expansion, Scheme K, which would do just that.

On top of this, Newall agreed on a proposal by Air Marshal Sir Wilfrid Freeman, the newly appointed Air Member for Development and Production, for the ordering of three types of heavy bomber not yet in service. These orders were for a considerable level of production. The bomber was very much disproportionately prioritised by both sides, but for the Germans, despite the aerial siege during the Battle of Britain, the bomber would always be a tactical aircraft more relevant to interdiction and the support of advancing ground forces. The concept of the strategic bomber was essentially the cornerstone of British air policy. But in the late 1930s, German air power was, much like its army in comparison to the British, growing to a greatly disproportionate size and strength in comparison to the RAF.

CHAPTER 2
Rising Eagle:
The Second World War

On 1 September 1939, the German Army had rolled swiftly into Poland. On 3 September, having received no response from the government in Berlin to Neville Chamberlain's ultimatum '... that unless we heard from them by 11 o'clock that they were prepared at once to withdraw their troops from Poland, a state of war would exist between us,' a solemn Chamberlain went on air fifteen minutes after the deadline to announce to the nation that '... no such undertaking has been received and that consequently this country is at war with Germany'. A similar ultimatum issued by the French government likewise received no response and it too was at war by 5 p.m.

On 3 September 1939, the day of the declaration of war on Germany, the RAF mounted its first sortie of the war. Bristol Blenheims of No. 139 Squadron of Bomber Command were tasked to carry out a reconnaissance mission over the Schillig Roads. The RAF was also called upon to dispatch a Tactical Air Force in the form of the Advanced Air Striking Force. It was not much, despite the grand title, being made up almost entirely of Fairey Battles, an obsolete large monoplane powered by the Rolls-Royce Merlin.

In addition to the Battles, four squadrons of Hurricanes were dispatched to provide the air defence element. This was by the standards of the Luftwaffe an inferior proposition. The Battles were big, ungainly and slow. They had none of the dive-bombing qualities of the Ju 87 Stuka nor the ceiling performance, range or bomb load of the German and RAF bombers in service at the time. But if the Advanced Air Striking Force (AASF) lacked the required capability to meet any future German aggression, the Army was far more significantly out-gunned and out-matched by the *Heer Korps* and *Waffen-SS* units. The Army received the lowest priority in expansion. Before 1939, policy towards land rearmament was based on one of limited liability. In other words, sending an expeditionary force to Europe would not be necessary. Instead, the emphasis was to be placed on 'Imperial Defence'. This meant provision for coastal defence and anti-aircraft guns based in the UK. It would not be until as late as spring 1939 that the cabinet would accept that a 'Modern British Force' might very well have to fight on the Continent. In March, the decision was taken to double the size of the Territorial Army, and conscription was introduced in April. This sudden and massive expansion, plus the fact that many of the Army's own expansion programmes, just like those of the RAF, had not been completed, meant there was a considerable period to go before the Army would be ready for war.

The British and Canadian soldiers of the British Expeditionary Force (BEF) when deployed were armed with First World War-era Lee-Enfield .303 calibre bolt rifles. They had lacked realistic armoured support and the only automatic firearms available were Vickers and Lewis machine guns. These, again carried forward in service from the First World War, were large drum-like barrels, which in the case of the Vickers required a heavy tripod stand and water for barrel-cooling, and the trigger mechanisms were handle grips pushed inwards. This meant in almost every case the machine gun had to be carried by a three-man team, including someone to carry the ammunition and to take time to set the gun up with a pre-determined field of fire. Tactical manoeuvre was not a concept that the Vickers machine gun was well suited to.

By contrast, German infantry units carried not only First World War rifles such as the Mauser 98K but were also widely equipped with the MP40 Schmeisser sub-machine gun. These weapons were very well designed with pistol grip, adjustable butt and magazine clip feeding from below. In addition, German infantry units were well assigned with a superior light-support machine gun design. The MG34 was fitted with small bipod supports at the end of a long, narrow barrel and with rifled butts and pistol grips like the MP40. But most telling of all, the German infantry weapons possessed a frightening rate of fire, in the MG34's case, in the region of 800 rounds per minute. Some were belt-fed, others with a clip-on drum feed. The essential point is that the German infantry and panzer assault infantry were able to move, fire and lay down heavy rates of withering fire in a manner which the infantry of the BEF simply could not hope to match. This, together with the fanatical self-belief that typified the German soldier of the day, matched by a greater and alarming willingness to sustain losses, meant that the BEF and other European armies were never going to match their superior adversary. It may not have stood out over the intervening years, but this predicament is what led to the development of the RAF into a superlative air force while Germany had what can only be described as a superlative army.

The BEF deployed into France and the Low Countries with fourteen infantry divisions and the 1st Tank Brigade. The German Army units facing them alone numbered ten panzer divisions. In addition, seventy-five infantry divisions invaded France, divided into three army groups. The German armoured vehicles were a mix of Panzer 1 and Panzer 2 tanks with 20-mm guns, but also the Panzer 3 and 4, armed respectively with 50-mm and 75-mm short-barrel guns. The British 1st Tank Brigade was equipped with the much inferior Matilda II and Cruiser Mk I tanks, with 40-mm guns as the primary armament. However, the French Army, the principal Allied army on the field, also had three army groups, dwarfing the BEF. Altogether, the Allied side enjoyed numerical superiority. This was also the case with armour as the French fielded a large number of tanks, including the most heavily armed and armoured example, the Char B1, which had a chassis-mounted 75-mm gun and a 47-mm gun in the turret. This made the B1 the heaviest armed tank of the campaign.

The German victory was owed to the simplicity of the mobility and tactics of the *Wehrmacht* units against the static and inert posture of those of the French. As the Germans pushed through Belgium into the north of France, much of the French Army was quite powerless to respond adequately, as faith had been placed in the Maginot Line, which was now superfluous. Further, with both French and British tactics, the armour and infantry often acted separately and lacked the cohesion of German armour, infantry and, all importantly, devastating air support, which was fast and accurate courtesy of the Ju 87s and strafing from abundant Bf 109s. When the retreat reached the beaches of Dunkirk, Chamberlain had already stood down following the debacle that had seen the decisive failure of the British troops to secure Norway in April. And so, in the middle of this awful crisis, the government was pondering just who would lead Britain to victory, or as seemed increasingly likely, to an accommodation with Hitler.

Lord Halifax – the apparent favourite of the opposition parties to lead what would become the last coalition government before David Cameron's – was perhaps not the appeaser as common perception might have it, but the pragmatist who could not be wholly condemned for thinking that the situation was already lost and that the least ruinous path would be to seek terms. Winston Churchill succeeded Chamberlain as a result of Lord Halifax declining to stand. An accommodation would almost certainly have been agreed otherwise and doubtless on the most unacceptable terms for Britain and therefore democracy anywhere outside of North America. With the desperate evacuation of remnants of the BEF and French troops from Dunkirk at the end of June 1940, the situation must have appeared like the abyss. British soldiers of the BEF had done their duty and more, but the outcome was inevitable. With the BEF in no position to mount any serious challenge to the kind of army that could be landing by sea and air in the coming months, the government in Westminster faced a most frightful dilemma. The simple choice was to accept that in terms of land warfare, the odds were decisively stacked against any likelihood of a British victory or impasse in our favour.

The main land war effort against Germany came from the USSR in the East and to a lesser degree from the US in the western theatres. This is not to dismiss the British land campaigns as insignificant, but all things being relative there was no hope of a British victory single-handed against the Reich. The RAF contribution in the form of the AASF had been decimated, and the fighter units, having held their own against Bf 109s, were evacuated as soon as aircraft numbers and spares began to run dry. Rather than attempt to sustain the RAF squadrons in theatre, the decision was taken to withdraw the remaining personnel and aircraft back to the UK. Air support for the Allied ground troops from mid-June would be provided by RAF squadrons operating from bases in the south of England. Despite this, the French government had been assured by Churchill that further aircraft would be deployed. This is where AOC-in-C Fighter Command Sir Hugh Dowding, with the support of Sir Cyril Newall, presented the case against further air assets being sent over to France simply to be squandered when a pending German invasion was looking increasingly imminent. Thus, the Army being evacuated by hook or by crook, all available aircraft would be needed in order to provide the best possible chance of repelling such an invasion. In all probability, this refusal by Churchill, while not likely to attract any praise for Dowding, arguably set the stage for the RAF to prove itself as an imperative component of the military structure and confirm why the air force should exist as a separate power.

The resulting Battle of Britain, however, remains a unique example of how a military campaign with decisive results was waged between two air forces. Had the fighter squadrons been sent to France so late in the Battle of France at Churchill's request, the likelihood of the RAF holding the Luftwaffe at bay until the onset of winter would have been severely damaged. Even had Britain survived, the damage sustained may have altered Churchill's strategy for prosecuting the war thereafter. The credibility of air power could well have been destroyed, at least in the eyes of the British political establishment, resulting in a far more costly policy, in terms of manpower and emphasis on land warfare, with a drastically increased loss of life and an outcome that might have been less conducive to the survival of democracy. In short, Churchill, for all his defiance of Nazi Germany and resolve to confront the foe every step of the way, knew only too well that the Army, equipped with inferior weapons, was thinly spread across the Empire, and that the prospect of expending the country's young men on the plains of Europe, in the same way as just twenty-two years earlier, was not one which the country could support again so soon.

The answer to being capable of hitting back at the Reich lay in the development of weapons technology, science and a variety of unorthodox operations involving deception, intelligence and all manner of initiatives. The development of a superior level of air power was, on the more conventional level of activity, undeniably the favoured approach to taking the fight to the enemy. This was how it had to be until such time as Churchill could expect to see an army of a size and shape that was capable and ready to confront the *Wehrmacht*. The Royal Navy remained the strongest of the three services. It was able to meet the task of protecting the sea lanes and could match the *Kriegsmarine* on any terms. However, Germany was destined to flood the Atlantic with wolf packs of U-boats. While the Royal Navy operated often single-handedly, the degree of success against German surface ships and against the wolf packs would not have been possible without RAF Coastal Command.

In addition to the expansion of and greater reliance on air power, Churchill was keen, despite the doubts about likely success against the Germany Army, to present some form of realistic proposition with which to confront the enemy. This meant taking a leaf or two out of the books of some of Hitler's more able military commanders. With a view to again meeting the Germans in a more decisive strategic theatre, the UK would follow the example of Hitler's panzer supremo, Heinz Guderian. Armoured divisions would be formed and the tanks would operate more cohesively with infantry, artillery and air support, the very tactic that had served the Germans so well. Luftwaffe General Kurt Student's concept of the *Fallschirmjäger*, the paratrooper, was at the top of Churchill's list of priorities. Following on from this theme, and drawing from his own experience during the Boer War, he proposed the development of units within the Army and conversion of the Royal Marine Corps into hit-and-run assault troops – Commandos. It could be argued that the rise to pre-eminence of air power, and the arrival of the Special Forces soldier on the battlefield were of equal importance. This then was Churchill's plan to begin the task of bringing about the absolute defeat of the Third Reich. The RAF from the outset remained operationally engaged: from early leaflet drops over Germany's towns and cities; providing close air support of troops on the ground in every theatre; round-the-clock strategic bombing of German industry; and fighter sweeps over Fortress Europe. It also provided the means with which to mount many of the various SOE (Special Operations Executive) operations in occupied territory. Units within Bomber Command were assigned to this very role.

By the time the last of the Allied troops were evacuated from Dunkirk, a two-week respite followed before the air siege began, Hitler having been assured that the destruction of the RAF was necessary in order to ensure a successful land invasion. There have been a number of revisionist theories since. One theory is that a German invasion was doomed as there was no available coastline suitable for the landing of assault troops and heavy equipment. Another more recent claim suggests that the existence of the Royal Navy ensured that any realistic expectations of an invasion were not truly entertained by the German High Command. These are all practical points to consider. For example, if a German invasion could have successfully made the coast of East Anglia, the banks of the Thames Estuary or the coastline of Ayrshire where flat lands and sand dunes exist, like the Normandy landings, a covert geological survey would have been required to determine whether heavy vehicles would have sunk as soon as they rolled ashore. However, what is certain is that a German landing force would have been an overwhelming challenge for the frantically put together Home Guard (Local Defence Volunteers) and the few available units of the regular Army that were rebuilding themselves in earnest.

In light of this certainty, soft and unmanageable beaches or sheer cliff faces with extensive beach area below would not have spelled the end of the *Wehrmacht*'s ambitions to put a sizeable force ashore before constructing and defending a wider assault landing area for a main landing force. The Royal Navy, of course, would have presented a far greater threat to an invasion. Such an engagement would doubtless have been at a tremendous cost, leaving the Navy practically destroyed, but it might have been successful. The return on this would be that Hitler would have seen his *Kriegsmarine* severely crippled. In the long term, this would lessen the impact of German naval operations against supply convoys across the Atlantic; on the other hand, Karl Dönitz's growing U-boat fleet would become successful and highly feared. A successfully thwarted invasion might also have cost Germany dear in terms of its superior ground units – infantry, panzers and parachute assault infantry – and certainly hamper future strategic planning. Any level of a sustained siege/invasion against the British Isles would depend on the Führer's determination to neutralise Britain and its ability to continue to resist, against his much greater ambitions to colonise the East. But any such success against a German invasion would depend upon all available air power to support both the Royal Navy and, in the event of landings, to provide fighter cover and close air support for the troops on the ground.

The Battle of Britain remains a unique phenomenon in military history. The successful invasion of Britain, or at least the destruction of Britain's ability to protect its sea lanes and therefore ensure the country's survival, hinged essentially on the outcome of a straightforward three-month intense aerial battle between two air forces.

In terms of fighter aircraft, the RAF was reasonably well served in 1940. This was as a result of personal innovation that succeeded despite an atmosphere lacking political will and inclination. Reginald Mitchell's fighter derived from a racing seaplane design, the Supermarine Spitfire, was the first aircraft to meet the Luftwaffe's Bf 109. Despite being larger and heavier, it had a comparable performance thanks to the Rolls-Royce Merlin 12-cylinder engine. The drawback for the Spitfire and the RAF's other and more numerous fighter type, the Hawker Hurricane, was their light armament: eight Browning .303-inch calibre machine guns versus the Bf 109's two 20-mm high-explosive cannon and two 7.9-mm machine guns. The Hurricane, while larger, heavier and slower than the Spitfire, was highly manoeuvrable and was not found wanting in its ability to reach a respectable ceiling. The Hurricane was the easiest and safest aircraft to land due to the wide gauge on its main undercarriage, and its fabric construction meant that it could absorb huge punishment. Otherwise, with a noticeable edge in overall speed and acceleration in favour of the Spitfire and Bf 109, the general performance of all three put them in the same class.

However, the real advantage the RAF had over the Luftwaffe was being the defending party. The Germans had to navigate twenty-two miles of sea at the narrowest point between Dover and Calais. This allowed the RAF Sector Controllers to launch fighter formations of varying size according to the requirements. To engage an incoming raid of bombers and fighter escort with their limited range reduced significantly before reaching the Kent and Sussex coast put Fighter Command in a much valued position of advantage. This advantage would have been severely limited but for the ready availability of radar.

Radar was extensively deployed throughout south-east England in the early summer of 1940. Ventnor and Ash were two of the better known early warning radar locations. The basic process involved the use of radio signals from the transmitter aerial. These signals would reflect off any physical presence in their way, the signal bouncing back like a squash ball to be collected by a receiver antenna. The signal would be fed down through the aerial to an amplification processor and via a wave guide to the display unit, the cathode ray tube, and from here displayed on a monitor via an electronic beam. The information derived indicated to the radar operator that there was a physical airborne presence at a given range and bearing to the position of the radar station. This information would be cross-referenced and displayed by fighter plotters on a large snooker-like table. The fighter controller would direct fighters by HF radio accordingly as the plotters updated the aircraft positions on the table. In later days, fighter controllers sat in front of the radar monitor and were presented with a plan view surrounding the origin of the radar signal with the electronic trace beam rotating in line with the rotating radar aerial. This in turn transmitted the signal and collected it again instantly, thus painting a plan view of airborne activity out to a certain range. Later technical updates have included the provision of electronic overlay displays such as coastal outlines, georef map referencing, electronically displayed ancillary information pertaining to individual tracked movements and enormous amounts of clutter caused by high-static ground objects close to the radar head, bad weather and flocks of birds further out. But despite the primitive nature of radar at the time of the Battle of Britain, it was to prove as vital a component part of the air defence force as the fighter squadrons themselves.

In due course, the Chain Home radar stations stretched from Trelanvean in Cornwall, along the coast all the way east and north to Tannach in Caithness. Fighter bases were ranged from St Eval and Predannack in Cornwall to Wick in Caithness. Fighter Command was divided into four groups: No. 10 Group covered the south west of England, the south west approaches and South Wales; No. 11 Group covered the south east and London; No. 12 Group the Midlands and East Anglia; and No. 13 Group covered the north of England, North Wales, Northern Ireland and Scotland. From 10 July, the German raids concentrated on Channel convoys and targets of military value in the south of England, with the bulk of attacks in the south east. No. 11 Group was, therefore, the most severely tested of the four fighter groups, and Dowding was to rotate the squadrons out of No. 11 Group to the more northerly airfields for rest and training. Nevertheless, all squadrons remained on an operational footing.

As is often the case with any plan of action, the level of operational tempo was imbalanced for a number of squadrons. For example, No. 3 Squadron, having been deployed in France and seen heavy action, had been sent to Wick in northern Scotland before 10 July. There, the squadron saw very little action save for the odd intercept of a long-range reconnaissance patrol. On the other hand, No. 17 Squadron was continuously deployed in No. 11 Group's area and was constantly under pressure throughout the two most intense months of August and September. No. 19 Squadron, while deployed on the border between Nos 11 and 12 Groups, tested the cannon-armed Spitfire 1Bs from 20 July in place of the .303 gun-armed 1/1As. This proved to be a lethal bugbear for the squadron as they discovered that the cannons were unreliable, having a tendency to jam, evidently a result of the wing not being sufficiently sturdy and, of course, found out at rather critical moments. The squadron were much relieved to be told on 3 September they were to be reissued with the eight-machine-gun-armed Spits. During this short but intense period, No. 19 Squadron was issued with forty-two Spitfire 1Bs.

Despite the public perception of Fighter Command and the high esteem that followed, the greater weight of casualties, even in this early stage of the war, was sustained by Bomber Command. But exactly as history has recorded, the outcome of the air defence campaign across the south of England was what mattered, to the exclusion of other operations before the start of winter. Respite came following the change from bombing airfields and radar sites to bombing heavy concentrations of the population, which was largely the result of an unintentional release of bombs by a single German aircraft over London at night. This was met by a suicidal and otherwise ineffectual reprisal raid by Bomber Command over Berlin, to which Hitler responded by mistakenly shifting the emphasis onto city raids. The result was that pressure was eased on the airfields in No. 11 Group's area. Despite the intensity of the German onslaught during the months of September and August, the Führer's priority was to concentrate on preparation for his planned conquest of the East. By the start of October, and with the Battle still officially in progress, the operational tempo slackened off considerably. At the end of the month, an intercepted signal indicated that Operation Sea Lion, the planned German offensive, had been postponed indefinitely. That the UK was left in a position to make use of the time ahead to eventually begin offensive operations in earnest is seen as a crucial factor in bringing about the ultimate and decisive defeat of the Third Reich. All three armed services expanded, and the desire to take the war to Germany was exploited.

For the RAF, operations by Coastal Command were in high demand to protect convoys which were preyed upon by the U-boat wolf packs and surface fleet in the North Atlantic. In a reversal of the situation in the early stages of the Battle of Britain, Fighter Command were sending up large formations to breach the airspace over what was Fortress Europe, in the immediate period following. In 1940, the mighty Allied bomber offensive over the Third Reich was still in its infancy and far from the scale reached later in the war. Just the same, the RAF remained the sole military arm that could and did attack German forces on the European mainland and German soil. Sir Cyril Newall would remain CAS until 24 October 1940, a week before the recognised close of the Battle of Britain. He lent his support to Sir Hugh Dowding over his decision to deny Churchill's request for an additional six squadrons of Hurricanes to be sent to France in June 1940. Whether this may have had an undesirable effect on his future is far from certain and is the subject only of speculation. However, Dowding was also asked to clear his desk before the end of the year, his advanced years possibly working against him. That said, it does seem coincidental that two of the most able senior officers with such positive handling of the Battle of Britain should find their services no longer required so soon after the outcome.

The two men to replace the outgoing Newall and Dowding were respectively Sir Charles Portal and Sir Sholto Douglas. Portal had originated from Bomber Command and would hold the CAS appointment until after the end of the war. Portal was possibly the youngest CAS the RAF had appointed since Sir Frederick Sykes in 1918. It was clear from the outset that Portal was as outstanding a choice as any to lead the RAF through the Second World War. He was particularly important from the RAF's perspective, given that it would be catapulted to the fore as the service with the greatest and, at times, the sole means of taking the fight to heart of the Third Reich.

As the winter of 1940/41 approached and the crisis of the Battle of Britain passed, the emphasis on RAF operations shifted towards a broader versatility of roles. In some cases, such operations were unique yet imperative and in other cases, were devised to provide vital support to the other services and their lead operations. With regard to the latter, the ability of any one service would never suffice to bring victory single-handedly.

An effective campaign required the support of the Royal Navy, the most pressing priority being the Atlantic sea lanes. Coastal Command was continuously hard-pressed in hunting U-boats and providing intelligence on *Kriegsmarine* surface movements so that vital supplies of food and raw materials could enter the UK. Bombing raids over the Continent continued in earnest, but in no way comparable with those being flown two years later. Then, as 1940 gave way to 1941, Fighter Command began mounting an offensive campaign of its own. The fighter sweeps consisting of squadron and even wing strength flew daylight sorties over occupied France with the intention of doing just what the Luftwaffe had attempted in the early stages of the Battle of Britain: to draw a response from their opposite number and to attack targets of opportunity. Operation codenames such as Circus and Rodeo referred to this process of drawing the enemy aloft in order to try and shoot them down in an act of bloody attrition.

Bomber and Fighter Command operations mounted from stations across England were seen as the rightful area of responsibility of the RAF by the other two services; however, the Navy wanted control of all maritime-related air operations. Likewise, the Army felt that the provision of close air support of its troops in the field, once they deployed in North Africa and the Mediterranean, should be brought under its direct command. In other words, the RAF should lose Coastal Command, the Desert Air Force and later the 2nd Tactical Air Force in Normandy. According to the Admiralty and Imperial General Staff, they would be absorbed as respective arms of the other two services. It might be considered simple enough to swap a service to another, especially at an early and underdeveloped stage, but it is unlikely that these operations would have been given the same degree of priority for resources, development and operational tasking as they had had as RAF units. The Navy would be far too preoccupied with winning the war with ships and submarines, the Army with infantry, armour and artillery. The full potential would be far from exploited. As it was, the combined might of Coastal Command and the Navy, including a surface taskforce of four aircraft carriers, failed to destroy the German pocket battleship *Tirpitz*. It was Bomber Command that was called upon to drop 12,000-lb 'Tallboy' bombs at high altitude from Avro Lancasters of Nos 9 and 617 Squadrons on 12 November 1944.

Flexibility might well also have been lost. Tactical aircraft with a substantial attack capability assigned to the Army would be less available to alter roles and assignments to take part in other operations – they would possibly be reassigned to another command and re-equipped. This has been a far more typical characteristic of the RAF than the Army or Navy. That is the re-role of units/squadrons, for example requiring them to be moved from close air support to either heavy bomber of defence interceptor duties under a different command. Many of the tactical squadrons assigned to the Desert Air Force were formed out of the growth of Fighter Command, with many squadrons reassigned from air defence to the tactical ground attack role.

A letter from the War Office addressed to Sir Charles Portal a few months after he took over as CAS effectively ordered the RAF to hand over thirty Blenheim Mk III aircraft to Army Co-operation Command at once. The letter was addressed to 'Minister of State' and unsigned. With this came the caveat that they must be checked for signs of poor maintenance:

The Air Ministry will deliver to the Army Co-operation Command the Blenheim III type. Many of these airplanes [to quote the letter] will come from operational units. Care should be taken by the War Office to see that they are in satisfactory condition when received. Many Blenheim III aircraft in the operational units are not in satisfactory condition.

Whether the author was speaking from first-hand knowledge or simply being blunt with a casual prejudice about the RAF would not have made any difference to the reaction from Portal. The letter ordering the release of the Blenheims was issued on 27 May 1941 and a response was sent by Portal to the Secretary of State for War the next day:

I consider that the wording of these paragraphs conveys two gratuitous and unwarranted imputations against the Air Ministry and the Royal Air Force by implying:

a) That their operational aircraft are not kept in a serviceable and efficient condition. This is belied by the splendid operational record of Blenheim units;

b) That the Air Ministry would seek to provide, if possible, inferior Blenheims for the Army Co-operation squadrons, and that the War Office need to be warned against this.

As the minute is unsigned and displays an extraordinary lack of knowledge of service organisation by implying that the War Office are entitled or qualified to criticise the condition of RAF aircraft, I can only suppose that Lord Beaverbrook did not actually see it after it was drafted.

Portal went on to 'suggest' that '… these offensive and unnecessary imputations be withdrawn from the official records of the War Cabinet'.

The further rapid expansion of the RAF was the result of Churchill's belief that the German Army was in the long term never likely to be challenged decisively by the British Army alone. It was becoming ever more apparent that air power offered the opportunity to deliver the most destructive force against Germany while limiting the cost in manpower. The effect of landing an infantry division on enemy-occupied soil would be disastrous. But the destruction brought to bear by a single squadron of medium bombers would far more likely bring disaster to the enemy.

Churchill understood the need to be able to reach into the heart of Germany's industrial complex and destroy it. While Britain stood alone, this was to be the only way that the war could properly be prosecuted against Hitler's Reich with any hope of a successful conclusion. The means by which the Reich's factories could be reached ultimately lay with Bomber Command, but as of 1940, Bomber Command was not realistically capable of waging such a campaign. The most capable bomber available was the Vickers Wellington, a twin-engine, long-range and sturdy aircraft that could carry a comparable bomb load to that of the German bombers of the day. The Luftwaffe's He 111s, Ju 88s and Do 17s could carry no greater bomb load, but were superior to the Wellington, affectionately known as the 'Wimpy', in overall airframe and engine performance. Also, their defensive armament was much superior. The lack of the latter significantly influenced the shift towards night-time bombing by the RAF. The much heavier defensive armament on American bombers such as the B-17 and B-24 later in the war equally influenced the American belief that they could, with fighter escort in addition, carry out daylight raids with a realistic chance of achieving greater accuracy while holding off unacceptable losses. This proved not to be the case and the US 8th Air Force between 1942 and 1945 lost nearly half as many men as Bomber Command had between 1939 and 1945.

Despite these heavy losses, the air war over Germany would be far less costly regarding the amount of casualties if the UK, the US, the Commonwealth and their Allies such as France, Poland and other Free Forces engaged in an expanded army to replace the strategic bombing offensive. Churchill knew this only too well. The British people were not prepared to sustain such a haemorrhage of their young men, with the bitter memory of the First World War still fresh and traumatic.

The Navy and Army were expanding to meet target strengths with which it was expected that the armed forces as a whole would be capable of confronting Germany. The Army was to expand to a strength of 2,195,000 as of May 1941. This goal, a Prime Minister's Directive, was deemed difficult to achieve. In order to alleviate this, the Army put forward a plan to replace 100,000 male personnel in ADGB (Air Defence of Great Britain) and the RAF with female personnel, but this failed to be achieved due to a shortage of volunteers. But again, while the service of female personnel cannot be underestimated, for the Army to suggest such a plan says more about its regard for the credibility of the RAF as a military force than pragmatic thinking on its part.

The arrival of Air Chief Marshal Sir Arthur Harris at Bomber Command in February 1942 marked a change in the capability and use of military air power. Harris was indeed ambitious and believed in absolute power to completely destroy an enemy state from the air. Harris's belief in defeating Germany through aerial bombardment was over-ambitious and neglected the ultimate need to put the Army ashore to exploit the work of the bomber force. But what he could genuinely offer was a far lower casualty rate for the amount of damage inflicted. Harris did have the Prime Minister's backing in this regard. As a result, aircraft production accelerated to a point which gave the RAF an unexpected degree of prominence.

The need for new and more capable aircraft and the subsequent demand for personnel in the RAF were increasingly felt overseas. Even before the US entered the war, its assistance to Britain, as good as declaring war on Germany in all but name, saw RAF trainee air crew dispatched across the Atlantic to avoid training in the increasingly congested airspace over and around the British Isles. It was also deemed to be highly dangerous, courtesy of the ever likely chance of bumping into fighter patrols from the Luftwaffe searching for targets of opportunity. An increasing demand for air support was also demanded by the Navy and Army. A memorandum from the First Sea Lord, Admiral Sir Dudley Pound, on 15 May 1942, referred to the recommendation for the strategic bombing of industrial targets in Germany and occupied countries. His view was that such a policy should be adopted only after certain extensive and essential naval and military requirements, to meet the new situation regarding the outbreak of war with Japan, had been met. To this end, two minimum requirements needed addressing: the provision of larger air forces for co-operation; and organisation.

A third issue of extreme concern to the Admiralty was training. Increased air support for operations at sea was a view shared by the Air Ministry, and plans were being drawn up for a substantial increase in the number of aircraft capable of working at sea in co-operation with the fleet. None, however, had been made with the involvement of naval staff. Training and organisation was centralised, as it was in the Luftwaffe, but questions were raised as to what ends the RAF and Air Ministry were aiming for. The Admiralty was of the opinion that the Luftwaffe was a more successful arm, as its functions were primarily designed to support the operational effectiveness of the *Kriegsmarine* and the German Army. To this end, the Admiralty believed that RAF crews were essentially trained for overland operations, resulting in poor results in maritime operations due to a lack of specialised training.

A Board of Enquiry report by Mr Justice Bucknill on the matter of poor results regarding air support of maritime operations effectively suggested that the RAF should divert from what was seen as its primary role of bombing and concentrate more on daylight attacks on shipping if it was expected to take a more decisive role in control of sea traffic. Additional training in maritime operations was recommended as necessary, even if at the expense of bombing operations. The thinking at the Admiralty was that since flying was necessary over both land and sea theatres of operations, the emphasis should be placed on the more difficult circumstances of operations over the sea. The logic was that crews trained essentially for maritime air operations could perform equally proficiently over the desert if called to do so, but the same was not the case if the training syllabus was concentrated on air warfare over land. As far as the Admiralty was concerned, all aircraft taking part in maritime operations should be placed under naval control in order to achieve the best possible results.

Sir Dudley Pound now recommended that the types of aircraft suitable for anti-ship and anti-submarine operations should be increased and that Bomber Command should be organised to provide squadrons capable of locating and attacking moving targets at sea with success. Altogether, the Admiralty wanted control of some 2,000 front-line aircraft including reconnaissance, bombers and fighters. The Army requested control of over 4,000 aircraft, proposing that they should be 'specially designed' for support of ground troops and form an integral part of the armed forces. Essentially, the Navy wanted a home Coastal Command and an overseas one, both under its direct control. If these demands were agreed, the RAF would be finished as the principal air arm, a point that would not at all have been overlooked by the Admiralty and War Office. It would certainly have ended any chance of orchestrating the bomber offensive to anywhere near the level of intensity that was achieved. Or as Portal himself wrote: '… to meet them would automatically extinguish any hope of development of that bomber offensive which has been postulated by the British and American Chiefs of Staff as one of the essential measures for winning the war, as oppose to merely losing it'. Portal also dismissed notions held by the other two services that this was how the Luftwaffe was organised and successfully so. The Luftwaffe had no equivalent to Coastal Command or Army Co-operation. It did indeed support the German Army and with devastating effect during all its successful drives against foreign armies including the British and French. But for this, aircraft were not uniquely assigned and were an integral part of the Luftwaffe under a central command, and would be dispatched to attack radar stations in mainland Britain just as they would to support advancing panzers in France. German torpedo bombers were part of the Luftwaffe bomber force and not that of a maritime unit under the control of the *Kriegsmarine*.

Portal's key objective was that the aforementioned bomber offensive, when combined with the US 8th Air Force, should be the most effective power to bring to bear on Germany's ability to wage war. 'To achieve this, the RAF must be held together. To do otherwise would at least push victory further away into the future, or worse, deny it altogether.'

So far the RAF had rendered effective close air support to the 8th Army in the desert. This had been provided largely by later variants of the Hawker Hurricane, the Mk IIc, armed with 20-mm Hispano cannons and 250-lb bombs. In addition, there was the Bristol Beaufighter, a jack-of-all-trades type, not unlike the legendary Mosquito, and also heavily used in North Africa. The Luftwaffe had not developed its close air support capability beyond what was used in the *Wehrmacht*'s swashbuckling advance through the Low Countries and France. The Ju 87 dive bomber was very much the German workhorse – in close air support, interdiction and anti-shipping. That said, the Stuka, as it had proved earlier in the Battle of Britain, was highly vulnerable due to its slow speed and was mincemeat to fighters such as Spitfires and Hurricanes. The Army's request for some 4,000 aircraft was to have been divided thus:

Fighter Reconnaissance (sixty squadrons)	720 aircraft
Light Bomber Reconnaissance (thirty squadrons)	360 aircraft
Air Observation Posts (twelve squadrons)	144 aircraft
Specially Designed Transport Aircraft	2,484 aircraft
Inter-Communications (five squadrons)	60 aircraft
Ambulance Duties (four squadrons)	48 aircraft
Total:	3,816 aircraft

This amounted to 850 aircraft more than the Germans used to support 178 divisions across a 1,000-mile front during Operation Barbarossa. The British Army in total had about a quarter of that strength, which was spread across the globe: the Far East, Mediterranean, North Africa and at home. Yet despite this improbable shopping list, the Chief of the Imperial General Staff (CIGS) still found the need to insinuate that the RAF in the western desert had at no time reached the irreducible minimum. In summing up his response to the Chiefs of Staff and Minister of State, Portal outlined the priorities of the RAF and the purpose of air warfare more comprehensively:

> The first principle of air warfare is to concentrate the maximum air strength on whatever task may be of decisive importance at the time.
>
> The extension of the war thus calls for the utmost flexibility in the development of air power if we are to win general air superiority over the Axis Powers and create the situation in which other forms of offensive effort will become effective. The Admiralty and War Office proposals would involve the segregation of some 6,000 first-line aircraft in the form of specialised components, the greater part of which would be transferred to Naval and Army control. If these proposals are approved, the Air Force will be virtually divided into three parts, to the fatal prejudice of our capacity to concentrate and with disastrous consequences to the development of our offensive strategy.
>
> The need for full-scale air co-operation with the Army and Navy was not in dispute. Only a flexible force, under commanders whose profession was air warfare, could offer the full assistance required.

Portal had his own list of proposals designed to achieve the maximum air assistance to both services. These included an increase in aircraft assigned to maritime duties. Expansion of Coastal Command was in hand due to the strength of the U-boat threat to Atlantic shipping, especially when the Americans were transporting enormous quantities of men, machines and supplies.

The Army's requests were harder to meet. A response to demands by the CIGS for the expansion of Army Co-operation Command and No. 2 Group of Bomber Command was experiencing delays due to the need to obtain supplies from America. In addition, there was a growing need for air reinforcements in the Far and Middle

East and the provision of fighters and bombers together with crews to assist the Soviets. The expectation of the Army for ninety front-line squadrons in addition to permanent Army control was viewed as 'excessive by any standard'. However, for home-based operations, other than that afforded by the metropolitan squadrons, Army Co-operation Command could provide twenty squadrons for close air support. A further twenty squadrons of light bombers were available from No. 2 Group of Bomber Command, and fifteen day fighter squadrons of Fighter Command. The first twenty squadrons listed above would be assigned to specific formations within the Army while the remainder would train for the battlefield support role as required.

As for the pressing requirements of the Middle East, essentially the North African deserts, air support was to remain the same. There were Army Co-op squadrons already assigned and supported by whatever other air force units were available. A further requirement was for sufficient air transport to deliver an airborne division and a separate, independent airborne brigade. Ideally, the RAF was still to gain sufficient numbers of appropriate transport aircraft. This would not be too long in coming and would be the excellent Douglas DC-3, better known in military parlance as the C-47.

Whatever the requirements of the other two services with regard to air power, and whatever the level of support for such the RAF could provide, especially once Air Chief Marshal Sir Arthur Harris took the post of AOC-in-C Bomber Command, the main objective was the flattening of the German industrial base. Long before any US air chief coined the phrase 'We'll bomb 'em back into the Stone Age,' Harris was on course to single-mindedly do that. Harris genuinely believed that a sizeable bomber force could win the war against Germany without the need to employ another force. He was about to be proved wrong. That the strategic bombing offensive against Germany rendered dividends is, I believe, unquestionable. That if pursued, it could have eventually destroyed the enemy's ability to fight on is at best a seriously flawed argument. If strategic bombing had been relied upon to such a degree by the Allies, and assuming the point was proved in the fullness of time, the country left behind would be a charred desert. There are many who are always ready to provide a sweeping response to such concern of the 'so what' mentality. But to salt the earth throughout the German nation would be to destroy the Allied aim at the same time. The aim was to bring about the unconditional defeat of Germany, not to wipe out its population such as the Nazi regime was attempting with the Jews. Harris said he did not consider the sum total of Germany's cities worth the bones of a single British grenadier; however, the round-the-clock offensive certainly cost more than the bones of a single British airman.

Ultimately, the Allied aim in the Second World War came down to the comprehensive defeat of the Axis powers. Whatever the reliance on sea and air power to achieve this, the point of all military effort was to put the infantry soldier on enemy soil unopposed. The defeated state has then to be administered by the occupying force and the economy reconstructed, if only to be able to make good war reparations, but as is always the case, unless a policy of genocide is being pursued, then the occupier faces the task of reconstruction of infrastructure, economy and the forging of new alliances. To achieve this, the land force element has to fight its way through to that point. The Air Force and Navy do not oversee the governance and maintenance of order in a vanquished land; that is essentially the Army's remit. Certainly, Harris must have been only too aware of this, and one can only imagine that his theory of smashing the Reich from above was simply a means of making the job of the boots on the ground as simple as possible.

The capacity of the UK to produce aircraft and other weapons was limited and way behind that of Germany in the period up to the start of 1942. Other than a quick victory over Italian troops in North Africa, much of the British arms left a lot to be desired. The situation in the deserts of Libya and Egypt was soon turned around with the arrival of Rommel's Afrika Korps. The war presented a series of reversals and setbacks for the British, with no sign of how Britain could possibly prevail. Before Hitler launched Operation Barbarossa, the British had been thrown out of Crete and driven across North Africa. British shipping was being sunk at an alarming rate by U-boats in the Atlantic, and the bomber offensive relied on obsolete aircraft that suffered an appallingly high rate of attrition for little impact on German industrial output.

The invasion of the Soviet Union took the pressure off for the first time since the Battle of Britain. The level of military expansion in all respects was not showing promise of reaching the kind of levels that would be needed to orchestrate a fully comprehensive campaign against the Reich. But in order to build on what had so far been achieved and to seize every opportunity to prepare an army to free occupied Europe, Churchill had to approach the US for assistance and materials. The opportunity to do this successfully came when Japan entered the war with its surprise attack on Pearl Harbor. Prior to this, the US was a source of supplies and materials to boost the equipping of the the Army back home. America was to provide much needed materials, food, aircraft, tanks and other weapons. While its armed forces were considerably limited in strength prior to the attack on Pearl Harbor, it was developing and bringing into service some first-rate aircraft which would play a decisive role in the war years ahead. The two European-based heavy bombers of the 'Mighty 8th', the B-17 Flying Fortress and B-24 Liberator, were already in service but existed in small numbers and had yet to be developed to their full potential.

On the day when Japan launched its surprise attack on the US fleet at Pearl Harbor, the US armed forces, having been scaled back significantly since the armistice of 11 November 1918, stood at a manpower strength of 178,000. This is the same as the number of British forces at the time of the recent SDSR announcement. The British

Expeditionary Force sent to France in 1939 was nearly twice the size. Yet three-and-a-half years on from 7 December 1941, the US forces had reached a peak strength of some 16 million.

Isolationism in the US allowed some quite unsympathetic attitudes to develop among the wider population. There was even the suggestion that far from supporting Great Britain, the US should seek an accord with Germany. This did not attract a great deal of sympathy, but wider opinions favoured keeping out of the war. President Roosevelt was, fortunately for one and all, a most pragmatic man and sympathetically disposed towards the British position. At the time of the Battle of Britain, while unduly negative reports were dispatched by the US Ambassador to London, Joe Kennedy Snr, Roosevelt opened up a parallel line of communication with Colonel Bill Donovan, future head of the Office of Strategic Services. Donovan had been dispatched to London as the President's personal representative and fed back reports of a contrasting nature to the content of those Kennedy was sending to the White House. Indeed, Donovan was confident enough to state that 'England could and would withstand a German invasion'.

An interesting anecdote concerns an article in the *Daily Express* on 19 January 1947, written by Commander Noel Gayler of the US Navy, who claimed that only 20 per cent of RAF pilots shot down a German plane during the Battle for Britain. This caused no outrage on the British side, perhaps in no small part due to Anglo-American relations at that particular time. Those in authority were also anxious not to start a conflict with Gayler or representatives in the media. That said, there was a request from Fighter Command to clarify Gayler's assertions. His claims were based, he said, on gun camera footage. However, it seemingly had not occurred to him that only 15 per cent of fighters during the conflict were installed with gun cameras …

It was in no small part thanks to this second reporting line that Roosevelt received a more balanced appraisal of the RAF's progress during the Battle of Britain. It has been argued that this indeed led to the increasing support for Britain from the US government. This may in part be the case, but the idea that Roosevelt would have been more favourably disposed towards Hitler as it looked increasingly as though Britain faced defeat and occupation is difficult to imagine. But America remained neutral just the same. American journalists freely reported from Berlin with impartiality on the progress of the war up until the attack on Pearl Harbor. During this time, and in contrast to the position of neutrality, Roosevelt signed the Lend-Lease agreement in March 1941. This in turn can be regarded historically as the true beginning of the end of Britain's imperial status. In return for immediate assistance, in the form of a handful of obsolescent ships, Britain agreed to hand over control of a number of overseas bases to the US.

As the Lend-Lease agreement progressed and American armaments manufacture geared up, an increase in arms to Britain began to gather momentum. The real mobilisation to a war economy in the US, despite growing indications that they could not remain neutral for much longer, did not get going in earnest until after the Pearl Harbor attack and the subsequent declaration of war on the US by Germany. While the RAF benefited immensely from the Lend-Lease arrangement, the bombing of industrial Germany relied essentially on three superb home-built aircraft: the Halifax, Lancaster and Mosquito. By the time of the D-Day landings, Bomber Command deployed some forty-three operational squadrons equipped with Lancasters with a typical unit establishment of the order of twenty-one aircraft. The de Havilland Mosquito, a true master of all trades, was serving in practically every operational command at home and abroad.

It is incomprehensible to think that the reliance on the round-the-clock bombing of Germany, which absorbed so many men and material, was the preferred less costly alternative. The level of manpower that made up a British army comparable in size to that of Germany was clearly so far beyond the pale for the government to even contemplate. The cost in materials and the degree of skilled training to put a Lancaster into the air with a seven-man crew and sufficient fuel and upwards of 22,000 lb of bombs may have made a much lighter demand on human beings, but it certainly did not make for a reduced consumption of material and resources. Considering that the RAF was pressed to train legions of bomber air crews for operations, there was a desperate need for flying training schools from the elementary through to advanced stages, as well as pilots, navigators, flight engineers, bombardiers, wireless operators and gunners.

The arrival of the heavy bomber in the war brought the creation of all these new air crew positions. This in turn placed a heavy demand for resources to train personnel for the new specializations. Training schools were established from Canada and the US to British protectorates in Africa and the Middle East. The Royal Navy had its work cut out ferrying thousands of trainee airmen from the overseas training schools to and from the UK.

Rhodesia and South Africa were not the easiest or cheapest locations to get to, and the cost of moving future air crews to and fro came with the likelihood that a number of trainee airmen would either fail the course or be lost in action. Therefore, an enormous strain was placed on the Navy to ensure that the RAF was able to take the war to the Reich in a decisive fashion. Then there were additional resources to consider such as the training of ground crew in the various disciplines of aircraft airframe and engine maintenance, electronic aids, flight instruments and radar. In addition, there were the demands of dealing with bombs encasing 10,000 lb of high explosives, phosphorus sticks and all manner of materials designed to burn anything they came into contact with. To expend this amount of ordnance week after week using several hundred bombers, each typically carrying 13,000 lb of explosives and incendiaries, was incredibly expensive. When adding the hefty cost of training the personnel to make it all happen, one might sympathise with the schools at the time which questioned not only the logic but the morality.

As the author of this book, I do not feel it my place to judge the policy of heavy bombing of Germany's industrial complex and suburbs during the Second World War. The policy and operational directives, such as they became under Air Chief Marshal Harris's command, existed as a result of the perilous circumstances of the time. Nazi Germany promised medieval butchery, pitiless genocide and limitless slave labour. The air commanders can no more be blamed for the destruction of German cities any more than army commanders on the ground could be held to account for the destruction of French towns and villages when this was necessary to prosecute the war on land.

In Bomber Command (and those from the myriad of nationalities which flew with the RAF) and its American counterpart, the 8th Air Force, the number of sorties that constituted a tour of duty on ops was thirty and twenty-five respectively. Bomber Command crews faced a slightly lengthier tour on operations, of thirty ops (sorties flown in anger) than their American counter-parts in the 8th Air Force, who were ordinarily returned to the States after flying their twenty-fifth mission. From this follows the matter of crew fatigue and its inevitable effect on Bomber Harris's young men who were in some cases succumbing to a great sense of diminishing chance of survival as the sorties over enemy territory grew. Just as shell shock for soldiers in the field has become recognised as a genuine psychological condition, the tally on air crew nerves, through relentless forays into the breach, was a matter that needed to be addressed. A memorandum from the Air Ministry dated 19 September 1941 set out to clarify a matter raised by the Air Council a year previously, stating '… disposal of members of Aircrews whose conduct may cause them to forfeit the confidence of their Commanding Officers in their determination and reliability in the face of danger and to inform you that the time is ripe for the procedure to be brought up to date in the light of further experience'. The new memorandum outlined three categories under which serving air crew were deemed 'unable to stand up to the strain of flying'.

As of March 1942, there were five categories under which air crew could lose their brevet and be declared unfit to fly. These were contained in the RAF's Disposal Policy: air crew who refuse or are unfit to fly. Such conditions outlined were medical unfitness; inefficiency or misconduct; failure to reach the productive stage in the training or operational sphere; and forfeiture of the confidence of the C.O. The final condition was the infamous 'Lack of Moral Fibre' (LOMF) classification. One further condition was on compassionate grounds. All of these were classifications through which the air crew badge or brevet worn on the left side of an airman's chest could be withdrawn, along with consequent grounding. A review of LOMF after the war resulted in a new provision whereby any officer or airman categorised as unfit on account of nervous illness would hence be examined by a neuro-psychiatrist before his disposal would be finally determined. The reason given for this revised process was that an officer or airman might possibly be suffering from a temperamental handicap that he had tried unsuccessfully to overcome. In this case, it was deemed unfair to ignore the possibility of a favourable discharge. In an Air Council letter dated 28 September 1940 such air crews in operational units were described thus:

> As having displayed conduct which may cause them to forfeit the confidence of their Commanding Officers, placed the onus of determining whether an airman or officer was a Lack of Moral Fibre case, or not, on the Medical officer. This was challenged some months later (9 June 1941) by the Air Member for Personnel. This decision was instead, that the Station medical officer and specialists in neuro-psychiatry should only determine whether an individual case was a medical one or not. An Air Ministry memorandum, issued on 29 September 1941, determined that even consultants in neurology could, in the event of a case where the airmen/officer has been determined medically fit, not say anything else beyond stating that the individual was lacking in confidence.

In other words, the medical branch having determined an individual's physical fitness to not be in question but lacked confidence, should not be assumed to be a case of LOMF. This ultimate judgement would be made following all medical reports and assessments from the individual's commanding officer. If the judgement was that the airman/officer lacked moral fibre, the subsequent disposal was determined according to rank and experience. Officers were to have their services dispensed with forthwith. If the officer in question was on probation, his commission was terminated. If he was substantive in rank, he was called to resign. Airmen so classified were not to be employed in any circumstances as air crew again. Further, it was to be made clear to the individual that they would be re-mustered to the lowest rank of AC2 (Aircraftman 2nd Class) in the trade of general duties. This is effectively a nondescript trade with no recognised skill or training required beyond basic military training.

Reporting to the station warrant officer (the RAF equivalent to the Army's regimental sergeant major), as an AC2 GD (General Duties) the airman would be available for every kind of menial and uninspiring task which the SWO and his staff could throw in his direction. His previous service was not to count towards any reclassification to the rank of AC1, however, and this is the part that tends not to be included in any horror stories about the wartime RAF and the LOMF rule. Subject to having completed three months' satisfactory service as an AC2 in general duties, he was once again eligible for re-muster to a ground trade. Furthermore, if the airman was serving in a ground trade prior to being selected for air crew, he would be returned to that trade and reinstated at the rank held had he not been selected for air crew. This last point is a curious one and can only refer to timed promotion rather than on merit and availability of post. Timed promotion was a common process in the RAF for many years after the war, whereby an individual who satisfied the qualification requirements for promotion would in time be promoted, the logic being that rank was often seen as a trade qualification as much as an authoritative rank. Also, no reference was to be made to the reason for re-muster in personal documents other than the Service Form 1580. This form provided guidance to anyone involved with the airman's future movements and would be stamped with a red 'W' in the right-hand corner. He was also no longer entitled to wear his air crew brevet. Such measures could only be regarded as a way to bolster the resolve of air crews who were to climb aboard their aircraft and fly into danger against such terrible odds. By the end of the war, RAF Bomber Command alone had lost over 50,000 air crew on operations. Added to other RAF losses, the service, by a slim margin, sustained the highest ratio of personnel killed or lost in action of all British forces, and Bomber Command the highest loss as a recognised military unit for the whole of the Second World War. Care must be taken with such figures as they are relative to the numbers who served, and the reliance on Bomber Command and the RAF's other operational commands in various theatres stemmed from the British desire to avoid the greater carnage and loss of life that would ensue with what would be the corresponding requirement of ground forces to achieve the same end.

The American administration's mindset was no different when contemplating the public reaction at home to the inevitable day when American boys would be off to foreign fields once again to preserve its interests. As of 1940, America was not expecting to be drawn into the war in Europe. On 7 December 1941, the day when Japan launched its attack on Pearl Harbor, the US was not prepared for any kind of protracted military engagement. There is a slight paradox in the comprehensive state of the US preparedness for war with the Axis. The US was ahead of Britain in the design of heavy bombers, as the B-17 Flying Fortress and B-24 Liberator were in service with the US Army Air Corps as it then was. The drawback, needless to say, was the very small yet professional military force that America had. The attack on Pearl Harbor was met by a demonstrative attack on Japan. The best that the US could manage at the time was a makeshift and rather suicidal air raid launched at sea. The B-25 Mitchell was a superlative design for the age, but the circumstances under which it was to be used in retaliation for the Pearl Harbor raid which entailed severe risk. Sixteen B-25s were launched from the USS *Hornet* on 18 April 1942. The plan was to bomb Tokyo, their fuel taking them sufficiently further on to land at airfields in China. Although the amount of damage inflicted was negligible, all sixteen bombers reached the target and surprisingly not one was shot down. However, all aircraft were lost due to a lack of fuel after reaching Tokyo. Of these, three airmen were killed attempting to bale out, and another three were tried as war criminals by the Japanese and executed. As far as strategic interests were concerned, any armchair general would accept it had no merit. As a morale booster, it was a grand gesture. But once again, the only way to strike at the enemy was by air by launching aircraft designed to operate off concrete runways, not the deck of a carrier. Tests had proved that an aircraft of this size could operate from a carrier the size of the *Hornet*, and the operation was approved, organised and carried out in just three months.

The galvanisation of the US into a war economy was swift and dramatic. From the incredulous sight of US Army recruits drilling with flour bombs and wooden drill rifles in these early stages, the US armed forces expanded and equipped with unbelievable speed. Much of the South West US was a hive of construction in building airfields and associated infrastructure in order to churn out the massed ranks of operational air crew for the various air forces which would exist under Army command for the rest of the war. An advance headquarters unit for the 8th Air Force was set up at RAF High Wycombe on 23 February 1942, alongside HQ Bomber Command of the RAF. This had happened so quickly due to Churchill's continued persuasion on Roosevelt to prioritise the defeat of Germany over Japan.

On 17 August 1942, the first of many American air raids in daylight were launched from the UK against targets in Europe. Twelve B-17Es of the 97th Bomb Group operating from Polebrook in Northamptonshire was, by comparison with British raids at the time, a small but significant step. By the following year, a typical bomb group of the 8th Air Force consisted of four squadrons, and in some cases a unit establishment of seventy-two aircraft per squadron was not uncommon. The 'Mighty 8th' is often thought of in terms of four-engine heavy bombers, but as its description has it, this was an air force, not a command. The 8th Air Force comprised three operational commands: Fighter, Bomber and Air Support. Just the same, the primary mission was that of strategic strike. By August 1944, the bomber element of this now numbered nine bomb wings, each consisting of either three or four bomb groups. In addition, there were two similarly deployed fighter wings. All were deployed on thirty-eight airfields predominantly around East Anglia and the East Midlands. Also, within the North West European theatre alone was the 9th Air Force. It was based in England up until D-Day when the bulk of the 9th deployed increasingly alongside the RAF's 2nd Tactical Air Force.

The 9th originally deployed to North Africa in support of the first American troops when Rommel's Afrika Korps was finally driven out of the desert in 1943, the 9th then transferred to the UK in preparation for D-Day. By 6 June 1944, it had grown to five fighter wings, three (light and medium) bomb wings and three troop carrier wings (Troop Transport and Glider Assault Force). The RAF was organised somewhat differently. Starting at squadron level, the progression up the scale went next to the wing, usually anything from two to four squadrons. The wings were organised into groups, a reverse of the American terminology for numbers at this level. Thereafter, groups formed commands and they in turn formed the air force. The overseas commands tended to be known as air forces. The Far East, Middle East, Desert and 2nd Tactical Air Forces were, despite the title, regarded as operational command level organisations. Each of these commands was fully engaged against the Axis forces whether mounting bombing raids, reconnaissance flights, air-landing special agents or resupplying isolated forces on the ground such as the Chindits in Burma.

Air power may not provide the ultimate means of securing and holding the ground so vital to the total defeat of an enemy, but without it forces on the ground are severely disadvantaged. During the Second World War, the Allied armies would have been defeated in any theatre without the depth and comprehensive air support that was always available and in heavy demand. Similarly, no navy of any repute goes to sea on a war footing without adequate air cover, although traditionally the Navy relies on its own mobile air base: the aircraft carrier. To this end, the only truly offensive campaign waged by the Western Allies against Germany was the round-the-clock bombing raids by the American 8th during the day and RAF Bomber Command at night. The Normandy landings marked the beginning of the Western Allied land offensive against the Third Reich. Even so, it was no more than a sideshow in terms of the demand it placed on the German war effort for even with the offensive in the Normandy, two-thirds of German forces were engaged on the Eastern Front.

The fruits of victory could never have been achieved without the Allied air forces and the singular contribution made by the RAF throughout the Second World War from the very first day. Had the RAF been returned to its origins as arms of the Navy and Army, as had been advised from the end of the First World War, it would have been impossible for such sizeable operationally focused elements as Bomber and Fighter Command to have come into being. Their remit would have been too far outside the primary focus of Admiralty and War Office thinking. There would, in all likelihood, have been far greater resistance towards and lack of enthusiasm for purchasing so many thousands of so many varied but vital aircraft and to invest in the crucial pains taking development. As for the development of the heavy bomber force, the other services were never wholly convinced that this was the right path. Any senior army officer would have preferred to sink the resources expended on Bomber Command into the land offensive. Had this been the case, German concentration on the air defence of its cities would have been a much smaller priority and greater concentration of air support for its own land warfare effort resulted.

The last air raid over Germany, mounted by Bomber Command, was on the evening of 2 May 1945. Aircraft from Nos 8 and 100 Groups participated and at this late stage in the war, fourteen RAF air crew were killed in action. The crews of three Handley Page Halifax III aircraft from No. 199 Squadron based at North Creake were brought down during an attack on the port at Kiel, while a Mosquito from No. 169 Squadron based at Great Massingham, was lost while attacking a German airfield at Jagel.

The fact that German forces were still prepared to put up an effective resistance despite the utter futility of the situation is testimony to their resolve, if nothing else. The remainder of the bombing force returned in the early hours of 3 May. By this stage, however, such raids would have been hard to justify. The Allies had advanced across much of North West Europe and much of Germany's shattered industrial centres were under Allied occupation. The next day, General Admiral Hans-Georg von Freideburg, head of the Kreigsmarine, surrendered German forces in the north of Europe to Field Marshal Bernard Law Montgomery on Lüneburg Heath. On 7 May, Colonel General Alfred Jodl surrendered at the headquarters of General Dwight Eisenhower, with the surrender to come into effect at midnight on 8 May. Field Marshal Wilhelm Keitel, the Chief of the *Wehrmacht* High Command, surrendered to Marshal Zhukov in the East. This came into effect on 9 May, hence Russia has always observed this date as the day of victory. Thus the war in Europe was at an end.

Now the war in Europe was over, the government could begin the rolling-up of its forces in earnest. Even though the war was still being fought in the Far East, where plans were afoot for a large scale invasion of Japan, significant reductions were already under way with demob notices handed out and entire units across the services disbanded. For the RAF, demobilisation had taken place as early as June 1944, but only if units were available to take over the role and function. Wherever possible, those squadrons that had been formed since the start of the war were disbanded. So while all was still to play for on continental Europe and with the bulk of American armour and infantry yet to arrive, the following Air Ministry policy for 'rolling up squadrons' was in the process of being agreed and in some cases acted on, the priority for disbandment being as follows:

1. Squadrons with number plates which have only come into existence during this war.
2. Squadrons with number plates which have been revived and were in existence prior to this war.
3. Squadrons which have been in existence prior to this war. (It should never be necessary, in point of fact, to roll up these squadrons.)

Let the last category roll around your mind for a while!

Of some concern, while the policy was being communicated to commands, was the fact that while those units in the first category were by now the majority, many had distinguished themselves to such a degree that to dispense with them altogether would be a loathsome task. The responsibility in the meantime for deciding where the axe should fall went to DGO (Directorate-General of Organisation). Initially, it was felt that only the overseas commands should be prepared to lose units, but before this could happen it was urged to communicate this message to the home-based units that they may be affected. Also, a further minute defined in greater detail

Battle of Britain At Home Day at Church Fenton on 15 September 1945, scarcely two weeks after the formal end of the Second World War. (*National Archives*)

that no squadron formed during the First World War should be disbanded except in exceptional cases. Those squadrons formed prior to the 1914-1918 war which had enjoyed a continued existence since were not under any circumstances to be disbanded. As spring 1945 loomed, however, various squadrons were selected to stand down. A number of what were termed 'gift squadrons' were also protected from disbandment as far as operations and circumstances allowed, including the reallocation of number plates to less distinguished units. The 'gift squadrons' were those sponsored by colonies, states and provinces of the British Empire such as the Madras Presidency, the Federal Malay States or the Straits Settlements, often carrying an imperial provincial name such as No. 74 (Trinidad) Squadron. This was the famous 'Tigers' squadron of RAF folklore and was on the initial list of forty-five 'gift squadrons' to disband if not already having done so as of 7 June 1945. All would be expected to go by December regardless of arguments supporting the retention of some units. In addition, at least thirty-six squadrons were formed during the First World War, thus falling within the other category that was expected to save them. There were so many squadrons listed for disbandment that when a command proposed squadrons to be 'rolled up', Air Ministry approval had to be sought. Squadrons which had existed before the war and those identified as 'gift squadrons' were typical of those needing approval before being disbandment.

The Pacific War came to an abrupt end for those involved and expecting to take part in the invasion of Japan. The invasion was avoided courtesy of the Manhattan Project and the dropping of 'Little Boy', the first use of an atom bomb in anger. Thus the Second World War became the first and so far only nuclear war in history. The bomber that dropped the atomic bomb was *Enola Gay*, a B-29 Superfortress of the American 12th Air Force, flown by Colonel Paul Tibbets and his crew of ten. They averted a bloody invasion of Japan estimated to have cost over 100,000 Allied lives. The Japanese War Council, otherwise referred to as the 'Big 6' and who were determined to fight on to the bitter end, attempted to negotiate a separate treaty with the Soviets. This was incredible wishful thinking, as the Soviets, hardly allies of the Japanese, had previously agreed to a treaty with the UK and US at the Potsdam Conference. The agreement was to declare war on Japan, and on 8 August, Stalin did so and invaded the state of Manchukuo the following day. On the same day, not having received any signals of acceptance of surrender terms, the US dropped 'Fat Man' – the second atom bomb that possessed a greater yield of destruction, 22.5 tons to the 12.5 tons of 'Little Boy' – on Nagasaki. This combination of seismic events forced the Emperor's hand to accept surrender terms. Even so, this was delayed by diehard officers with a wilfully different take on circumstances, believing the Emperor to have been misadvised by a coterie of traitors within. They planned to storm the Imperial Palace, save the Emperor from cowardly traitors and seize the tape of the Emperor's Surrender Message which was to be broadcast to the nation, but were, thankfully, too late and the attempted coup failed. The Emperor announced to the Japanese people later that same day, 15 August that the war had developed in a direction not necessarily to Japan's advantage, and on 2 September 1945, onboard the USS *Missouri*, the final articles of surrender were signed by the Japanese government delegation before US General Douglas MacArthur.

CHAPTER 3

Post-War and National Service

As described in the previous chapter, long before the end of the war in the Far East, the Chiefs of Staff were outlining their provisional personnel requirements expected in the post-war era. At a meeting held on 7 June 1945, papers were placed before them from their respective government ministries: the Admiralty, War Office and the Air Ministry. Each of the papers was an estimate of the level up to which new personnel might be recruited. The limit was intended to allow the retention of skilled and irreplaceable trained personnel who might be attracted to remain rather than leave the services. The earliest of the papers had been circulated by the Chief of the Air Staff on 8 May 1945 and asked the Chiefs of Staff to record the provisional view that the post-war needs of British security would require an air force of not less than 200,000 regular personnel, whilst the minimum requirements of the Navy and Army were stated in subsequent papers to be 170,000 and 275,000 respectively.

It was pointed out on 7 June by Sir Douglas Evill that the figures for the Admiralty and the War Office had been calculated somewhat differently from the basis adopted by the Air Ministry. It was important that such figures were calculated on the same basis to avoid the risk of an unintended advantage to any one individual service. The request for a common basis of calculation was later deemed unattainable due to uncertain factors, such as insufficient knowledge of the post-war strategic requirements and how the responsibility for meeting these would be apportioned between the three services. The figures being considered at this stage did not include conscription, but to reach a decision on the provisional requirements for personnel, conscription would have to be included to provide a comprehensive review of personnel levels.

The three services had carried out individual studies into peacetime conscription and each came up with different degrees to which they felt they would be reliant on conscripts. Conditions and length of service were where the fundamental differences arose. If, for example, conscript service was to be set at twelve months, the Army could regard about half of its conscripted personnel as effective. For the RAF and the Navy, that effective reliance was to varying degrees less so. The amount of time to train naval personnel in a wide number of roles meant that an average of one-third or less of recruits would be effective for such a duration. All three services, however, were agreed that eighteen months would make a considerable difference. The Ministry of Labour had calculated that about 65,000 men would volunteer for regular service in the armed forces each year. On this basis, the total peacetime military strength of some 645,000 personnel would not be sustained, even with a lengthy minimum term of service, hence the considerations given to peacetime conscription.

The post-war manpower estimates for the Navy were greater than the strength of the service at the outbreak of war in 1939, which then stood at 133,000. It was, of all curiosities, the advances in technology that had brought this about in order to counter the threat of air attack, with the need to increase the complement of ships as well as providing crews to man radar-warning equipment and large numbers of anti-aircraft weapons. Among the points set out by the Navy was the requirement for carrier-borne air forces, which were now considered to be fundamental to sea warfare. Therefore, a large proportion of naval manpower should be devoted to this end. As well as its carrier-borne aircraft, the Navy should maintain airfields for flying training and accommodating disembarked aircraft. The necessity for all these increases including minesweeping, coastal and amphibious forces had been proved during the war. It would also be necessary to maintain training organisations and to provide scope for technical development.

In considering the policy for the post-war active air defence of Great Britain a report from the Chiefs of Staff Committee was issued on 7 July 1945, examining the said requirements for Britain's air defence during the ten years following the defeat of Germany. The report assumed that two years' warning could be reasonably expected of any major conflict in the future, but that a sudden attack at shorter notice could not be ruled out. It was also assumed that the scale of any air attack was unlikely to be less than that levied by Germany during the period of 1940-1941. On the basis of this, plans were already drawn up dividing the country into a defended area and a shadow area.

The defended area was to be manned by a nucleus force that could be expanded to provide a reasonable active defence at short notice. The shadow area would contain an air defence framework, capable of expansion to full operational efficiency within two years. The major conclusions were that it would be essential to organise a non-regular reserve that would be used to bring the nucleus force up to full operational strength. It was further considered that such a force would remain inoperable until such time as the reserve was recruited and trained, so it was an imperative to recruit and train the necessary personnel without delay. Finally, a large proportion of existing air defence equipment was obsolescent and the re-equipment of defences should not be deferred.

The type of aircraft to be employed in air defence would be influenced by several factors, notably the development of new weapons technology and revised methods of attack arising from the previous war. It was expected that any future war would see 'very high performance' bombers employed with large-scale and continuous attacks from V-weapons or ballistic missiles. Among the technologies expected during the early post-war period was that of rocket-propelled fighter aircraft in addition to jet power. At the time, the piston-engine fighter was still the backbone of the RAF's air defence effort. Jet aircraft performance was not that advanced beyond the piston types available to warrant any immediate concern, but it was expected that developments in jet technology would see performance improve dramatically, necessitating large-scale re-equipment in the near future. This would entail readjustment of the air defence organisation in the air and on the ground.

defence organisation in the air and on the ground, as far as possible threats and military alliances were concerned. The decade following the defeat of Germany was expected to see no return of a German air force, and a French air force would be unlikely to pose any kind of threat, even from the point of view of prevailing strength. However, the continuation of and increased threat from a strong Russian air force was most predictable. Of further concern to the Chiefs of Staff Committee was the post-war layout in Europe and how it was seen to develop. The Soviet Union was expected to be in occupation in Germany to a point of eleven degrees longitude east, 660 nautical miles east of the Greenwich meridian. Attacks from airfields in Germany east of this line could realistically be expected, even though Russia had not as yet developed long-range bomber aircraft. Putting all into perspective, this was why an attack no greater than on the scale of those sustained from Germany in 1940-1941 was envisaged.

The most binary-like shift in air defence provision was the obvious realisation that the principal threat to UK airspace in the years ahead would come from the East. In 1945, the RAF early warning radar system, which had played such a critical role during the Battle of Britain and thereafter, was strung out along the south coast and continued up the east coast. By the early 1950s, the south coast radar stations were all but closed down and, increasingly, new early warning radar heads were sited along the east coast up as far as the Shetland Islands. The new heads were, in some cases, sited at different locations to those which had formed a part of the Home Chain during the war. The old concept of the transmit and receive lattice structures was now gone. The new radar systems had the transmitter and receiver combined in the same antenna. A feeder horn fired the signal at the antenna dish and then bounced out to reflect anything in its path. The signal return was immediately collected by the receiver and fed down a wave guide to an amplification unit before being painted onto a plan position screen by means of an extra high voltage/tension-derived beam of electrons, also known as the Time Base. This has been depicted in numerous war films, with the radar operator sitting in front of a rotating pencil of light highlighting blips on the circular screen.

The MRS (Master Radar Stations) were, with the new Type 80 primary search, Control and Reporting radar, eventually able to cover the approaches of the North Atlantic and North Sea. Together with their satellite Control and Reporting posts (subordinate radar stations whose function was largely to provide a continuation of radar cover along the coast), they also provided a fighter control and airspace monitoring service but with less capacity. In addition, the HPRP (High Power Reporting Posts) covered outer extremes of the North Atlantic and worked in conjunction with Danish and Norwegian air force radar stations on the Faroe Islands and at Maakeroy and Reitan in Norway. This was due to the belief that the threat of air attack from the north-east approaches to the country was far more likely than through Central Europe. The new radars had considerable range and were positioned as close to the coast as possible in order to gain the earliest possible warning of an inbound attack. The most distant location of an RAF early warning station was at Saxa Vord; this sits at the most north-easterly tip of the Shetland Islands and is closer to Norway than to the UK mainland.

Meanwhile in 1945, detailed planning for the future was still far from determined. It was already accepted that both light and heavy anti-aircraft guns would be of increasingly little use in the future and it was expected that major equipment replacement programmes would need to take place more than once in the next ten years. By 1947, British defence policy was yet to settle on the peacetime level of the armed forces. The government was to make an announcement later in the year. The strength of the RAF was expected to be 315,000 as of 31 March 1948. In preparing for this, an operational squadron strength of 150 was envisaged as a conservative estimate. Peacetime National Service was about to come into effect in the meantime, and young men were still being called up under the wartime draft that had yet to be replaced. A clear and firm structure about manpower requirements had be agreed upon and no one thought the circumstances presented such little concern that an immediate cessation of abundant recruits could be dispensed with. Nevertheless, there was a disproportionate allocation of personnel in certain trades within the RAF and a lack of experienced personnel was the basis of a manpower level of 315,000. Therefore, the RAF was going to have to reduce its expectation of a front-line force of 150 squadrons to ninety. Even assuming that the government would impose no further cuts on the RAF, it was expected that beyond 1948, the strength of the RAF would progressively fall until January 1950, by which time a forecast manpower level of 250,000 would hopefully be reached.

The proportion of GDP being spent on defence in the period 1952-53 was in the order of 11.1 per cent. This had peaked in 1944-45 at just over 50 per cent and would reduce to 6.6 per cent by 1960. The RAF was hopeful that from 1951 to 1952, the front line would expand again beyond the level of ninety squadrons. In the meantime, any loss of overseas bases or redundancy of overseas units was expected to result in the bolstering of front-line units at home. Until then, the intervening period was regarded as a transitional phase during which the definitive framework of the RAF of the future would be determined. This framework included a planned heavy bomber force of thirty squadrons by 1952 with a unit establishment (UE) of eight aircraft and two squadrons deployed in the Middle East. This would increase the total 1948 bomber force by the equivalent of eight squadrons. The plan to source the manpower for this additional operational strength would be found by dismantling much of what remained of the RAF in India and Japan. This amounted to seventy fighter aircraft in five squadrons and a further eight transport squadrons, one of which would come from the Far East Command. The transport units would join the UK-based RAF. The plan was just that, to transfer the redundant personnel of this restructuring to Bomber Command. If this practice proved insufficient, the next move would be to disband some or all of the eight transport squadrons, again transferring them to the bomber force. The proposed future fighter squadron size was to be a unit establishment (UE) of sixteen aircraft. The rank of the squadron commander would remain at the appropriately titled rank of squadron leader. The typical corresponding squadron strength at the height of the war was sixteen and twenty-four.

A wider-ranging raft of proposals for changing the structure of the RAF was put to Prime Minister Clement Attlee on 10 June. As a result of experiences from the Second World War and trials carried out since, a change to the organisation of operational stations and squadrons was put forward for consideration. The experiences in question primarily concerned the increased complexity of operations within the service and the gradual increase in the day-to-day responsibilities of station commanders. To be more specific, the typical station commanding officer having responsibility for signals, armament, personnel issues and general works service provision, in addition to flying, meant a redistribution of duties was required. These duties would be farmed out to officers filling existing posts without creating new ones. Further, each RAF station would be organised into three wings: Flying Wing (Squadron Operations, Air Traffic Control, Signals and Station Defence & Security); Technical Wing (all maintenance of aircraft and supporting equipment); and Administration Wing (all other support functions including catering, supply, motor transport and personnel management). Obviously, some of the responsibilities in the latter two crossed over into operations management depending on circumstances. Likewise, a number of squadron functions went the other way. So essentially the station became the air base with squadrons consisting of aircraft and their air crews and maintenance engineers directly assigned. The reduction in squadron size was something the Air Council was keen to put across to the Prime Minister when considering the number of squadrons and future structure of the RAF.

The immediate period following the end of the war brought little change in many aspects of how Britain functioned. Rationing was still in force due to the poor state of food production. A housing shortage demanded immediate attention and was being addressed with the mass-production of prefabricated homes. The country was on the verge of bankruptcy and owed a vast fortune to the US, and young men were still being called up in large numbers under wartime draft requirements. This was necessary in order to provide replacements for those wartime service personnel based around the Far and Middle East and across the European continent.

Another issue was the withdrawal over the next three decades from Britain's remaining imperial responsibilities. From India through to Singapore, British forces would be required to garrison a roll-call of emerging independent countries stretching from Africa to Hong Kong. This last outpost was not handed over to China until 1997. In the meantime, while there was a continued rundown of the various post-imperial dependencies and a subsequent rundown of military units, there was a necessity for a continued supply and rotation of military personnel to maintain essential security and defence obligations.

Often a benign handover was the order of the day, but many locations for a number of reasons presented various difficulties from general maintenance of law and order to guerrilla warfare or terrorism as we call it now. This and the emerging threat from the Soviet Union ensured that while the armed forces were to be significantly reduced from their wartime standing, the need for a larger than otherwise necessary force never dissipated. Therefore, conscription would have to continue, but under new legislation with changes to specific requirements. The Ministry of Labour and National Service was responsible for managing what would be the first ever peacetime national call-up. Given that throughout the period that post-war National Service was in force not a single year would pass when British forces were not engaged in shooting and being shot at in any number of overseas hotspots, the term 'peacetime' was rather inappropriate. That said, there was no war and the British people did not feel threatened by a Russian invasion as they had done previously with Nazi Germany. Russia was far away and we were not at war with them, but over the years ahead the proliferation of nuclear weapons on either side of what Churchill named the Iron Curtain was going to face humanity with an uncertainty future. Public acceptance of this seemingly endless knife-edge peace was going to be mixed to say the least.

On 1 January 1947, a new bill received its first reading in Parliament. Originally announced by Clement Attlee in 1946, it was intended to build up a large, well-trained reserve that would be ready for operational use in an emergency without the need for a lengthy period of further training. This was the bill to introduce, for the first time in Britain, peacetime National Service. The bill was not properly introduced for a further two years, but those conscripted from this point forward, while still called up under the original wartime draft, were largely considered peacetime conscripts. A seamless continuity of the call for military service was maintained, but officially now to meet the peacetime requirements for maintaining the standing Army, Navy and RAF as well as various overseas commitments. Anyone called up prior to the implementation of the National Service Act 1947 was still subject to the wartime call-up regulations. In other words, length of service was officially indeterminable. But a minimum of two years could be envisaged, while some had in excess of three years to look forward to before the new act was properly functioning. Those called up were divided into four medical grades. Those who fell into Grades 3 and 4 were not required by the armed forces. This was the case until May 1951, shortly after the start of the Korean War.

A manpower shortage had developed and a way to alleviate this problem was by accepting those who fell into the latter two medical grades. The Army and the RAF were to accept certain men in Grade 3. By May 1956, the Royal Navy was accepting those with Russian language skills, and the RAF was required to accept only those needed to fill technical or specialist positions. The RAF was taking 2,000 Grade 3 recruits a year, while the RAF Regiment was not taking any. The Army, which was obliged to accept the RAF's rejects and Grade 3 recruits assigned to it in the first instance, took about 76 per cent of all recruits as an overall share of National Servicemen, it being the most manpower-intensive of the three services. The RAF took 21 per cent and the remainder went to the Navy. During the Korea emergency, the Army was obliged to take Grade 3 recruits, it simply wasn't possible to fill its quota with fitter men of similar intelligence. By 1955, with the demands of the Korean conflict no longer a concern, the Army was happy to dispense with all Grade 3 recruits.

Ironically, National Service was least popular among MPs of the Labour Party who happened to be in government when the bill for peacetime National Service received its first and second readings in Parliament. The country had no other way of maintaining its post-war obligations and with a large vote in favour, the length of National Service was limited to a mere twelve months. Even in an era comparatively far less reliant on erudite technical thinking than today, this left at least two of the services in a difficult situation. The training of RAF National Service personnel did not provide much scope. With only a year's service from the first day of basic training through to the last day of demobilisation, such recruits, without existing applicable skills, were limited to less demanding service trades.

The result of this was that while the RAF was obliged to take by far the second largest number of conscripts, it could only assign them to those ground-based trades that followed a short training programme beforehand. As a general rule of thumb, the closer one gets to the core of RAF operations, the greater the demand for recognised skills from those involved, both in the air and on the ground. Ultimately, this ends up with the pilot. Therefore, a large number of RAF conscripts were allocated to various duties which rendered them productive in the shortest time frame. Those who were not fussy and had no readymade skills that could be exploited, developed or sharpened expeditiously, could find themselves serving as an officer's batman or

A 1954 Air Traffic Control room scene. This is one of the early Second World War era control towers, which at the time rapidly were being replaced with the more familiar all around glass Visual Control designs. Note the Very pistols and cartridges stored at the far end of the room, available for immediate use. (*The National Archives*)

working under the direct orders of the station warrant officer, nicknamed the 'SWO's Commandos'. On the other hand, many with the requisite aptitude could just as well find themselves training in a more relevant field that required more specialist skills.

Before the National Service Act came into force on 1 January 1949, the tariff of twelve months' service had been sensibly raised to eighteen months. In 1950, it was set at two years in response to the services' growing commitments abroad. The allocation of conscripts to a broader range of ground trades was therefore made possible as well as the opportunity to post trained National Servicemen further afield, more specifically to the Middle and Far East. Anyone who has studied the history of Britain's only peacetime era of National Service will be aware that conscripts were not all recruited into the ranks of the enlisted, not even by the Army, who like the RAF put time and effort into selecting those with ability, aptitude and qualifications for a short-service commission.

In the earlier stages, particularly with regard to the Army, after having been forced to take officer candidates during the previous two World Wars from a variety of backgrounds, the services had reverted to type. National Service officer candidates stood a much better chance of being considered if a public school background was listed as part of their profile. The RAF had from its earliest days found difficulty in maintaining such a selection process. The Army, to be fair, had found itself reflecting society in its recruiting requirements. At the start of the twentieth century, British society was very much polarised along class lines. This division was deeply ingrained in an army that needed leaders and cannon fodder. Therefore, the officer corps recruited, more or less, exclusively from public schools and universities. The rank and file found its manpower among the nation's factories, coal mines, tin mines and the household staff of the landed gentry. The idea of an erudite knowledge and rare technical grasp of newfangled things such as aeroplanes was never an issue. Men led and were led according to background. The First World War had shaken the status quo initially due to the heavy losses within the officer corps. This led to officers being recruited into the Army from middle-class backgrounds. Sons of tailors and doctors began to appear with pips on sleeves and shoulders. The situation reversed after the war, but alas, the die was cast and the long-term future would be different.

The Second World War and the demands for technical expertise and talent, particularly in the RAF and the Navy, altered the profile of the typical British military officer for good. However, the Army – having been affected by the changing nature of war – looked back at the early post-war period for traditional sources for its future leadership. Therefore, National Service recruits with public school backgrounds were ushered in its direction. However, originating from a good home and being educated at a good school as a pre-requisite for a commission was increasingly less significant. In the 1950s, a shifting society and new demands of modern warfare required an aptitude that did not necessarily come from the playing fields of Eton. The Army, with the need for more engineers, bomb disposal officers and demolition experts, relied more on professionalism and less on aristocracy. The popular perception of the British officer class would appear to be indelible in the public conscience and perception, but it was the RAF and the Navy who set the least store by whether or not a man's family were listed in *Debrett's* and were more concerned about the qualifications he had left school with. Otherwise, the RAF had the fewest prerequisite demands of potential officers but perhaps the most difficult mental agility requirements, particularly regarding air crew.

From the foundation of the Royal Flying Corps, military flying has carried a well-deserved mystique. As with joining the Special Forces, flying a modern sophisticated high-performance jet fighter and strike aircraft demand the most exacting standards of physical fitness, dexterity, synapse reflexes, academia, clarity of thought and single-minded commitment. For this reason, those National Service recruits who were regarded early on as potential officer material, or indeed potential air crew material, faced a most unforgiving selection process. Air crew candidates went to the then Aviation Candidate Selection Board at the former fighter station at Hornchurch, Essex. All air crew candidates had to sign on for at least three years' service to allow sufficient time for training and a short productive period of operational flying should all go well. None other than Lord Tebbit followed this very path when called up, becoming an operational fighter pilot before embarking on a commercial flying career. Ideally, those air crew applicants with appropriate qualifications were offered an eight-year fixed regular service engagement followed by four years in the reserve in the first instance. Those accepted as pilots or navigators could also be offered a four-year fixed engagement followed by a further four in reserve if they would not accept the longer one. There was a further ruling that pilots and navigators in training had to be unmarried unless 'exceptionally qualified'.

The required education standard for pilots *circa* 1953 was a General Certificate of Education O Level pass in English and two other subjects. Otherwise, the candidates were to produce a written statement from their headmaster that they had attained the educational standard required. In such a case, the candidate's general education must have included a study of elementary algebra, geometry and science. Where a candidate was unable to produce any such certificate or statement from their headmaster but was in other respects suitable, he could be sent to the air crew selection centre with letters explaining the absence of educational qualifications and confirming educational attainment included in the candidates papers. Not that the education hurdle had been successfully negotiated at this point. Before being sent to Hornchurch, the candidate would receive the Matrix 1938 test and would take what was described as the Science IV graded interview. A score of forty-three in each was required. Applications for air crew began with an interview form that contained six points for initial assessment with three gradings against each question and the automatic points score according to the assessing officer's take on the candidate:

1. What is his educational history?
   (a) No formal education after 15. (0)
   (b) Claims School Certificate or equivalent. (8)
   (c) Some formal education after 15 but did not obtain School Certificate. (5)

2. Does he strike you as a go-ahead?
   (a) Little sign of ambition; seems to take life very easily. (0)
   (b) Moderately enterprising. (3)
   (c) Seems to have made himself opportunities and profited by them. (8)

3. Does he get the sense of spoken questions quickly?
    (a) Yes. (5)
    (b) Neither quick nor slow. (1)
    (c) Definitely slow. (0)

4. Are his spoken answers clear and to the point?
    (a) Decidedly clear. (5)
    (b) Fairly, but not outstanding aptitude. (2)
    (c) Muddled and woolly. (0)

5. Do his motives for volunteering strike you as sound ones?
    (a) Displays outstanding enthusiasm for air crew duties. (16)
    (b) Seems genuinely keen on flying. (8)
    (c) Suspect strong secondary motives, such as prestige and glamour. (3)
    (d) Suspect strong desire to avoid other kinds of service. (0)

6. Did his bearing and personality impress you favourably?
    (a) No. (0)
    (b) Yes. (8)
    (c) Mixed (favourable and unfavourable elements). (4)

There were many who regarded service in the RAF or Navy preferable to service in the Army, and it was clear that the services were not too keen on National Servicemen. One senior army officer, Major-General E. H. W. Cobb, having read reports from interviewing officers at the Ministry of Labour centres at Acton and Birmingham (which recorded 10 to 22 per cent of the men interviewed for the Army had been rejected by the RAF), wrote: 'Are you really convinced that the RAF can't find sufficient low-grade men to sweep out hangars, etc, from amongst those who have expressed a preference for the RAF? Is there no possibility of the problem being solved by RAF interviewing officers being briefed to accept a quota of low-grade men from amongst their applicants?' Cobb wanted it made clear to those called up that failure to make a preference would mean automatic selection for the Army, as was the case. However, they would then be given the opportunity to make a final decision after being given a clearer insight into which way the land lay. Another problem was the number of young men rejected by the RAF being disgruntled and prejudiced towards service in the Army that had to accept them.

There was certainly a hefty number of recruits turning up at the main gates of the various recruit training camps each week. To put matters in perspective, compared to today the RAF alone had five recruit training centres: Padgate, West Kirby, Wilmslow, Bridgnorth and Hednesford. Typically, basic training lasted eight weeks. There is a

Canberra of 21 Squadron at Khormaksar in 1955; the soldiers on horseback are Aden levies under the command of the RAF regiment. (*C1764, IWM*)

single such location today that trains male and female candidates. One can imagine the level of basic training of new recruits managed by the much larger Army. As the 1950s wore on, National Service air crew, particularly pilots, became less likely, owing to the complexity of the new generation of front-line aircraft. By 1953, the next generation of front-line types were starting to arrive in the form of the Supermarine Swift, Hawker Hunter and English Electric Canberra. The first of the V-bombers would begin to arrive, aircraft that required an operational crew of five, each man a higher than average-rated airman whether pilot, navigator or air electronics officer. There were misgivings about the aptitude of air crew to cope with the demands of the new aircraft that would soon equip Bomber Command in particular. For example, the demands of an air electronics operator/officer (AEO) would represent quite a jump from that of an air signaller or WOP/AG (wireless operator/air gunner) who were the most likely antecedents of this new air crew category. Many such NCOs and officers had seen operational service during the war and it was hoped they would transition naturally to provide the initial cadre for the new AEO requirement.

Churning out the required level of manpower remained a headache even though the immediate period following the cessation of hostilities in Korea meant that the period of re-expansion was now in reverse. In 1955, the manpower projection for 1

April 1956 was expected to be 783,000 for all forces, of whom 287,000 would be National Servicemen: 200,000 of whom would be in the Army, 77,000 in the RAF and 10,000 in the Navy. The RAF, like the Army, was increasingly dependent on National Servicemen. Its radio fitters, for example, consisted of 25 per cent conscripts, whereas half the strength of the Army were National Servicemen. Prior to the Suez crisis, the government was looking to reduce the number of personnel from the projected 1956 figure to 700,000 by 1 April 1958. In order to achieve this, it was proposed that the length of National Service should be reduced to eighteen months from 1 January 1956. Even with 25-30 per cent of conscripts signing on to become regulars, the shortened length of service was expected to have a serious impact on the size and number of military units. The RAF did not expect to be too seriously affected in terms of numbers, but it would be hit rather drastically in the more skilled areas. Furthermore, the number of personnel in training would increase in relation to those trained with six months taken off the length of service. The original National Service Act also had a time limit that was supposed to have expired on 1 January 1954. It was believed that opponents of the Act would table an amendment if it were left open-ended. For the bulk of National Servicemen, service life was typically two years in duration, most of which was spent at the posting they received following trade training and a possible tour overseas. Bases from Malaya to the Dutch-West German border consumed much of Britain's military manpower and assets up until well into the 1960s.

From the signing of articles of surrender aboard the USS *Missouri* in September 1945 through to 1967, not a year passed without UK forces being engaged in some form of aggressive military action. 1968 remains the one unique year when British military personnel were not engaged in combat. The milestone was short-lived as Northern Ireland descended into civil disorder in 1969 and some 30,000 British Army personnel were deployed by the Wilson government to protect the Catholic minority from the excesses of a largely Protestant-run component part of the UK. Following this would come the all too familiar peripheral wars brought about through internal uprising and religious intolerance in the Balkans and the Middle East.

The National Serviceman's post-war tour began with Palestine followed by Korea, Malaya, Cyprus, Borneo and Aden, all of which brewed into emergency situations at various times, not to mention messy withdrawals from various African dependencies. On top of all these pressing problems, the British government from the outset, and under the Labour administration of Clement Attlee, sought to ensure that Britain retained its position in the world by developing its own atomic bomb. Meanwhile, the hard-pressed economy had to support an expanding force following the early decline of the wartime strength.

The bankrupt state of Britain's economy took a long time to reverse. Long after the Korean conflict, the lot of the National Serviceman remained austere due to the expansion of the military and the residual demand on resources. Enlisted airmen

HM Queen Elizabeth inspects the Guard of Honour before departing RAF Leuchars, 4 June 1957. Many on parade here would be national servicemen. (*The National Archives*)

could expect to put up with their fair share of screaming and shouting from basic training instructors. The RAF had from the Second World War through into National Service one particularly notorious location: Padgate. It was typical of airmen during the war once basic training was complete to ask if they had been posted to Padgate. If they had been, it often spurred interest to ask if it deserved its bad reputation. It is unfortunate that National Service seems to have been coloured by this. The lasting image of this era of British military history in particular is one of polishing boots, brasses, scrubbing urinals with steel wool, and waxing linoleum floors with broom-handled floor bumpers. Fizzers, a term used to describe the summary offence charge under the RAF Form 252, were often issued for the most innocuous offence: uniform and kit failing to meet inspection standards, hair length unacceptable, and so on. Typical awards from the officer hearing the case could mean several days of 'jankers', a common term for extra duties taking up the bulk of an offender's free time and often entailing various menial but laborious tasks.

Often put across humorously in the popular media, this process was not a game. A charge was a recordable offence that could follow someone into civilian life. For example, a string of offences could adversely appear on discharge papers if an individual was incapable of maintaining the minimum acceptable standards of uniform presentation or enough self-discipline to keep out of trouble. While many military offences were not taken too seriously by employers in the National Service era and many have no equivalent in civilian life, they can and do follow service personnel into civilian life. More recently, former servicemen/women looking to follow a career in certain fields, perhaps joining the police, can find it difficult if summary convictions under military law to declare.

'Bull' is short for bullshit, and is an accepted form of reference in British service life when speaking of some of the pettier regulations enforced such as polishing boots, putting creases in tunics, polishing floors and brasses, marching and saluting. All have always been a part of military life, most specifically for the enlisted man and everyone going through training. The image of 'Bull' is one that has typified Britain's military establishment, or more specifically the junior ranks, far too disproportionately and seems to have been especially characteristic of the National Service era, so much so that the RAF, more than any of the services, has for good reason tried to scrub itself spotless of this reputation over the years since. This era, in particular, has branded this impression into the public psyche far more indelibly than earlier austere periods. Speaking as someone who joined the 'force for good' in 1977, I would claim that it had not progressed too far at all. Today's RAF, certainly on the face of it, appears to have engineered a radically changed image for public consumption. However much this is the case, life in today's armed forces and the RAF in particular, remains the subject of future books.

As Britain pulled out of India, Palestine, Malaya, Kenya and Borneo, and faced conflict in Cyprus and Korea, the country had less of a need for its mass forces. Together with Britain's independent nuclear deterrent and a reliance on what was described as the 'trip-wire strategy', large numbers of tanks, tactical aircraft and capital ships were replaced by the strategic bomber, submarine and land-launched missiles. The trip-wire strategy referred to NATO plans to respond to armed aggression by the Soviet Union with overwhelming firepower, to wit an immediate response with nuclear weapons. Before the last National Serviceman had completed his term of engagement, the world came scintillatingly close to doing just that. The Cuban missile crisis of October 1962, which brought the world perilously close to Armageddon, had not surprisingly prompted the government to reconsider the length of National Service for the last remaining conscript personnel who were looking forward to being demobbed that December. Their service was extended on the 'just in case' rule for a further six months, meaning that the last British peacetime conscript handed his uniform back to stores in June 1963.

A popular dinner-party and pub debate, that National Service should be reintroduced as a cure for society's ills, has done the rounds for more than forty years. The argument for National Service is that it would help combat high unemployment among young people and entail ex-servicemen instilling discipline into difficult adolescents. This very much bears the lasting public perception of the rationale behind the National Service Act – that it was an extension of youth custody and correction. The idea of young men being ordered about, trained to march and make their beds seems to have obscured the original aim of taking large numbers of young men from across the country and putting them in uniform in the first place.

CHAPTER 4

Cold War Rising

With the end of the Second World War came the resumption of enmity between East and West. The USSR and the US had emerged as the two major powers, replacing Britain's imperial reach that was now rapidly contracting. Britain then, however, was unwilling to let past glories go easily and despite the parlous state of the country's finances and the growing demand for independence throughout the Empire, His and latterly Her Britannic Majesty's government was determined to play as great a role as possible. The difference between then and now is that then, whatever the state of the nation's finances, Britain still fielded the kind of military might which, although overshadowed by the two new principal superpowers, was prominent enough. Furthermore, the new polarisation of the democratic and capitalist West and the totalitarian and communist East, with nuclear weapons technology thrown into the mix, on both sides, ensured a focus on military preparedness which admittedly would not have been quite so prominent among most of the Western Allied countries otherwise .Because of the concerns felt in both camps about the designs of one side towards the other, for the next four decades, the northern hemisphere would sit on a nuclear knife-edge, something quite unprecedented, and with only one imagined outcome that would break the stalemate.

This new situation, very much like that of the Second World War, placed the RAF in pole position militarily, particularly with regard to home defence. The war had brought about the Home Chain of radar stations together with similarly placed fighter stations which covered the country quite comprehensively, but with the emphasis on the south east and south coast. Now with improved technology the focus on the air defence apparatus would be more clearly defined and in order to prepare for the likely direction of the new airborne threat, this new emphasis was moved away from the south entirely, perhaps not wholly advisedly, to run along the east coast from East Anglia north to Aberdeenshire, with pre-warning radar stations sited in the Outer Hebrides and the Shetland Islands.

Air defence fighter stations were likewise closed down further south and some bases previously assigned to Coastal and Bomber Commands were reassigned to

Before the Sandys review, a good many operational RAF stations still included old wooden huts. This is the Station Headquarters at Acklington in about 1954. (*The National Archives*)

Fighter Command. Wattisham, Binbrook, Leeming, Leconfield and Leuchars have all since become synonymous with the latter. Subsequent Defence Reviews saw to it that those which were in vital locations during the previous war were now, in this regard, surplus to requirements. Middle Wallop, North Weald, Biggin Hill, Tangmere and Hornchurch were all prominent during the Battle of Britain but, by the end of the 1950s, were either handed over to other commands or vacated altogether.

The new stations typically had the ready advantage of extra hangar space and, like those Bomber Command airfields selected to accommodate the V-force, were to receive significant improvements by way of runway extensions. The typical 'expansion period' airfield of the 1930s and 40s had two or three runways of equal length laid out in such a way as to avoid as many crosswinds as possible. The post-war operational airfield layout meant in almost every case the selection of an existing runway to be extended, inevitably into additionally acquired land. No further military airfields have ever been built from scratch in the UK since 1945, but many existing ones have been increased in size to accommodate near double runway extensions, often with new intersections and dispersals to take the forthcoming generations of heavy, powerful jet aircraft.

Aerial shot of Biggin Hill in 1966 revealing the Cold War era runway extension to the north-east. By 1958, like most airfields upgraded to take higher performance fighters, Biggin's runway was surplus to fighter command requirements. (*The National Archives*)

In all, preparations were being made to fight the next World War, or at least make it an unthinkable venture for the Soviet Union, increasingly seen throughout the late 1940s as hostile to the West. War between the Soviet Union and the UK was a distinct possibility prior to 22 June 1941, when the USSR was already deeply mistrusted for all the same reasons that it was after 1945. In the early stages of the Second World War, the Soviet alliance with Nazi Germany must have made bleak reading for Churchill and his war cabinet. It is impossible to overstate the importance of the eventual German attack on Russia, and the enormous relief it had brought in London at a time when there was quite some chance of Britain standing alone against the two countries. This supreme act of folly secured victory for Britain and the West.

In the summer of 1945, while the process of setting up military governorships was taking shape, divisions were beginning to appear. The US, perhaps in the interest of maintaining good relations and of course balancing the zones of occupation, obligingly withdrew from certain parts of Germany and allowed the Russians to take their place. This was a most ominous development for the local inhabitants but doubtless they

did not attract too much sympathy at a time when war crimes trials of the former
Nazi government were being prepared on some quite staggeringly shocking evidence
of systematic inhumanity. Furthermore, Eastern European countries, notably Poland
and Czechoslovakia, were inescapably consigned to spend the next forty-five years
behind the Iron Curtain with unrelenting austerity their reward for the exemplary
contribution made by their people while serving with HM Forces through the
war. Meanwhile, well-meaning but little-knowing Western liberals argued the case
for the Soviet Empire, accusing their own governments of being the merchants of
authoritarianism and challenging them to provide proof of the communist regimes'
inequities. It was while tolerating this delusional and potentially dangerously
influential agenda, that NATO was properly organised and made ready for the
eventuality of a Soviet-led military intervention in Central Europe. Those Poles and
Czechs who unwisely returned home after serving in their home country's Free Forces
in Britain were, in many cases, arrested and imprisoned by the communist authorities,
paranoid about the ex-servicemen's political leanings and subsequent influence. This
then was the principal concern of the West's defence and security planners over the
bulk of the second half of the twentieth century and, needless to say, the RAF would
be a prominent piece on the chessboard of the Cold War game.

In 1949, the Minister of Defence and the three Secretaries of State who held the
separate defence portfolios at the time, the First Lord of the Admiralty, the War
Secretary and the Air Secretary, had received a report from an ad hoc committee
under the chairmanship of Sir Henry Tizard. This report recommended the minimum
air defence forces considered necessary by 1957, to guard against the level of attack
envisaged on the UK. The report, however, did not take into consideration 'weapons
of mass destruction'. And this was the very expression used. The Secretary of State
for Air reminded all that under earlier proposals for the size and shape of the armed
forces in the period 1950 to 1953, the RAF, which of course would have had the
responsibility of meeting the demands for the already foreseen increased air threat in
the future, would be no more than a 'shop window' force and would not be backed
by adequate reserves of either aircraft or air crew. The Secretary of State for War,
who would logically be expected to fight the corner for the land force requirements,
surprisingly agreed that fighter and anti-aircraft forces were the priority for
resources, which gives an indication of how serious the matter of the defence of UK
airspace was becoming once again. Plans to increase the size of the RAF from 1951
were already in hand, but were now due a further increase and against the backdrop
of Britain being still far away from the much needed post-war economic revival. The
arrival of the Cold War, the conflict in Korea, the development of the Soviet bomb,
the need to stand ready against the growing Warsaw Pact forces, and the remaining
demands of Empire all ensured that the RAF, like the other two services, needed to
expand yet again.

Even by 1954 when this photograph was taken, the Gloster Meteor was still in widespread service, however, it was increasingly deployed in various support roles, such as target tugs, like these examples here at Acklington. (*The National Archives*)

The strength of aircraft originally planned for December 1952 stood at 1,775. This was to be increased to a standing strength of 2,539 and related to all front-line and operational support squadrons. The biggest single increase would be in the number of Meteor day fighters, set to be increased from 520 to 718. There was to be a total of 400 North American F-86 Sabres, a stopgap to bridge the arrival of the next generation of British fighters, the Supermarine Swift and Hawker Hunter, with 264 of these making up the figure of 2,539. The RAF of this period was nothing if not unsettled, new aircraft quite often bringing as radical a step forward in design and performance as that experienced when the leap was made from biplanes with open cockpits to Perspex sliding canopies, mono-wings and retractable undercarriages. Ten different types of fighters and bombers were in service along with five maritime patrol and three transport types. The latter were proportionately very few in number alongside the front-line command assets. The new expansion plan made provision for older obsolete aircraft to remain in service with a large number of squadrons, which were to be regarded as directly operational but as second-line units. This was thought prudent as all incoming new aircraft would go straight to front-line units with nothing left as a reserve. This then meant a figure of 30 to 40 per cent of obsolescent types remaining in squadron service. The day-to-day task of these would be to train additional air crew in order to have a ready reserve available on

Gloster Meteors of 74 Squadron still operated as Front-line Interceptors in 1956. (*Air Historical Branch*)

mobilisation. Some twenty years later, the RAF did something similar on a smaller scale when it regenerated two squadrons of Hunters not long after that aircraft's withdrawal from operational service, all in order to maintain a pool of ground attack/strike fighter pilots which would provide a substantial flow of the same to the then newly forming Jaguar squadrons. In due course a reserve of new aircraft would build up, these aircraft could transfer forward and the second-line squadrons would become front-line as well. The accelerated production of new aircraft necessitated the proposed opening of three more production plants (in addition to four new ones already planned) to build the new Roll-Royce Avon and Ghost jet engines.

Among the Chiefs of Staff's other recommendations were the development of Centimetric Early Warning and Control and Reporting equipment (radar) as essential. Also of overriding importance was the urgent need to improve the UK radar chain, and resources were to be diverted from civilian use for this. The development of radio systems, latterly referred to as electronic countermeasures (ECM), to resist radio and radar signal interference was another priority. This all represented a significant step beyond the tin foil chaff of the Second World War and jamming as it was then called. Despite these recommendations, it was still imagined that Mk III and IV Meteor fighters would be relied upon in 1957.

A further concern was low-level attack, which had been used most skilfully

Biggin Hill's Meteors flypast for Spitfire and Hurricane investiture ceremony in 1954. Although it wasn't yet decided, the base's operational days were numbered. (*Air Historical Branch*)

during the previous war by the RAF in its determination to find more effective and less costly ways of hitting enemy targets hard, and with the all-important element of surprise. Now the fear was that this form of air attack was something to guard against. Indeed, Sir Henry Tizard's report on this was thought to underestimate the threat. While anti-aircraft guns were seen as adequate at the time, guided weapons were considered the most cost-effective and promising guard against the threat of air-launched atomic weapons. Sir Henry's report suggested that an increase in conventional weapons would not be an effective defence against the atomic bomb, guided weapons not being classed as conventional at the time. An air defence fighter force of 1,150 aircraft was recommended as opposed to a figure half this which had previously been envisaged. This was viewed with scepticism by the Chiefs of Staff, as this kind of number would have to be partly found by other Allied air forces. Among the guided weapons under way in 1949 were two air-to-air missile designs: a pursuit-course missile (Blue Sky) promised by 1954, and cancelled shortly after the due date, and a collision-course missile (Red Hawk) which it was hoped would be ready for 1957, but was handed over in 1953 from Folland to Vickers by the Ministry of Supply due to difficulties in resolving problems with the guidance system. It too was ultimately abandoned. Following Red Hawk came a retread known as Red Dean, which was cancelled as well on account of the abandonment of the supersonic version of the Gloster Javelin fighter project in 1956.

The size of the fighter force of 1957 was now expected to be seventy-five squadrons, of as yet undetermined types. There were plenty of promising prototypes in the pipeline, but the mix was not quite certain beyond the new types currently being delivered, with a unit establishment of sixteen aircraft each. The cost for this was thrown into confusion when it only latterly came to the attention of the Chiefs of Staff that the Parliamentary Defence Committee were equating the cost of a fighter squadron to that of an MAA (Medium Anti-Aircraft) regiment, and that the cost of the future Control and Reporting radar system was to be included in the cost of the fighter force. A further critique of the chiefs' report by Sir Henry Tizard was the suggestion that an increase in conventional forces, beyond that in his report, would not render any greater defence against the use of nuclear weapons. Even so, mass is all, and as was also pointed out on the Chiefs of Staff's Committee, a force of 100 squadrons would shoot down significantly more enemy aircraft than seventy-five squadrons. So much store was placed by such an expanded air defence fighter, missile and radar force in 1953, following the end of the Korean conflict. The need to find the means of funding this super sky shield and the debacle over Suez culminated in a report by Duncan Sandys, the Dr Liam Fox of his day, which would prove a turning point for the RAF and Britain's position as a world class aerospace manufacturer. The role of Fighter Command by the mid-1950s had become primarily that of Defence of the Deterrent. Determining the exact number of fighter aircraft required in the future was impossible as it was difficult to pin down the actual effectiveness of fighter aircraft against an attack of any kind, the aim being to convince the Kremlin that the UK had a deep enough capability as to make an assault a costly and pointless adventure. By 1956-57, the air defence fighter force in the UK had been built up to a strength of thirty-six squadrons comprising 560 aircraft. By the middle of 1958, the number had been reduced to thirty-four squadrons (not as a result of the Sandys Defence Review) comprising 480 aircraft made up of 192 Hunter F6s and 288 of the brand-new, purpose-built, all-weather fighter, the Gloster Javelin.

The Air Defence Committee, as of July 1956, envisaged that no further reductions below this number should take place until truly all-weather supersonic fighters with collision-course missiles were fully operational. At the time this meant buying American fighters, seemingly little faith being placed in any of the British projects at the time, including the English Electric P.1 programme. Indeed, while the P.1 and another project, P.177, were expected to enter service from 1959 (P.1) and 1961 (P.177), the Air Defence Committee regarded this as some kind of second best to getting an American fighter type, which seemed unlikely. In the period immediately before the infamous Sandys White Paper, there appears already to have been a feeling

56 Squadron Hunters – four in a loop. (*C2756, IWM*)

The proliferation of Hunter aerobatics teams in the 1950s was not restricted to fighter command squadrons. Here, Germany-based 93 Squadron Hunters reach the top of a loop with additional aircraft from their neighbours 118 Squadron. (*C2383, IWM*)

HM Queen Elizabeth II on a visit to RAF Leuchars in June 1957. In the background is a newly delivered Gloster Javelin, the irony here being that the infamous 'Sandys White Paper' was published this year. (*The National Archives*)

that a significant shift in government policy lay just around the corner. The scrapping of the English Electric P.1 (Lightning) was seen as a distinct possibility, in which case the Hunter F6 fighters would have to soldier on. Had it come to this, Fighter Command would have been left well and truly on the quayside as far as having a comparable interceptor fighter was concerned. Much smaller NATO air forces in Europe were looking forward to receiving the first Mach 2-capable interceptors from the US with which to replace their own Hunters and F-86s.

The best bet with regard to the UK's own unique geographical circumstances lay with the purchase of some 400 Javelins which were on order. Of these, 177 were being financed by US aid. This all formed part of the Plan K air defence structure. One cost-cutting measure was to reduce the overall number of Javelins by not deploying a planned 48 aircraft with 2nd Tactical Air Force (TAF) and instead assigning them to Fighter Command, but this was expected to meet with problems with NATO and the Americans.

The Javelin evolved through many updates along the way from its entry into service. Between 1956 and 1958, the RAF took delivery of seven different marks. It seemed to some that they were being used as a test and development facility for

Heralding its arrival at Leuchars, a formation of sixteen Javelins, drawn from Nos 141 and 41 squadrons, fly past on the occasion of the Queen's visit to the station in 1957. (*The National Archives*)

this one aircraft which still had a couple more variants to go before the end of the decade. Not only was there no definitive mark of Javelin but the aircraft had proved to be troublesome in development, with one test pilot killed after he entered a deep stall and another having to abandon the aircraft during a spin. The most famous test pilot associated with the Javelin, Bill Waterton, nearly died bringing one prototype into land after the tail section detached itself from the fin. One of the reasons why so many unnecessary versions of this aircraft were built in small handfuls was due to Ministry of Supply pressure to get it into service.

The result was a farrago of aircraft still under development going to production run. By 1960, one trainer and all eight operational variants were in service with seventeen squadrons at home and overseas. Gloster stood accused of not making corrections recommended by Bill Waterton and others. Waterton was gaining an undeserved reputation as a troublemaker, but that the Javelin was a tricky aircraft to fly was beyond question. By the time Gloster accepted that there were problems, in particular with the fin-mounted tail, they had been put on notice by the government to get a production version in service. Hence the fiasco of the many different marks.

Original in-service marks were distinct according to whether they had the British or American airborne intercept radar fitted. The Mk 1 had the British AI.17 radar, the American Westinghouse AN/APQ-43 radar type was fitted only to the Mk 2, 6 and 8. The next phase saw the introduction of a two-seat trainer version, two more upgrades of the British radar-equipped Mk 1, the Mk 4 and 5, the first fitted with an all-moving tail section and the latter with a modified wing to accommodate additional fuel internally, and next came the Mk 6, the US radar version of the Mk 5. The Mk 7, regarded as representing the kind of standard that the Mk 1 should have been at the point of delivery, had the all-moving elevator tail, the uprated Sapphire engines and the ability to carry Firestreak infra-red homing missiles. Penultimately, the Mk 8 was the Mk 6 with the uprated Sapphires further uprated with afterburner to 12,390 lb thrust. The ultimate version, the Mk 9, which was the Mk 7 with the augmented engines of the Mk 8, latterly fitted with an inflight refuelling probe (to some airframes), but by the time it was being delivered to the squadrons in earnest the Lightning was also available, and in five years the Javelin units were receiving the later Lightnings. By then the majority of RAF air defence and tactical squadrons active when the Sandys White Paper was being leaked by the press had been stood down and the colours cased.

CHAPTER 5

Trip-Wire Response, V-Force and Missile Defence

The House of Commons defence debate held on 16/17 April 1957 was opened by the presentation of the now infamous White Paper by the Defence Minister, Duncan Sandys. He hoped that the House would forgive the delay in presentation and went on to explain that, unlike previous statements of defence, this particular one was different in so far as it was a broad reappraisal of future defence policy. 'We have endeavoured to place before Parliament our conception of how Britain's defence system should evolve over the next five years.'

Sandys also felt the need to prepare MPs for what had been accepted abroad (i.e. the US and other NATO countries), in the main with understanding and respect, that Britain was cutting its air and ground forces stationed in Germany. The reason why this particular defence debate needed everyone to brace themselves was because of what was being described as its revolutionary content. The paper had already caused a press reaction over the future of the RAF. Newspapers had been carrying stories on the proposals since early February, which the Chief Information Officer had urged the Ministry of Defence and Air Ministry to officially deny with supporting data to fortify the denial. The section of the paper which caused the greatest response was the chapter titled 'Defence of the Deterrent'. In this section was the following paragraph:

> Although the country as a whole cannot be protected against nuclear attack, the defence of the very much smaller target presented by an airfield is a feasible task. A manned fighter force, smaller than at present but of adequate size for this limited purpose, will therefore be maintained and will progressively be equipped with air-to-air guided missiles; these fighter aircraft will gradually be replaced by a ground-to-air guided missile system.

It is that last bit which got so many people upset, a very clear statement of intent to bring down the curtain on the manned fighter. It went further, indicating in the longer term the same outcome for the bomber force as well. Significantly, the government now formally recognised that under the present circumstances there was no way to

The Black Arrows, the first of what can be described as a super aerobatics team. Drawn from 111 Squadron, they performed sometimes with as many as sixteen aircraft. Their greatest moment was to loop twenty-two Hunters over Farnborough in 1958. They're seen here over Biggin Hill. (*Air Historical Branch*)

defend the country, or for that matter any other country, against a nuclear attack, or as the paper said, 'Hydrogen Bombs'. Furthermore, the country was unable to devote as much manpower and other resources to defence. What this was leading to was the suggestion that the British people were not prepared to see resources squandered on the pretence of defence. Preparation to prevent war rather than to wage it was a logical goal to which all would surely agree, regardless of political opinion.

Although a Tory, Duncan Sandys could have sat quite comfortably with the members on the opposite bench. He had been to Russia the previous year and spoke admirably of the work they were doing to forward their own social and industrial programme. This had given him the impression that the Kremlin was no more interested in military engagement with the West than vice versa. But the complete mistrust between both sides was such that neither would lower its guard. That the guard would be lowered someday was one thing that Duncan Sandys was to be proved right about. However, his White Paper made one claim which was particularly radical: the replacement of the manned fighter and manned bomber with missiles. He explained on this occasion that discouraging comments made in some quarters about the future of the RAF were misleading. He reiterated his belief that

Britain was moving unquestionably toward a time when fighter aircraft and bombers would all be replaced by guided ballistic weapons. Interestingly, despite his vision for the future of the RAF, he detailed in the same White Paper that the Royal Navy's greatest contribution was the provision of a powerful element of the mobile reserve, in particular, air power. To this end it was decided that the Navy would be organised primarily around a small number of carrier task forces. To read this correctly, he meant maintaining a number of sizeable aircraft carriers quite some distance into the future, the idea being that a smaller Navy would be adapted to deal with any number of overseas emergencies. This was not such an unrealistic proposal at the time; the Fleet Air Arm fielded some fourteen fighter squadrons together with about eight anti-submarine and anti-ship squadrons equipped with Douglas Skyraiders and Fairey Gannets. Overall, the armed forces would be reduced from about 700,000 personnel to about 375,000, effected largely by the running down of National Service to the point at which it was no longer required. That is to say, the military structure was to be run down with the closure of bases and units to the stage where an all-volunteer service throughout was possible. This was going to be a reduction in strength of nearly 50 per cent, the largest cut this time being borne by the Army (two-fifths), with the RAF cut by rather less than two-fifths and the Navy by about one-fifth.

Every now and then, it becomes apparent in the speech and actions of politicians and military chiefs alike just how biased towards one or more of the armed services or disregarding of another they can be. Sandys was no different. His twisted concerns for the Navy and its personnel above the other services led him to state openly that the Army and, to a lesser extent, the RAF would need to greatly increase the number of long-service recruits, in other words rely less on National Service, while on the other hand:

> ... the Navy and the Marines will almost certainly be able to attract, on 9-year engagements, more men than they will need under the new plan. It would really be a great pity to have to turn away any of these long-service naval and marine volunteers, most of whom would probably not be willing to join either of the other services instead.

Not content to leave the matter at that, Sandys further remarked (speaking, you will notice, of only potential recruits not real ones) that 'suitable' responsibilities currently being performed by the Army and RAF might be transferred to the Navy and Marines, so as to avoid disappointment and despair for some unknown quantity of young men who might select the Senior Service should they feel like answering the call to the colours.

Before the White Paper first appeared in drafts issued to the service chiefs for comment in March 1957, the long-term defence policy of the UK was looking at a reduction to an overall figure of 450,000, a figure that the Chiefs of Staff objected strongly to dropping below. For the RAF this meant a reduction from 155,000 to 135,000. The losses were to be applied without impacting too heavily on the operational front line. Therefore, the following reductions were proposed:

Abolition of the RAF Regiment	1,000
Savings from abolition of National Service	9,500
Disbandment of Airfield Construction Branch	1,000
Savings on Fighter Command Control and Reporting System	3,500
Relinquishment of Nicosia	1,000
Savings in HQ Far East Air Force	50
Savings in Administrative units	3,500

These figures were produced by the Assistant Chief of the Air Staff (Policy) and were instantly criticised by the Secretary of the Chiefs of Staff Committee for managing to avoid impinging upon the actual fighting strength of the RAF, save for the RAF Regiment. The Secretary was playing Devil's advocate, because the other two services had proposed quite significant cuts to their front-line strength. But the point of the criticism was that while the defence chiefs were trying to make the case for persuading Sandys not to reduce their numbers below 450,000, here was the RAF inadvertently making the case for reducing their numbers to 380,000. Because the front-line strength scarcely suffered at all in ACAS's proposed cuts, which were put forward to accommodate the reduction from 450,000 to 380,000, no doubt the Defence Minister would argue that the RAF fighting strength could be maintained as well with 135,000 as it with 155,000. The argument therefore went that the reason why there was such a small difference in fighting strength with a reduction of 20,000 personnel was because the RAF had already reached rock bottom. It went further in suggesting that abandoning the airfield construction branch, for example, would reduce the flexibility and mobility of the RAF. The abolition of the RAF Regiment would mean a significant risk taken with airfield security, thinking particularly at the time of places like Cyprus, Aden and even Northern Ireland, unless such tasks were lifted by the nearest Army garrison. The introduction of Thor missiles, which were initially going to run alongside the V-bombers for a good while, would also require additional manpower to be recruited.

The White Paper compared UK defence expenditure (9.3 per cent) with other NATO countries at the time, the highest being that of the US at 11.2 per cent and the lowest, Denmark and Luxembourg, 3.6 per cent each. Sandys wanted savings in the front line in any case. The British Army of the Rhine was to be reduced from 77,000 to 64,000 and the 2nd Tactical Air Force reduced by half by March 1958, as part of the move towards the all-missile defence force. However, some 2TAF squadrons would be armed with nuclear weapons in order to make good the losses. The effects of the rundown of fighter squadrons following the Sandys review meant a restructuring of Fighter Command itself. As of 1957, Fighter Command was split into three operational groups – Nos 11, 12 and 13. They covered UK airspace from south to north in numerical order. As of 31 December 1960, there would be just two – Nos 11 and 12. To avoid confusion among the remaining bases and other installations, the decision was taken to renumber 13 Group as No. 11 and subsume what was No. 11 Group into No. 12 Group. The alternative was to renumber 13 as 12 and 12 as 11. Some may think that simply standing down 13 and making it part of 12 would have been simple enough but, by this time, the original No. 11 Group possessed so few bases and squadrons, and no active radar sites, that the south of England could no longer justify being recognised at group status. Air defence resources were now concentrated further north and east of the United Kingdom; this early warning screen stretched as far as the radar station at Saxa Vord on the north-eastern tip of the Shetland Islands.

From 1949 to 1954, the UK military establishment had enjoyed something of a renaissance, largely on account of the Korean War. The irony of this for the RAF was that it had scarcely got involved but received due consideration in terms of armament and expansion. While it made little difference to what was happening on the Korean peninsula, where General MacArthur was threatening to take the matter a stage or two further, the RAF was building up again nicely with a raft of various projects for new cutting-edge fighter and bomber aircraft. There were indeed far too many promising and radical-looking new designs to run with that, Sandys White Paper or not, some would never get beyond the prototype stage or others leave the drawing board, but of all the quirky sleek-looking new designs, the proposals for a new bomber capable of carrying a nuclear bomb to the heart of Russia were seen as of the utmost imperative. Whatever the arguments regarding other defence issues, the bomb had heralded a new age in world diplomacy, and the next chapter in the Cold War after the conflict in Korea was about to centre far more closely on the nuclear stand-off.

The British government, when Clement Attlee was Prime Minister, had committed to an independent nuclear capability. The expectation at the time was that this would be an air-delivered weapon, a free-fall bomb. The technology for a sea-launched guided missile was far removed from the stage matters were at on 9 August 1946 when the first Air Staff operational requirement OR.1001 was issued for the development of Britain's own atomic device. The Attlee government accepted the need for a British bomb despite a backdrop of severe austerity; the country simply could not afford it, but the need to acquire its bargaining power and to retain Britain's world prestige were no doubt the overriding arguments in favour of its development, with the decision to proceed taken in 1947.

This is where the story of the V-force begins. The RAF's bomber fleet of the day had as its ultimate platform the Avro Lincoln. The Lincoln could just about range as far as the western reaches of Soviet Russia. Despite having been developed from the highly regarded Lancaster, this was a four-prop conventional bomber designed to attack targets in Central and Eastern Europe but no further afield than that. The interim answer was to be the B-29 Superfortress, or Washington B.1 as it became known in British parlance. In the meantime, a purpose-built bomber to carry the nuclear weapon to be designed and built indigenously was, as of 1947, just a draughtsman's drawing. The height of the Cold War, as far as the RAF was concerned, became iconised by three world class and radically new aircraft designs to fulfil a requirement that frankly had not existed before. Not only this, but the fact that they were designed and built by British aircraft companies alone, with no prior existing design on which to build and improve, gives some indication of just where Britain's place was in the world at that time, when many would eagerly like to point out that the country was a spent force. Truth be known, the circumstances regarding the country's slide down the scale to a position whereby the UK is effectively outclassed by Sweden took a lot of hard work on the part of our elected 'great and good' over the forthcoming years. But for the time, this was the last word in cutting edge and pushing back the boundaries.

None of the previous four-engine bombers that had served with the RAF from Stirlings to Lincolns and the American Washington (B-29 Superfortress) could lend much of a clue as to what sort of airframe and engine design should meet the new specification. Four companies got to the stage of building flying prototypes. The first of these came from Short Brothers, originally built in response to specification OR.239. Their aircraft, the Sperrin, did not provide anything quite like the revolutionary airframe design that the other three did. Vickers-Armstrongs, Avro and Handley Page produced airframes that, unlike the Sperrin, departed from the design concept which more closely suited the prop-engine aircraft of earlier years. Short Brothers had originally been invited to tender to meet the requirements of the new bomber on 18 January 1947. The next tender went to Vickers-Armstrongs on 19 July 1948. The SA.4 Sperrin prototype (one of two built) first flew from RAF Aldergrove in Northern Ireland on 10 August 1951, and the first prototypes of the Vickers design were nearing completion at this time. The Air Staff were more impressed with the Vickers design which was yet to fly but was already mooted to have a superior performance. In any case, financial cuts put paid to any further development of the Short SA.4, and the project was cancelled following an Air Staff meeting on 11 October 1951. This was prompted largely by the amount of progress now being made by the Vickers prototype B.9 and two further prototypes from tenders to Avro and Handley Page. The two design concepts from Avro and Handley Page, which were further behind in development, were bigger and heavier and promised a higher level of performance. They both flew for the first time in 1952.

The entire project to design and build even one aircraft to meet the specification required was quite frankly an astonishing undertaking for the UK, staring down both barrels of the bankruptcy gun. The Britain of 1947, playing its part on the world stage despite simultaneously coping with post-war austerity and its obligations to meet the emerging threat to national sovereignty, contrasts markedly with the Britain of today, where regardless of the international security situation the government has acted bombastically on the one hand while finding ways to cope with each crisis with diminishing military assets. The inability to maintain a comprehensive military posture, much less an in-depth one, despite the amount of money spent on defence seems to be constantly at odds with the present-day government's strategic aspirations. The demand on resources from the public purse we see now may not translate directly to what was faced sixty-five years ago, but it begs the question, just how can affairs of state today be so badly managed when compared to the far more dire circumstances of the earlier period? With all the pressing demands of post-war debt and the introduction of the welfare state, the Air Staff still issued operational requirement OR.229 for an aircraft capable of delivering a nuclear weapon of some 10,000 lb against a target as far away as Moscow. In less than five years, the first three prototypes were taking to the air.

For the coming move toward the V-force, the Air Ministry had identified a number of existing airfields across the country to be developed as the main operating bases for the new generation of bombers. Some but not all were in use by Bomber Command during the war; others had been in use by Transport and other commands. The airfields were concentrated in Yorkshire, the East Midlands and East Anglia. At first sight, this appears not to be a particularly prudent arrangement from a security point of view. But while each of the new stations would provide quick reaction dispersals and slipways onto the lengthened main runways, the process in the event of deteriorating diplomacy between Washington and Moscow was to disperse the V-force across the UK. This included a further list of selected airfields from Wick in Caithness to St Mawgan in Cornwall.

The UK defence statement of 1955 planned for a front-line force of 240 aircraft by March 1959, assuming production forecasts were correct. Back in 1952, the Valiant had been expected to become the mainstay, but by 1955, both the Vulcan and Victor were being seen very much as urgently needed successors to the Valiant. Forecasts further into the future were fairly accurate. Beyond 1965, not much hope was held for the survivability of the V-force against what would by then be a more effective in-depth Soviet air defence screen. Political opinion in the press was both alarmed but, surprisingly in some quarters, constructively supportive if also critical. *The Manchester Guardian* (*The Guardian* as it is today) exaggerated in a leader column about an immense bomber programme to build 400 aircraft, while at the same time observing the need for the Vulcan in particular, which was constructed

Vulcan B2 XH534. (*ZZZ 99654, IWM*)

nearby. The paper criticised concentrating on building a bomber force rather than a ballistic missile force, the like of which would not meet the threat any time in the foreseeable future no matter how much store was set by research in this area. The *New Statesman* was less accommodating and spoke of 'delusions of grandeur'.

Vickers were first off the blocks with their aircraft, the B.9, later known as the Valiant. In common with the following two, the Valiant was a four-jet-engine design with a five-man crew of pilot, co-pilot, navigator-radar operator, navigator-plotter and air electronics officer. Despite similarities, the Valiant Mk 1 was quickly overshadowed by the other two designs. Powered by four Rolls-Royce Avon engines developing in the region of 10,000 lb thrust each, it made a hell of a difference over all that preceded it. The first two aircraft for the Operational Conversion Unit (OCU) arrived at Gaydon near Royal Leamington Spa in Warwickshire on 8 and 19 February 1955. No squadrons re-equipped from one V-bomber type to another; the entire force of three types was deployed simultaneously. The Vickers Valiant survived to see operational service in place of the Sperrin as the more clearly advanced of the two.

With the V-force as the jewel in the RAF's post-war crown, the 1950s was the decade that saw aircraft development, both commercial and military, reach its nadir in Britain.

Left: Aerial photo of the first V-Bomber Base, Gaydon, taken while nearing completion and with sketched detail indicating some of the new infrastructure. (*The National Archives*)

Below: 232 O.C.U. staff parade alongside their pristine new Vickers Valiants for the first Annual Formal Inspection at Gaydon, following the base's development as the first for the V-Force. (*The National Archives*)

HP Victor Prototype at Farnborough, *c.* 1956. (*C1181, IWM*)

As well as the clear military and commercial objectives, both airline and air force were eager to showcase their wares annually, and the manufacturers and the RAF were equally aware of the merits of publicly demonstrating not just what they had but also what was in the pipeline. The then annual Farnborough SBAC Exhibition and Flying Display was the venue for such proud flag-waving. No other such theatre provided a comparable stage for the Army and Navy – the demonstration of armoured vehicles, infantry equipment, ships and submarines was simply impracticable by comparison. As a result, the Air Council found a small degree of its time involved in overseeing RAF involvement in public events through sheer demand for its presence. In 1950, the RAF commandeered Farnborough to stage a public air show separate from the SBAC event, solely to present the spectrum of assets, roles and capabilities which the RAF could field. This was a huge success, but efforts to restage this spectacle never got off the ground, to use a shameless pun.

In 1956, the matter was revisited with a view to holding another such show the following year, again using Farnborough as the venue, but was abandoned on the grounds that the RAF was keen to show off its new V-bombers in as impressive a manner as possible. As 1957 was right in the middle of putting the V-force together and crews lacked sufficient experience for any particularly ambitious levels of display flying, let alone operational deployments, what was described as an 'impressive display of V-bombers' at that date seemed unlikely. What was being considered must have been very impressive, as the Valiants, first displayed in the hands of RAF crews publicly in 1955, were expected to be able to provide much more polished and impressive displays in 1956. The then Secretary of State and the Under Secretary both felt, from the political perspective, that in view of the importance of the deterrent in the public mind, RAF participation at any public event without a display of V-bombers would rebound to the Air Ministry's discredit. Once again, the SBAC show was to be the main event for presenting progress in aircraft design and development. In particular, the desire to get the Vulcans flying publicly by September 1956 had been suggested by the Vice Chief of the Air Staff, Sir Ronald Ivelaw-Chapman, though this had depended upon the arrival that year of the first eight aircraft. If they could be delivered to the RAF prior to mid-June, then it might be possible to organise an acceptable display in time. The Secretary of State for Air, Nigel Birch, was keen to avoid incurring criticism of the Vulcan at Farnborough and elsewhere, as had happened following the Valiant displays in 1955. Namely, that they were done badly. Otherwise the demand for RAF aircraft to pitch up at public displays had to be addressed specifically and the Air Council had by now set up a Participation Committee in order to deal with the relentless demand. Limits were imposed: no more than two items allocated to each local display. The committee also had the authority to expand any contribution in a limited number of events which were deemed to merit special consideration; the ration in this case was not to exceed four or five items. Limits were imposed on formation size as well, and use of operational squadrons was kept to a minimum. Auxiliary units, which existed in quite some number still, were to be used instead. The public attraction to such events was demonstrated in September 1955, when three out of forty-six RAF stations holding displays to mark the anniversary of the Battle of Britain reported crowd control problems. Biggin Hill had enjoyed an attendance figure of 275,000; Thornaby, 100,000; and Castle Bromwich, 145,000. Not all followed a prescribed standard for crowd safety. The display committee at Castle Bromwich set the crowd barriers 150 yards from the runway's edge; at Thornaby the barriers were set 90 yards back.

The crews for the inaugural flight of the first Valiant squadron, No. 138, started training on 21 February. By May 1957, all the Valiant squadrons – 7 Bomber, 1 Strategic Reconnaissance and 1 ECM – had stood up. The Vulcan squadrons were next to start; in their case, the OCU had been formed some months in advance, but when the first Valiant squadron had started forming, the OCU was yet to stand up and get to a state where it was fully functioning as such. With the Vulcan programme, the OCU was formed a year before, in May 1956. With the first operational Valiant

RAF Gaydon hosts the general public for its final Battle of Britain Display in 1969 before being put on care and maintenance the following year. (*Warwickshire County Records Office, Reference no.: P4 (N) 600/1073/30*)

The mighty Vulcan explained to visiting school boys. (*Air Historical Branch*)

squadron stood up at Wittering, equipped to carry the Blue Danube bomb, the rest followed quite quickly considering the lack of familiarity with aircraft of this complexity, and by January 1960, a total of eleven squadrons variously equipped with all three V-bomber types, including an ECM and a reconnaissance squadron, were now based mostly around Lincolnshire, South Yorkshire, the East Midlands and East Anglia. Over the next three years a further ten squadrons stood up. Thus the RAF V-force was more or less complete by the time of the Cuban missile crisis. Once again, to compare such an output of operational manpower and aircraft of such advanced design with the recent leaden progress of introducing the Typhoon into service perhaps says more about the sense of urgency of the time than anything else.

The envisaged role of the V-force was exactly as you would imagine: to strike, not in isolation or carry out covert attacks on selected high-value targets, but with immediate and overwhelming force at all the high-value targets that could be reached. This would include maritime targets, i.e. the principal naval docks as well as Russian bases, main centres of communications and government. Therefore the force had to be capable of surviving a pre-emptive strike by the USSR. The minimum size of the force therefore had posed a critical question. The need to deploy as far and wide as possible to bases from which it could launch quickly meant dispersal was to be to airfields with over 2,000 yards of runway available. Not a great deal of length, but it posed something of a limit as civilian airports were not used.

If there was one thing about the V-bomber programme which seems puzzling, certainly from a modern perspective, it is why, given the state of Britain's solvency at the time, the government still pressed ahead to the point of having three such aircraft types in operational service together. Originally the Valiant was the nuclear bomber of choice; however, the other two designs showed promise of considerable improvement, while much attention was given to the progress being made with Soviet air defence technology and nuclear weapons stockpiling. As time passed and the shortcomings in the capability of the Valiant appeared more significant, the view was taken, much to the consternation of the Treasury, that only when both the Avro and Handley Page aircraft were flying operationally could a firm decision be made as to which was the better aircraft and therefore the one to proceed with overall. In the meantime, the Valiant effectively became a much needed stopgap. Somehow, the argument with the Treasury was won on the logic that any additional cost would become a saving in the long term. This was a minor miracle to achieve, as the pressing need for yet more defence cuts raised the question that the latter two bombers should be cancelled and progress concentrated on the Vickers aircraft as it was cheaper and nearest production. However, as early as August 1955, the expected total of V-bombers had already been reduced from 240 to 176, and of this eventual figure the number should be tipped against the Valiant by at least twenty.

The arrival of the latter two aircraft prompted a slight change in deterrence policy.

Pinecastle, Florida. Vulcan and Valiant, *c.* 1956. (*CAM 2665, IWM*)

The Vulcans and Victors when deployed in numbers did not join the Valiants but rather replaced them, enabling the older jets to be assigned to the operational battle order of SACEUR (Supreme Allied Commander Europe) as part of his Strategic Reserve. This essentially meant that while the Vulcan and Victor would stand ready to scramble in the event of British nuclear retaliation, the Valiant would be deployed to carry out what would be tactical strikes on Soviet tank formations rolling across the North German Plain. For this latter role, the RAF desperately needed a new and more realistic aircraft, which by 1959 was a series of concepts proposals and at least one flying prototype, the latter being something of an outsider. So the primary deterrent was maintained by the latter two types alone, a proportion of the available aircraft being maintained at the highest possible readiness. By 1960, this meant three or four at any one airfield. This was the Bomber Command round-the-clock minimum readiness. The USAF Strategic Air Command, the nearest comparison, went a step further and maintained bombers armed and airborne on a continuous basis, ready to react.

The weapons carried by the V-force were upgraded constantly as new warheads and casings became available. The original Blue Danube bomb was carried only by the Valiant, had the smallest yield, 12 kilotons, and was soon replaced by the smaller but more powerful Red Beard. This free-fall nuclear device was designed more as a tactical weapon and was to be carried also by the smaller Canberras and in the Royal Navy by Scimitars, Sea Vixens and Buccaneers. The next stage was the delivery of Yellow Sun Mk 1 and 2 bombs fitted respectively with Green Bamboo or Green Grass (Mk 1) and Red Snow (Mk 2) warheads. Yellow Sun was, unlike Red Beard, a strategic device, its warheads varying in yield from 400 kilotons to over 1 megaton for an all-up weight of 7,000 lb. The Red Snow warhead was eventually fitted in the Blue Steel missile delivered by the Mk 2 Vulcan and Victor.

The Yellow Sun Mk 2 fitted with Red Snow warheads presented no special problems regarding storage, servicing and movement around the country. But, the Blue Steel air-launched rocket system presented a bit of a predicament. Blue Steel equipped two V-Wings: Scampton, with Vulcans; and Wittering, with Victors. As the Blue Steel stand-off bomb carried the Red Snow warhead. There was considerably greater risk here as the Blue Steel contained 80 gallons of kerosene and 400 gallons of HTP (High-Test Peroxide) as propellant for the missile. If HTP comes into contact with a foreign body, such as dirt or another chemical, it can burn very easily. On top of this, a thermal battery activated by heat was used to provide power for the warhead. This posed a dilemma. In the short term until further steps could be taken to resolve this concern, when Vulcans and Victors stood QRA (Quick Reaction Alert) equipped with Blue Steel missiles, the propellant was removed. This may not make sense, but the Blue Steel could in this case be used as a free-fall bomb. However, in the long term this was hardly a satisfactory solution. The Blue Steel Joint Ordnance Board/A&AEE Safety Committee's advice had been sought by the Ministry of Aviation on this matter and had been told that all modifications affecting nuclear safety had been incorporated. Furthermore, special precautions had been taken in the design of the missile to avoid contamination and to keep the HTP and kerosene apart, even in the case of a leak. The Blue Steel was designed so that fuelling, loading of the warhead and fitting of the thermal batteries could take place in an emergency. The QRA requirement meant that a live weapon should be able to remain on board an aircraft for up to thirty days.

It is worth reflecting upon the kind of undertaking this represented at the time, fulfilling a requirement which frankly had not existed before. There was still concern over the insertion of the thermal batteries. These were left out in periods of rising tension, such as the Cuban missile crisis, until as late in the preparation for take-off as possible. How this played with a scramble order which could be signalled at any time was resolved as best as possible by having the batteries close at hand to be inserted. However, emergencies were excluded from this process. Clearly here the Air Staff were confident of some degree of notice or some form of alert prior to a genuine scramble order being issued in order to ensure that, were it necessary, Britain's nuclear deterrent got airborne with the ability to deliver Armageddon. The situation with the thermal batteries was resolved by July 1964. The batteries were placed in a semi-installed position in their housing in the warhead pod during standby on QRA. In this situation the contacts were physically separated. The batteries would then be thrust home in the event of an emergency.

Access to all V-bomber QRA sites was strictly controlled. The idea of sabotage, however, was curiously discounted. Special Safety Teams (SSTs) of between twenty and thirty people were set up and available within 30 minutes at V-bomber airfields and a number of others. The role of the SSTs was that in the event of a radioactive hazard resulting from any incident involving a nuclear weapon, they would isolate with a cordon the incident zone and further determine the presence and extent of contamination. Further control in such an event would be overseen by the Air Force Operations Room who would co-ordinate the response of the local emergency services.

Eight airfields, some already V-bomber stations, were selected for dispersal of the Blue Steel aircraft in particular: Bruntingthorpe, Burtonwood, Coningsby, Elvington, Gaydon, Kinloss, Lossiemouth and Wyton. Ultimately, the V-force could be held at 15 minutes' readiness for a period of seven days. A step down from here was 40 minutes' readiness for thirty days. In preparation during a rising period of tension, 75 per cent of the force could be dispersed to the other airfields within 24 hours but for no longer than 26 hours in any event. The requirement of the dispersal airfields was that sleeping quarters were to be provided within the vicinity of where the aircraft would be parked. By the time the force was at full strength, should a full dispersal be called, four aircraft would disperse to each of the dispersal bases and eight aircraft would remain at each of the main operating bases. During holidays and weekends, the level of response could be maintained only by retaining a number of officers and airmen on call in the immediate vicinity. This period, 1955 to 1969, was probably the RAF's post-war zenith. It carried the ultimate stage in defence against the Warsaw Pact forces and Soviet hegemony. At their meeting on 8 May 1956, the Chiefs of Staff invited the Air Defence Committee to prepare a report of the UK air defence requirements following a fresh development. This was on the appreciation that the assessment of a recent UK/US Guided Weapons Intelligence Conference was correct (see below). The Chiefs of Staff subsequently called upon the committee to examine the air defence of the UK V-bomber bases and, in view of the urgency of the latter study, it naturally took precedence. The whole question of the present and future size and composition of UK air defence was under examination by the policy review committee.

The concern exercising the Chiefs of Staff was that of medium-range Soviet ballistic missiles. The Ministry of Supply had put forward proposals for countering this new concern, making it clear that technology to carry out detection, interception and destruction of ballistic missiles was feasible, at least against a limited threat. But such a system was forecast to be at least five years away. Among the proposals to counter the new threat was the eventual integration of surface-to-air guided missiles. Air Marshal Sir Hubert Patch, Air Defence Commander, more widely known as C-in-C Fighter Command, prepared a report looking for a change in the air defence system to one that would be less reliant on reservists and auxiliaries, and was already under way with the arrival of a new long-range Control and Reporting radar, the Type 80.

The new early warning radar head would allow for increased defence efficiency without a corresponding need for increased manpower. Furthermore, Air Marshal Patch recommended that existing day fighters should be given a limited night capability, stating that it was illogical not to be able to use the full fighter force in conditions which the enemy might think were the most favourable time for initial attack. That said, the UK/US Guided Weapons Intelligence Committee had assessed the threat and believed that a short-range weapon would be available in 1956 to 1958, and a medium-range weapon in 1959 to 1961. However, the Ministry of Defence had not fully supported the assessment in this report. Of the Chiefs of Staff of the day, it was the Chief of the Imperial General Staff, Field Marshal Sir Gerald Templer, who suggested that it would be prudent for the Air Defence Committee to examine the air defence requirements on the assumption that the intelligence appreciation was right. Air Chief Marshal Sir Dermot Boyle, now Chief of the Air Staff, was more concerned with being able to counter the low-level air threat for which, with adequate early warning, fighters were most appropriate. However, the provision of low-level early warning was being held up at the time by, of all things, balloon-borne radar. Light anti-aircraft defences were therefore believed to be still necessary for targets likely to be subject to this form of attack. In the meantime, the first purpose-built, all-weather British jet fighter, the Gloster Javelin, was being delivered to the first operational squadron to operate the type. The Javelin, with a ceiling of 52,000 feet, was intended to intercept the high-altitude manned bomber threat from the Soviet Union.

By the end of 1958, Duncan Sandys was already back-pedalling on his all-missile defence shield, but there was no outright admission that events had been set in train which would greatly reduce the RAF fighter force. The Chancellor of the Exchequer was smelling blood. The fighter force was already down to just twenty Fighter Command squadrons, and the disbandment of a further twelve was sought. In the interest of balanced argument, a number of the promised SAM squadrons would be deployed, the first that year, and the additional fighter squadron reduction was to be carried out over the period 1959 to 1964, yielding £139 million savings. If this was to be the case, the Air Staff not surprisingly offered to lose the squadrons equipped with the earlier model Javelins before the drawdown got round to the Hunter squadrons.

Hunters of 92 Squadron's Blue Diamonds in steep climb in diamond formation. They were the second and last of the super aerobatics teams. (*C3275, IWM*)

The Sandys Defence Review had presumed a rundown of ten Hunter squadrons from the end of 1959, at a rate of one each quarter up to the end of 1961. However, no capital savings were envisaged here as the personnel from these units would need to be dispersed to other areas where deficiencies were expected. Boyle was advised by the Acting Under Secretary, R. C. Kent, to emphasise to the Treasury the minimum return from the short-term savings expected from disbanding these squadrons and the cost involved, as money had already been committed. Sandys was now saying he did not want to see the fighter force reduced any further, but he was critical of the allocation of fighter squadrons principally as a defence of the nuclear deterrent. The Air Staff had informed him that if no direct fighter defence of the V-force nuclear deterrent was planned, then the air defence of the UK with surface-to-air guided weapons would still require a fighter force of twelve squadrons which, by 1964, would be equipped with the new English Electric Lightning and armed not only with the Red Top missile, as they eventually were, but with the American Genie missile carrying a nuclear warhead capable of obliterating a large force of enemy strike aircraft. Defence of the deterrent would further require the retention of eight squadrons of the later Javelin marks. Sandys was prepared to accept this, but would not accept that the Russians would, for example, launch a surprise attack on the UK without simultaneously destroying all the US strategic bases.

Whatever the likelihood of this, that the UK should move further toward reliance on the premise that its defence was an integral part of US defence policy was ill-advised. The Secretary of State for Air had noted in a paper titled 'Air Defence of the UK', written in 1957, that 'we must expect an increasing danger that the concept of confining war to Europe, and ultimately of Fortress America, will receive growing American support'. In other words, rather than American forces becoming consumed in a war in Europe, the American people would feel it preferable to see war confined to the European continent and America out of it.

As an example, the Russians might calculate that a swift attack on USAF peripheral bases around the globe and in the UK would greatly diminish the possible weight of an Allied attack on the Soviet Union. To the extent that the US, itself under direct threat, might be willing to bargain, the UK might be forced to retaliate alone. Naturally, it followed that whatever the strength of the alliance through NATO, not just consideration but preparation had to be made in order to face, as best as possible, a more defined Soviet threat to British soil specifically. One of the most expensive elements of the RAF's Cold War preparations to confront an all-out Soviet attack was the east coast Control and Reporting chain of static radar stations. Trimingham, Watling, Bawdsey and Neatishead all clustered around East Anglia and their radar coverage overlapped with the antenna at Patrington on the spur of land that juts into the Humber Estuary. Up from here was Staxton Wold near Scarborough, which overlapped with Boulmer near Alnwick. The cover was maintained from here to Buchan in Aberdeenshire. The Control and Reporting chain consumed more resources than the deterrent, but was equally vital to the overall defence tapestry.

A brief on defence manpower policy prepared by the Air Ministry on 20 November 1958, referred to the phrase 'inevitable uncertainty about the future of manned aircraft' as being one which it was hoped would be avoided in future cabinet meetings. The uncertainty was again brought about by Sandys' earlier claim that the days of manned aircraft were numbered. The assessment now, less than a year on, was that there certainly were going to be manned aircraft in the future. The only question was how many and what type. Even so, were it not for Boyle's strong representations in defence of the future of manned aircraft, far more damage may well have been done, and it is not beyond question that Sandys could have brought about the still-birth of the English Electric Lightning. For what it is worth, Boyle also managed to get a stay of execution for the TSR2 while it was still at such an early stage.

So within less than two years, while a raft of military projects had been cancelled which would see the end of many aircraft companies in the UK, there was at

Hunter Squadron Bomb burst during aerobatics practice. The aim of aerobatics is principally to develop skill and confidence. (*Air Historical Branch*)

least some reassurance that the future was not entirely bleak, and perhaps some acknowledgement on Sandys' part that he had misjudged the situation. Of course, saving face is a preoccupation of politicians, if no one else, and to maintain some form of credibility about future defence planning, the RAF continued to deploy a significant number of Bloodhound surface-to-air missiles and Thor intermediate-range ballistic missiles, the latter on lease from the US. With the deployment of the former, the air defence fighter force wound down dramatically but on nothing near a like-for-like basis. The Air Ministry had just one major aircraft project left at the embryo stage and one which was regarded as crucial to improving the RAF's capability to strike at vital targets without resorting to all-out Armageddon. This was the decision to approve OR.339, the requirement for a tactical strike aircraft with a high chance of survival against the increasingly impossible Soviet air defence network, and was about the best thing that had happened since 1957. Manned aircraft and guided missiles were to be complementary, nothing more. The time when there was no longer a need for substantial numbers of manned aircraft could not be envisaged at this stage. And as far as the Air Ministry was concerned, it was most important to destroy categorically and authoritatively any idea that the RAF as a flying force had had its day.

The Sandys defence paper detailed some significant reductions to take place over the five years following publication. The UK fighter force was to be cut nearly in half, from 480 aircraft to 280, with the limited task of protecting the V-bomber bases only, but was to be replaced in due course largely by guided missiles. By 1962, this had reached a peak in terms of surface-to-air missile units, a total of eleven squadrons having been deployed around the UK, mostly in Eastern England. They were backed up by, or rather were backing up, twelve fighter squadrons. By 1965, they would have been reduced to a single squadron with six fighter squadrons. So not only was the increased reliance upon missile defence short-lived but the fighter force was further reduced in any case. This would be recognised as a problem to be redressed in later years, although not substantially so before the arrival of Margaret Thatcher at No. 10 Downing Street.

The bomber force itself was determined to be of moderate size, which in due course would be replaced largely by ballistic missiles and a stock of British bombs. These would be supplemented by US bombs which would fall under US control. Coastal Command was to see its force of twelve squadrons of Shackleton anti-submarine warfare aircraft reduced to seven. Transport Command would operate seven-and-a-half squadrons, a peculiar figure, but would include sixteen of the new Britannias and thirty-two Beverleys. Overseas, the current 466 tactical aircraft were to be immediately reduced to 216 and then further reduced to 104 by 1961. Four UK-based tactical bomber squadrons equipped with Canberras would, however, be assigned to SACEUR. Elsewhere, the Middle East force would be reduced from twelve to ten squadrons, with five aircraft concentrated in Cyprus, four fighter squadrons in Aden and a Maritime squadron at Luqa in Malta. The Far East would be cut back from 134 to 74 aircraft, with the RAF station in Hong Kong to be closed down.

This was to be the RAF of the future and how it would look by 1964. Yet further cuts were expected on top, with particular concern arising from the continued spending on training National Service pilots and on the University Air Squadrons (UAS) through which a good many RAF pilots were being recruited and from which the RAF received, by and large, recruits of the 'background and calibre' it could not do without. In search of further economies, the Inspector General was already looking at the UAS. The cost of pilot training at the time was £50,000 per student, the same as for those recruited through the UAS. As for National Service pilots, to be worthwhile they needed to be signing on for regular service at a rate of at least one in two. The figure was more like one in ten. This made the cost of training National Service pilots prohibitive, and with the loss of auxiliary squadrons there was no longer a need to seek pilots among the National Service intake anyway.

Shackleton bomb bay containing torpedos, depth charges and sonar buoys. (*HU 109897, IWM*)

Whirlwind Troop assault demonstration at Benson, 1962. (*Air Historical Branch*)

With regard to the missile shield and where it eventually stood, the Russian threat was expected to increase, and the purchase from America of the Nike-Hercules missile system was also considered as a ground-to-air system that would, like the air-launched Genie, carry nuclear warheads. Indeed, every weapon on Fighter Command's shopping list, despite the numerical rundown of current airframes, was considered a requirement. In a brief to the Secretary of State for Air and Sir Dermot Boyle, the Assistant Chief of the Air Staff (AD) advised that no further reduction in the manned fighter force should be planned due to the expected increased threat.

One scenario imagined that safeguarding the bomber force was impossible since the force could be exhausted through being scrambled from the readiness dispersals following a series of feint attacks and then be destroyed when back on the ground. Refuelling, the fighter would be needed. If the government was to be brutally honest with the public, it would admit that the reason for the sharp reduction in the fighter force, more specifically the UK air defence element, was because it had been rendered virtually superfluous, or was about to be, with the inevitable deployment of intercontinental ballistic missiles in the Soviet Union. The government's position was that the missile threat was impossible to counter. The bomber threat, supposing the missile threat never materialised, could be countered just as it had been during the Battle of Britain. However, the number of new fighters, rather than the current types, required for this was beyond any sustainable means, certainly if the country was to maintain a National Health Service and any existing or better levels of support for families without any other means of income. The situation in Europe was different despite the lesser levels of defence spending. Save for France, there was nothing of the level of overseas dependencies, and together with the heavy presence of American forces covering every spectrum, including those based in the UK, all of which were assigned to SACEUR, Britain's immediate defence against a separate overwhelming air attack placed the government in a serious predicament. The extent of reductions including tactically assigned squadrons in Germany amounted to not much short of abandonment. The replacement missile umbrella in the UK would indeed be considerably cheaper, but again this would not be expanded to any level at which the country stood a reasonable chance of at least countering the manned bomber threat.

By the time of the Cuban missile crisis in October 1962, Nos 1 and 3 Groups of Bomber Command were able to deploy some nineteen squadrons, not counting one dedicated reconnaissance squadron and one ECM. Two OCUs were also available as additional assets should operations dictate. If matters had got to such a state, the involvement of the OCUs would have been academic.

Airfields in No. 1 Group (HQ at Bawtry):
Coningsby
Finningley

Scampton

Waddington

Airfields in No. 3 Group (HQ at Mildenhall):

Cottesmore

Gaydon

Honington

Marham

Wittering

Wyton

In addition to the main operating bases, there were a total of thirty-two other airfields across the British Isles listed as dispersal airfields.

Over on the other side of the Atlantic, the USAF's Strategic Air Command maintained a permanent airborne nuclear retaliation force. For the RAF it was sufficient to maintain four aircraft at scramble readiness at each of the bases. Depending on the alert status, additional four-ships of bombers were deployed to the secondary dispersal airfields. While President John Fitzgerald Kennedy was relying on his resolve to stare down President Nikita Khrushchev during the Cuban missile crisis, the V-force was brought to this state of readiness. The crisis was resolved by a face-saving agreement for both sides. The Soviet contention had been that the basing of missiles in Cuba was a move to rebalance the state of affairs created by American missiles in Turkey. The agreement was, of course, that once the Soviet Union had clearly abandoned its programme to base missiles in Cuba, the US would withdraw its missiles from Turkey.

It is impossible to understate the teetering on the edge that the thirteen days of rising tension between East and West brought about. In truth, the general public, while aware that something was amiss, had absolutely no idea just how close to Armageddon the planet was. British service personnel, like those of other NATO countries, were being prepared to deploy. Leave was being cancelled and others were being recalled. The ramifications following the crisis meant that Britain's remaining National Servicemen who had been looking forward to their demob date in December would be obliged to remain in service until the following May.

The months following the crisis saw Fighter Command increasingly being called upon to scramble and intercept Soviet Bear, Bison and Badger long-range bomber reconnaissance aircraft. One RAF station featured in particular. Leuchars up on the Fife coast near the St Andrews golf links, spent the next twenty-six years at the forefront of the Cold War ritual of Soviet long-range flights testing the response of UK air defences to routine infringements. The Northern 'Q' never saw a week go by without a number of live scrambles and intercepts from the Scottish air base. Indeed, a regular unintended feature during the annual Battle of Britain air show there was a recess in the day's proceedings to allow the 'Q' aircraft to launch from the readiness shelter at the west end of the runway.

In 1960, on 1 May, a CIA-operated Lockheed U-2 flying a high-altitude reconnaissance sortie over Sverdlovsk was intercepted at an altitude of over 70, 000 feet by a Soviet SA-2 missile and brought down. The U-2 was operating from the Peshawar air base in Pakistan. The pilot, Gary Powers, baled out and was promptly picked up. He was sentenced to ten years' imprisonment for his part in espionage activities against the USSR, but was later released and exchanged with a Russian spy, Colonel Vilyam Fisher, on 10 February 1962. Nevertheless, relations between Kennedy and Khrushchev had suffered a setback which may well have made the situation regarding Cuba some months later rather more difficult to resolve than they proved. The incident proved something else as well – no matter what the ceiling performance of the Victor or Vulcan B.Mk 2, the chances of the V-force successfully penetrating Soviet air defences in order to deliver the stand-off Blue Steel, let alone a free-fall Yellow Sun, were now well and truly called into question. The British government was already negotiating the purchase of Skybolt air-launched missiles the same month that Gary Powers was shot down, and the incoming Kennedy administration, a year later, was keen to review the Skybolt programme. This was prompted by a lack of faith by the new US administration not only in Britain's but also its own airborne deterrent, a faith that been shaken by the Gary Powers incident.

In November 1962, immediately following the Cuban crisis, US Defense Secretary Robert McNamara approached the British government with the suggestion of not only cancelling the Skybolt but also standing down the V-force along with it. The option presented was for a dual-key nuclear deterrent system. Doubtless the Americans would be the overriding decision-makers if such an arrangement were to go ahead. In the event Harold Macmillan made it clear in no uncertain terms that the British deterrent would stay. McNamara had a point: the V-force had been rendered obsolescent, pretty much as had the USAF B-52s, B-47s and B-58s, by the advent of strategic missiles launched from silos and submarines. This was the solution to the airborne deterrent – submarine-launched guided missiles. Further meetings between Kennedy and Macmillan arrived at a sales agreement on 6 April 1963 for Polaris A1 missiles. In May 1963, the British government ordered four submarines to carry the missiles, and on 26 February 1964, the keel of HMS *Resolution* was laid down at Barrow-in-Furness. Launched on 15 September 1966 and commissioned on 2 October 1967, it became the first of Britain's strategic nuclear submarine force. The RAF V-force continued with an ever-dwindling number of aircraft until it had been wholly replaced by the Royal Navy's Resolution Class Polaris submarines on 4 December 1969.

A Vulcan in anti-flash white. This scheme was dropped in 1964 for low-level camouflage on all V-Bombers when low-level penetration was preferred to high-level, the risk from Soviet Air Defences being much greater against high flying aircraft. (*John Wharam*)

This was the last year that the Vulcans carried Blue Steel operationally, and then only the aircraft of Scampton-based No. 617 Squadron. Nos 27 and 83, the two other units making up what was hitherto the Scampton wing, stood down this year. No. 617 along with the remaining Vulcans of the Waddington wing was left to continue with the insurance policy role of standby nuclear deterrent. Blue Steel was gone and the aircraft now carried the WE177 free-fall nuclear bomb. This weapon was also being carried by the Blackburn Buccaneer from off the decks of the two remaining Audacious Class carriers and would be carried by the RAF Buccaneers from bases in Germany. It was also to have been carried by the American-built Phantom FGR2 in RAF service, but technical difficulties meant the RAF Phantoms were to be equipped instead to carry an American weapon. The decision to develop the forthcoming Jaguar high performance jet trainer, an early Anglo-French collaborative project, as a front-line strike fighter may well have been prompted in no small part by this.

While the Air Ministry was counting its blessings that at least one major aircraft programme remained in procurement after the Sandys axe fell, another aircraft escaped to see the operational light of day by the skin of its aluminium, and along with the Vulcan and Harrier, became one of the most charismatic RAF aircraft of the Cold War era. The English Electric Lightning was, and perhaps will remain, the sole

Vulcan carrying Blue Steel, the primary nuclear deterrent in the 1960s. (*Warwickshire County Records Office, Reference no.: P4 (N) 600/1674/25a*)

wholly British-designed supersonic aircraft to reach operational use. Along with the Bloodhound missile, it was going to replace the second generation Hawker Hunter and Gloster Javelin jet fighters. To the new fighter fell the responsibility primarily of safeguarding the V-force.

The English Electric Lightning was an equally radical design in terms of airframe as the Vulcan, possessing a 60-degree wing sweep along the leading edge and with two engines mounted vertically and staggered, the upper slightly further aft of the lower. The powerplant was the already in service Avon Turbojet from Rolls-Royce, this time with reheat. The Mk 1s had the series 211 engine. This provided 11,250 lb of dry thrust augmented to 14,430 lb with afterburner. This gave the 16-ton fighter the now benchmark Mach 2 capability and a 50,000 feet per minute rate of climb. A Ferranti airborne target locking radar system allowed the Lightning to engage targets beyond visual range, just as with the Javelin, but from the outset one of two notable drawbacks was the aircraft's limited option for carrying any kind of array of weapons and retaining its scintillating performance. A further bugbear was endurance. There would be little point in its getting off the ground but for the fitting of a non-jettisonable fuel blister under the fuselage. Even with this, the Lightning was notoriously short-legged, relying more than any other design on the presence of an airborne tanker. Later developments resulting in the Mk 6 brought uprated engines and an enlarged fuel pack, but range and weapons remained the Lightning's two very notable limiting factors.

The requirement as of 1957 was for a force of twelve Lightning squadrons. These were to have been supported by having 144 aircraft in service with a further twenty-eight as attrition spares to cover the period up to 1970. It was expected early on that of the earlier Mk 1 aircraft, forty-seven would enter service but would quickly be assigned to the operational training role. The rest, mostly the Mk 3 version, would become the principal interceptor. Of the twelve squadrons, eight were to be deployed overseas in accordance with Air Ministry plans. However, the Ministry of Defence was concerned about a high proportion of the intended units being permanently based overseas; two squadrons in the Far East, one in Cyprus and one in Aden, under normal peacetime conditions, with four doubtless in Germany. The issue was possible difficulties within NATO on the question of unified air defence with the Americans regarding air defence of their Strategic Air Command Bases (B-47/B-52 deployments) in the UK, and concerns over UK public opinion.

The proposed twelve-squadron force was later scaled down to nine in 1960, with a review to consider an increase by the autumn of 1961. The future fighter force was envisaged as being made up solely of Lightnings, which were not expected to continue in significant numbers beyond 1967. But the nine squadrons would need to continue until 1972, and this being so, the number of Lightnings on order would have to increase by eighteen. The Air Staff still felt that twelve was the minimum

Lightnings of 19 Squadron. (*John Wharam*)

Lightnings of 74 Squadron
run in and break to land,
Farnborough, 1961. (*Air
Historical Branch*)

settled number of squadrons adequate for the future, and that to drop below this
would pose 'very serious difficulties'. The Defence Secretary believed that twelve
squadrons could remain operational through to 1963 at least without exceeding
the estimates total for the Air Ministry. A further £1 million, however, would be
needed to retain two squadrons of Gloster Javelins which would otherwise have
been disbanded, but this was considered a relatively low additional cost. Part of the
concern about the long-term maintenance of Lightning numbers was due to there
being nothing in terms of a replacement available before the early 1970s. That such
concerns existed so soon after the all-missile future had been announced suggests
some rapid reassessment but, as expected, the Treasury was unenthusiastic about a
much expanded fighter force, not once it had been whittled down considerably, and
was not keen on an expansion beyond a future total of nine squadrons.

The high-end or big-ticket programmes for the immediate, and RAF-centred,
defence of the UK, the need for a field army on the north-west plains of Federal
Germany, and to police the still quite substantial post-imperial territories while
maintaining a blue-water navy to guard the trade routes and provide immediate

assistance and support all continued to demand a price which was becoming ever more difficult to justify to an increasingly sceptical public. Today's government is faced with a rather reversed case to make. There was a good argument to support the defence expenditure at the level it was at. There was also now a growing culture in western society that not only questioned the morals and judgements of military expenditure but also the concept of defence much more than before. This was coupled with a growing assertion that the West's democratically elected governments were actually the bad guys. The pacifists and their beliefs were nothing new; however, increasingly through the Cold War era, there was a growing culture, perhaps fuelled in part by the threat of nuclear annihilation, of radical political thinking and theorising. The Beatniks, a collection of radical artists, poets and writers and like-minded types, emerged from the 1950s as the vanguard of future western society which sought to challenge convention and, in no small part, conventional attitudes to the defence industry and military establishment. Together with the Beatniks came the more focused Campaign for Nuclear Disarmament.

Admittedly, none of these counter-culture and protest groups ever managed to rally public opinion sufficiently in any one country to drastically alter anything, but the simplistic arguments and feelings of mistrust and enmity towards the likes of the armed forces and other pillars of western establishment undoubtedly could not be ignored entirely. There were votes at stake, after all. Debate through the media, often with an alarming degree of misunderstanding and sweeping judgement, would affect defence policy in the long run and has increasingly been seen recently. But more about this later. Perhaps the peak of the effect of radical left thinking on defence policy in British politics came towards the end of the 1970s when the left-of-centre Labour Party, having lost the 1979 general election, swung wildly to the left and the following year elected Michael Foot to lead it into the 1980s, a decade which saw the focus on the nuclear issue become as intense as it had been in the 1950s. However, this time the polarisation affected not only public opinion but the mainstream political establishment as well. This was the story throughout much of the Cold War. The defenders of democracy were handicapped to a degree by the very accommodation of it, while Soviet intolerance and military hegemony were often excused by the West's home-grown critics.

CHAPTER 6

Flexible Response

As we have seen, the 1950s and 1960s period of the Cold War was characterised by the term 'trip-wire response', referring to the expectation that the conduct of a war between East and West would almost immediately reach the stage of general release of nuclear weapons. This was the era that the strategic bomber and ICBM (intercontinental ballistic missile) have come to represent; the era of V-bombers and the Strategic Air Command's B-47s, B-52s and B-58s; the era of the Aldermaston marches and of fall-out drills. The 1970s and 1980s were characterised by the term 'flexible response', which in effect reduced the tension of the Cold War. The aim, as the term suggests, was to avoid Armageddon by putting off for as long as possible the move toward that unthinkable scenario. Oddly, it was following this transition that some political parties, often ill-advisedly, sought to try and make capital out of public jitters about nuclear weapons.

For the trip-wire scenario, the RAF was well and truly established. Up until the end of the 1960s, the RAF had geared the bulk of its operational front-line inventory toward its ability to strike a nuclear blow in the centre of the USSR. In this respect, it stood only in the shadow of the USAF's Strategic Air Command. In addition, the air defence systems to counter the same kind of threat from the other side – long-range static early warning radar chains, quick response high-altitude interceptors and SAM missiles – had received considerable investment, up to a point. The Soviet air defence screen also had been invested in and by the time the V-force was fully assembled was so impenetrable that any aircraft trying to get through would have to approach very low below the radar coverage. This seemed to coincide with the shift in the military doctrine of Massive Retaliation in response to provocation otherwise known as the Trip-Wire policy. This pertained more directly to US defence policy but, by extension, spoke for NATO-wide policy. The British position fell into line. The term 'flexible response' is said to have been first used in this context by General Maxwell Taylor, who had commanded 101st Airborne Division during the Second World War. This was the philosophy brought about by the Kennedy administration. What this actually meant in practice probably changed very little, but the theory

A morning scene at a fighter station in the 1960s; these Lightnings appear to be ready for a squadron deployment. (*The National Archives*)

was a shift away from the expending of all nuclear assets in the first instance and seeing the V-bombers on QRA launched prematurely. This, while a Soviet armoured assault on points along the inner German border might be contained conventionally to one where those Soviet tank formations would be met by NATO conventional forces, then see how things went on from there. The trouble with this is that it is hard to imagine that the US administration and other NATO governments had not considered this possibility earlier. The truth is that doubt remained throughout the Cold War of NATO realistically contesting any Warsaw Pact offensive conventionally at all. But the new doctrine did coincide with a more realistic development of tactical air power. Here, the RAF of the 1960s fell behind somewhat.

The Fleet Air Arm possessed a tactical air capability superior to that of the RAF in the 1960s. The Scimitar, Buccaneer and Sea Vixen afforded the Royal Navy's aircraft carriers with a reasonably impressive tactical strike, fighter and reconnaissance air force. The RAF was, as of 1970, still relying upon the English Electric Canberra to manage the role of air interdiction from bases in West Germany. Close support was the responsibility of the Hawker Hunter, which possessed a respectable performance but was behind in most respects compared to the American late Century Series aircraft. American and French fighters of the same generation or slightly younger but with higher performance and greater versatility, and more readily adaptable to tactical ground attack, were well deployed among other NATO air forces in Europe by the mid-1960s. The F-104, F-100, F-5, F-101and F-4 were all second generation and later second generation airframes, all supersonic designs, and were able to carry a more realistic range of stores and refuel in flight. Apart from the Lightning, which was dedicated to air defence, the RAF had no other airframe which possessed similar credentials. There was an attempt to offer the Lightning as a multi-purpose fighter to the Germans, pitting it against the F-104. However, whatever its merits as a thoroughbred Interceptor, the idea of the Lightning fulfilling any other kind of role successfully never seemed to exercise the imagination much. Its lack of application no doubt harmed the overseas sales potential rather than shrewd American sales know-how, which is often given as the reason why the Starfighter became the mainstay of many NATO European tactical air forces. Alas, the Lightning as a ground attack fighter was not an idea that anyone was keen to pursue. There was still a pressing problem though, finding a replacement for the tactical strike force of Canberras which by the end of the 1950s was no longer suitable. As mentioned earlier, the Air Ministry was already looking for a low-level strike aircraft in response to the difficulties with high-altitude penetration. The answer was to try and penetrate enemy (Soviet) airspace beneath the radar shield. To meet this requirement, OR.343 was issued. This is where the infamous TSR2 saga begins.

The Northrop F5E was built as a cheap alternative to aircraft like the Phantom; it was supersonic, light, and highly manoeuvrable. It equipped some smaller NATO Air Forces when the RAF still had some time to persevere with the obsolescent Hawker Hunter. (*John Fisher*)

The iconic English Electric Lightning demonstrating the prowess which typified its public image. (*John Fisher*)

   The TSR2 project attracted contributions from all the companies which no longer had any projects of their own left, thanks to the 1957 White Paper. This is where the key criticism arose about the aircraft being designed by committee, as indeed it was: no one single design chief led the project but different contributing elements managed their own bit of it. Somehow, it seemed to work. Any literature about the TSR2 laments what might have been, and there is plenty of it about. But in the end it also became the original procurement project disaster which has given a bad name to many subsequent British military aircraft design projects. Even so, the TSR2, or whatever might take its place, was imperative to the high-altitude problem. The base for the TSR2 was to be Weybridge, with a design team of forty or so people bringing different areas of expertise to the board room. The requirement for it began in 1955. Only three years into the Canberra's operational service, its replacement was already being sought. With the first V-bombers still working up to operational acceptance, the ability to reach Soviet high-value targets with air-dropped nuclear bombs was already looking unlikely to last and was being addressed. New supersonic fighters, from the MiG-19 through to the MiG-21 and the Su-15 Flagon, were nearing initial operational capability in the Soviet Union, and surface-to-air guided missiles which could well exceed twice the speed of sound shortly after launching were inevitable.

The original Ministry of Supply specification for an aircraft to meet the requirement to counter the emerging threat from enemy air defence forces was designated B.126T. This required an aircraft capable of carrying the nuclear weapon under development for the first V-bombers, the Blue Danube. It would have a range of 1,500 nautical miles at a speed of Mach 0.85 at a height of 500 feet for at least 80 per cent of the sortie. Various companies submitted designs; however, they were all abandoned over the next three years, by which time the RAF was revisiting the requirement as the new air defence technologies were becoming more imminent. A design project, the Naval Air Staff Target No. 39 or NA.39, was already making progress to the point of development airframes being ordered, and on the face of it would be a realistic goal for the RAF to proceed towards. But, as always, inter-service politics was to the fore again and the RAF had no more interest in the development of the NA.39 than it had in submarines. To be fair, the NA.39 failed to meet the new specifications that the RAF had placed on the original B.126T specification. This now called for the winning design to be capable of supersonic speed at below 1,000 feet and with good supersonic performance at high altitude. The NA.39 requirement, as of 1955, was already being addressed by the Yorkshire-based aircraft company Blackburn, which had its main bases at Brough and Holme-on-Spalding Moor. The Blackburn NA.39 became the Buccaneer. As history would prove, it would have saved a hell of a lot of time and, most importantly, money, if the Air Staff had accepted it to meet their own requirements in 1955. But then again hindsight is a wonderful thing, so what happened was that the RAF pressed on regardless with its requirement separately. In the meantime, it regarded the Buccaneer as falling far short of its imperative requirements for supersonic speed at low level and an inertial navigation system for use in conjunction with strategic strike. Interim designs were submitted for consideration, but the whole project was thrown into disarray when claims about the White Paper were reported in the press in February 1957, outlining the future for aircraft design and manufacturing companies. They would only be invited to tender for new design projects following amalgamation into larger companies. Among the mergers were English Electric, Vickers and Hunting, which formed the British Aircraft Corporation, and Blackburn and de Havilland merging with Hawker, resulting in Hawker Siddeley Ltd.

Despite the dark cloud promising an ominous future for British aviation, general operational requirement GOR.339, issued in March 1957, still proceeded. English Electric already had a design concept, the P.17A, which was smaller but near identical to the TSR2. The more definitive operational requirement OR.343 was issued in May 1959. This called for a weapon system with the following characteristics: to obtain reconnaissance information for all tactical purposes including target mapping at low altitudes in all weather conditions by day and by night, using radar and/or photographic measures, and the ability to deliver tactical nuclear weapons, again from low altitudes at the 'maximum ranges obtainable' and with the least regard to prevailing weather conditions by day and by night. To deliver a conventional bomb load was also a requirement in order to increase the flexibility of the aircraft's availability, as was the ability to operate within the most up-to-date and able air defence environment against the latest high-performance fighters supported by early warning Control and Reporting ground environment (radar systems) together with surface-to-air missiles. Studies showed that by the mid-1960s, in order to overfly any such saturation, air defences would require an ability to fly at an altitude of 80,000 to 100,000 feet. Having received a number of proposals from various companies, English Electric and Vickers were awarded the government contract to design an aircraft to meet OR.343. English Electric had responsibility for the airframe, which would build on the design proposal for the earlier P.17A, but Vickers would be the main contractor. The British Aircraft Corporation (BAC) as a result of the above merger became the sole company with the contract to continue with the project.

As has been mentioned earlier, the Buccaneer had already been costed and was proceeding towards the prototype stage in 1955. By 1958, it was flying while the TSR2 was yet to exist as a government contract for the first stage of development. Lord Louis Mountbatten, the First Sea Lord from 1955 to 1959, had during this time approached the RAF to urge it to get on board the NA.39 project in order to meet GOR.339. The RAF remained unconvinced that this design could meet its more exacting requirements. By 1960, with the TSR2 starting to take shape and the engine specifications issued to Bristol Siddeley, Mountbatten was Chief of the Defence Staff and was still not keen on the TSR2. Not surprisingly, he had the Treasury on his side, even if unintentionally he appeared to use his influence to contribute towards the scuppering of the aircraft, together with the increasing line-up of sceptics and those who opposed the aircraft outright as an expensive and unnecessary luxury. Mountbatten was not entirely unaided by the project itself, as further expenses were difficult, indeed impossible, to avoid. The aircraft would be expected to be fitted with a TACAN (Tactical Air Navigation) system in the absence of an ICAO (International Civil Aviation Organization) approved navigation aid, as by the 1970s, the height of the TSR2 operational deployment, it would be denied overflight rights by many countries. So TACAN would need to be carried, and this, as late as 1964, was a new feature. Cost estimates on this short-notice addition were expected in January 1965, so time was of the essence. The Air Staff requirement was to be amended once the cost was agreed. While this was in hand, a report was expected which would recommend the development of a quite complex low-level sighting system, already being developed, that was optimised for dive attacks. This would of course suggest approaching the target at higher altitude and therefore rendering the aircraft

Above and below: TSR2, XR222, the fourth prototype, did not fly but was salvaged along with XR220, both airframes remain as a museum pieces. (*Peter R. March*)

particularly vulnerable to enemy air defences. Another unplanned extra that surfaced late in the day was the provision for long-range fuel tanks. The original Air Staff Requirement (ASR) did not specify additional fuel tanks, but that they were needed was beyond doubt early on. February 1965 was the date by which the Air Staff would be expected to reach an agreement for the provision of three additional tanks which could be carried in the fuselage as a ventral pack, with provision to fit one in the bomb bay. Elsewhere, an emergency arrester hook was awaiting the go-ahead from the Treasury and was expected to cost about £400,000 or about £1,500 per aircraft. The fuel would need to be jettisonable as well, as weight increase all around meant that the TSR2 could not land in an emergency with full internal fuel. This was actually included in the original specification but, as of December 1964, still needed to have the cost assessed.

Slightly later, but still before the first flight of the TSR2, the US General Dynamics Company was working on a project known initially as TFX and aimed at meeting pretty much the same requirements. This aircraft, to become the F-111, possessed the variable-geometry swing-wing design first mooted by Sir Barnes Wallis, and as the escalating costs of the TSR2 began to cause concern, the General Dynamics proposal was increasingly looked at as a cost-effective alternative. Thus the F-111A became the subject of a study, the Cottrell Report, which compared it not just with the TSR2 but also with the Buccaneer. The TSR2 was yet to get airborne but was beginning to make promising inroads to prove its viability. However, the Navy and Chief of the Defence Staff were eager to get the RAF to accept the wisdom of looking at cheaper options; more specifically, the Buccaneer.

On 26 January 1960, a performance comparison of the NA.39 (Buccaneer) and the TSR2 was published by the Assistant Chief of the Air Staff (Operational Requirements), Air Vice-Marshal R.N. Bateson. He had indeed made comparisons with the Mk 1 Buccaneer, the Mk 2 and a mooted supersonic version with reheated Rolls-Royce RB163 Spey engines, designated as the B.111. Bateson's opening comments stated:

> ... even disregarding range and performance considerations, the B.103 (Buccaneer S1) and B.109 (Buccaneer S2) cannot meet Royal Air Force requirements because they lack the equipment we consider necessary for navigating to and attacking the target in all weathers and over land. Their equipment is designed specifically for Naval purposes and is capable of attack against 'sore thumb' targets such as ships at sea and prominent shore installations.

In order to make the TSR2 a more economically viable proposition, the government looked to the export market and found an interested potential customer in the Royal Australian Air Force. The Australian government had first expressed an interest in

By no means comparable to either the TSR2 or F111, the Blackburn Buccaneer Carrier Strike Aircraft, seen here, nevertheless became the alternative after much hesitation and a sheer lack of political will regarding the former two. (*John Wharam*)

the TSR2 in 1959. Both BAC and the British government were then keen to get the Australians on board, with various annual presentations over the intervening years up to 1963. No matter, even as far back as 1959, the British press had been pouring the usual scorn on the project, reporting that the government was not interested and had no intention of going ahead with it. Mountbatten as Chief of the Defence Staff, who was not keen in any case, while pushing acceptance of the Buccaneer, is said to have added to the lack of certainty of the British commitment to the TSR2, having told the Australians that the aircraft was unlikely to materialise. Sir George Edwards had countered this claim some time later by pointing out that the teething troubles with the aircraft's development had mostly been ironed out and any remaining technical concerns could be eradicated. Even so, as late as April 1963, the Australians were less than reassured of the British service chiefs' intent to order their own home-built and superlative strike aircraft. The Australian Prime Minister, Sir Robert Menzies, seemed to favour the TSR2 as of the summer of 1963, and a report by their own CAS following a fact-finding tour of Europe made reassuring reading, stating that the RAF did intend to purchase the TSR2. As well as clear details on the total number to be built, he had also received details of the cost to Australia, delivery

TSR2 prototype under construction the loss of what promised to be a world beating design owes plenty to procrastinating lack of resolve on part of the Conservatives and Labour's priority of social policy ahead of Defence Policy. (*Peter R. March*)

dates and the operational standard for the production order. The Australian PM did, however, stress the importance he attached to expert advice. Four months later, on 11 October, the Australian Defence Secretary Athol Townley was on his way to Washington DC despite an assurance that the RAF had confirmed an initial order for thirty TSR2s, with a view to purchasing as many as 138 aircraft. Menzies announced on the 15th that there would be a general election on 30 November, and the future replacement for Australia's own Canberra bombers now became an election issue. Despite the recent encouraging reports, confusion over British intent to proceed, along with limp inclination and heel-dragging by the British government, helped to encourage the Australian government to look at the TFX (F-111) as a replacement for their Canberra aircraft instead.

The British High Commission in Canberra received a letter on 14 October 1963 from Menzies, stating that they were now looking to purchase the American F-111 in place of the TSR2, but that the TSR2 would be fully considered before a final decision was taken. Before this letter was received, the Australian Defence Secretary was invited to stop off in London on his return from Washington DC, but it was accepted that this might be impossible due to other commitments. The British government told Menzies that its Defence Secretary Peter Thorneycroft had offered to send a small mission to Australia to discuss proposals which would include the Australians participating in trials, evaluation, development flying and training. The facilities for this were expected to be in place by 1966. They could also expect delivery of the first twelve aircraft in 1968, and a further twelve in 1969. As a stopgap measure, the sale of a surplus twelve Valiants at a bargain price, refurbished and modified according to requirements and credit arrangements, was also on the table. Training facilities for the Valiants, which were to be made available 'almost immediately', could be provided in the UK or set up in Australia.

The same day that the draft letter containing the British government's fresh proposals regarding the sale of the TSR2 was approved by the Prime Minister, the opposition Labour Party in Australia were attacking that country's defence policy as one of 'Boomerangs and Broomsticks', which would take the same percentage of GNP (2.7 per cent) at the end of what was then a five-year programme for modernisation as it had at the beginning. The opposition's own proposals, should they win the upcoming election, included three new Army battle groups, the acquisition of a modern aircraft carrier, and among other things which required a considerable degree of expansion, an immediate replacement for the RAAF's obsolete Canberra bombers. The next day, newspapers in Australia were carrying reports that the Australian government had decided to take the American TFX and also to accept an offer of B-47E Stratojet medium bombers in the interim. The Australian Secretary to the Prime Minister's department was contacted and was told that while a decision on which aircraft to go for had not been decided, mention of the great advantage of the TFX over the TSR2 had been made.

Later, the British Prime Minister was sent a message via Australia House that Menzies would announce at 11:00 hours GMT, the same day, the decision to adopt TFX (F-111) as the replacement for the Canberra. Meanwhile, the Air Secretary wanted to know from the RAF, in light of the report from Australia, and more to do with the purchase of B-47s as an interim replacement for their Canberras, what we should say when asked whether we were taking any immediate steps to replace ours; and if not, why not.

What is all the more galling is that the lease of American B-47s was to be free of charge until the F-111s became available. The Australians had indeed signed up to a cracking deal with the Americans. The purchase price would include one year's initial spare parts, ground handling equipment, training aids, and initial and operational training of crews. The Americans had also agreed to integration of RAAF and US logistics patterns, enabling the Australians to draw future needs in spare parts and equipment from American stocks, with the advantage of lower prices. Furthermore, the aircraft would be delivered at the same rate as those going to the USAF. Finally, Townley had told the US Defense Secretary Robert McNamara that the Australian government had decided to acquire TFX as the 'incomparably best bomber' in the next decade. Some Australian airmen had their doubts about this, but the mood of the national press in Australia was to welcome an end to the delay in confirming a replacement. The decision was also endorsed by the opposition party. Because events had moved so quickly, the High Commission did not pass on the British Prime Minister's letter offering terms for the purchase of the TSR2. In response to the question about replacing British Canberras, the Air Staff issued a brief, explaining that the RAAF Canberras had been purchased in the period 1953/54 and were therefore older and less developed than those then operated by the RAF. More realistic, however, was the observation that the Canberra was the RAAF's only bomber, whereas the RAF's force was fleshed out in both conventional and nuclear roles by its Vulcans, Victors and Valiants.

The RAF had at this time the B(I)8 Canberra, introduced in 1956/57, and upgraded B6s designated as B15s and 16s equipped the Near and Far East air forces from 1961/62. There was further talking up of the Canberras, including comments on range and navigation aids, and how they met the requirements of NATO and CENTO in the respective theatres for which the two basic models had been specifically designed. Refurbishment and modernisations had continued with a view to maintaining the aircraft up to the arrival of the TSR2, of course. By the end of the month, the Australian press, while still generally supportive of the decision to choose the TFX (F-111), were raising doubts about the decision, as was the political opposition. A controversial television programme about the TSR2 was to be shown on Australian television on 22 November 1963, and it was believed in British circles that the sudden lapse in Australian interest in the TSR2 was brought about by the fact that the American aircraft emerged as a serious contender at the start of 1963. In September 1964, the TSR2 flew for the first time. Still the first choice for the RAF, it was now showing true promise.

The following month Britain had a general election and by the slenderest of margins, thirteen seats, the Labour Party became the largest party. The margin of victory was smaller than that gained by the Conservatives in 2010, but Harold Wilson felt confident enough to run the country without a working majority. On 9 February 1965, the new Defence Secretary, Denis Healey, made the annual statement on defence to Parliament. The government was being asked to provide just under £1.7 billion in order to cover the defence budget for the financial year 1965/66. This broke down as follows:

Central Defence Vote:	£28,459,000
Royal Navy (inc. Royal Marines):	£544,188,000
Army:	£555,600,000
Royal Air Force:	£561,770,000

Healey went on to say that the government had inherited defence forces that were seriously over-stretched and, in some cases, dangerously under-equipped. Expenditure of over £20 billion since 1952 had failed to provide the necessary incentive for volunteer recruits in some of the vital fields or to produce all the weapons needed for the then current tasks. He went on to claim that there had been no attempt to match political commitments to military resources, still less to relate the resources made available for defence to the economic circumstances of the nation. The 1963/64 estimates produced under the previous government provided for expenditure of about £1.8 billion, while those for 1964/65 provided for just under £2 billion. This represented an increase of 8.7 per cent, which in real terms came to 5.5 per cent. The inherited previous defence estimate from the Conservatives for the forthcoming period stood at £2.2 billion, representing a further real terms increase of 5.1 per cent, or 8.9 per cent with inflation taken into account.

What concerned Healey was that these estimates projected a steady rise in defence spending at a time when, according to the government, the US and USSR were reducing theirs. Healey further claimed there was no guarantee in the previous government's plans of value for money, or of provision of forces 'at the right time' with the arms they needed. The new government had therefore set in train a series of studies on defence policy. These would cover the effects on force levels and capabilities of a number of different possible courses of action. The principal aim over the next few years was simple: to reduce defence spending. This was a not entirely less than laudable aim, and there was a plausible rationale to the spending reduction. Britain was, by hook or by crook, dismantling its Empire, as fast as it could. From this, naturally, came the opportunity to reduce the defence budget. In the meantime, Healey said the government would ensure that the armed forces would have their immediate needs met, but at a cost which the nation could afford.

A political recap: the government in 1966 had said it would not

a. embark upon major operations of war without allies,
b. take part in the landing or withdrawal of troops against sophisticated opposition outside the range of shore-based aircraft, and
c. provide any country with military assistance unless it was prepared to provide Britain with the necessary facilities in time.

The Labour government's long-term ambitions and belief was that defence policy and Britain's security could only be assured through general and comprehensive disarmament under the United Nations and dependence on alliances with friends in many parts of the world. Interdependence could be the only basis for national security in a nuclear age. Strengthening the peace-keeping powers of the UN therefore was the principal overriding objective. However, until such time as this goal

Mark 3 Lightnings in formation. In 1965 they were perhaps the world's most potent Interceptors in terms of airframe/engine performance. (*The National Archives*)

could be achieved, Britain had to meet its obligations by maintaining the capacity for providing military assistance in many parts of the world.

Some figures pertinent to the era regarding the rising cost of defence spending make for interesting, if not too surprising, reading. The cost of running an armoured regiment was expected to double in the period from 1963 to 1968. Furthermore, the cost of purchasing, for example, the Mk 3 Lightning all-weather interceptor fighter was as much as six times the cost of a Mk 6 Hunter fighter aircraft. The Royal Navy's relatively new Sea Vixen carrier-borne jet fighter was seven times the expense of its immediate predecessor, the de Havilland Sea Venom. Meanwhile, of course, allowances would have to rise in line with wages and salaries in civilian life.

The position claimed by Denis Healey was a choice between renouncing certain strategic options and increasing further reliance on military co-operation with allies. Another concern was that the forces in Germany were placing a heavy financial burden on the defence budget. In the meantime, a list of new aircraft for the RAF was in the pipeline, so to speak: the Hawker P1154 (the supersonic Harrier) the planned medium transport S681 and, still hanging on of course, the TSR2. In addition to these development projects was the programme to replace the remaining Hunters

Blackburn Beverley. The 1950s saw the development of more realistic Military Transport aircraft; the Blackburn Beverley could carry vehicles and other heavy equipment and unload on the airfield after landing using its Short Field performance. (*Peter R. March*)

in the close air support and reconnaissance roles. This latter endeavour was already expected to be the American-built F-4 Phantom. These aircraft, arguably, were crucial to the new posture to be pursued by NATO, 'flexible response', and gravitate away from the trip-wire policy of massive retaliation pursued so far. But to the government of the day, they placed an unacceptable burden on defence. On top of this burden, the forecast delivery dates were so far ahead for some that the interim purchase of foreign aircraft would be necessary. At the time, the savings from cancelling these projects and purchasing off the shelf from the US over ten years was expected to be £300 million. Also, the TSR2 project was being viewed by Labour not as the answer to the RAF's desperate need for a new tactical strike and reconnaissance fighter but as a means of continuing and maintaining the capacity of the British aviation industry, in the interests of the domestic economy, for the research, development and production of other military aircraft. But, of course, at a cost the nation could afford. The new defence estimate for 1965/66 now had a revised increase to some £2.12 billion, a marginal reduction on the previous estimate.

Matters by now had also moved ahead in respect of inter-European co-operation on new projects. Still concerned about the eventual outcome for the TSR2, the RAF

Ground crew manoeuvring the bomb trolley of a Vulcan at Waddington, April 1969. The Blue Steel Missile was now redundant as this year the RAF handed over the Primary Nuclear Deterrent role to the Navy's Polaris submarines. However, the Vulcans lived on for another 13 years as a standby deterrent, and also as conventional bombers typically armed with the 1,000-lb HE bombs seen here . (*R64177, IWM*)

was now placing a considerable degree of priority on the development of the future Anglo-French variable-geometry fighter aircraft (AFVG) project, the first major one involving international co-operation and with France on this occasion, which was considered sacrosanct. The development and purchase of the AFVG was to pick up the shortfall from a reduced number of the TSR2. The first squadron, however, was not expected to make the front line until 1975. With a total of 150 Canberras to replace, and at the absolute latest by the end of the 1960s, a justification was made for rolling on the Vulcans and Victors. This was seen as only a stopgap until the arrival of the AFVG to make up the requisite numbers. The Buccaneer Mk 2 was considered again and dismissed as a candidate for this requirement as well. The

Armourer fusing bombs for a Vulcan, April 1969. (*R64178, IWM*)

AFVG was also intended as the future replacement for the English Electric Lightning. As of 1965, in order to secure the viability and effectiveness of the V-bombers and ensure enough would remain available, the unit establishment would need to be higher by the start of the 1970s in order to meet the reliance on numbers. Before the cancellation of the TSR2 and the reduction in the number of F-111s, the long-term plan up to the mid-1970s had been to retain fifteen Handley Page Victor B.Mk 2 aircraft in the low-level strike role and a further eight Victor SR.Mk 2 aircraft for strategic reconnaissance. The much-loved and much more charismatic Vulcans were to disappear in total by 1971. The likely reduction in F-111 numbers now prompted a proposal by the RAF to retain up to 96 V-bombers as far as 1975, assuming that the proposed two CVA-01 carriers for the Navy were going to be around. If, for whatever reason, they would not be, the idea was to retain just 84 V-bombers and twelve Buccaneers (nothing to do with F-111 substitution); the twelve fewer Vulcans and Victors would result from the need to convert some more to the tanker role, presumably in order to give the RAF the reach required to compensate for the carrier loss. This figure was arrived at by assuming that the Polaris A3 would take over the nuclear deterrent role from the V-force. But with so few tactical strike F-111s expected to replace the existing Canberras, and a number of V-force aircraft (forty) also to be assigned to CENTO (Middle East pact with Iran, Iraq, Turkey and Pakistan), an additional 56 V-bombers would need to be retained to make good the numbers. NATO examinations of the Vulcans and Victors had confirmed that they would be suitable interim aircraft before something like the AFVG would be available in sufficient numbers from around 1975.

Meanwhile, Britain's total deployable armed forces at the start of 1965 amounted to 392,000. This did not include 14,000 deployable Gurkhas. Of this overall figure, 240,000 were based in the UK. Among the overseas commitments were 62,000 in West Germany, including West Berlin, 23,000 in the Mediterranean and 67,000 in the Middle and Far East, plus the Gurkhas.

Among the more pressing problems for the government to consider, with regard to ensuring that the armed forces were equipped at the right times with the right arms, was the recent disbandment of the Valiant element of the V-force. This had seen five operational squadrons – one reconnaissance, one tanker and three bomber – all disbanded with no evident replacement. The Valiant squadrons were assigned directly to the forces under the command of SACEUR and therefore did not form part of the UK nuclear deterrent. The loss of the Valiants left a considerable capability gap. They were also the principal force to be replaced by the TSR2 should it have made it into service, although, no matter what was done now with a view to filling the Valiant gap, there was no way that the first production TSR2s or, as would very soon be the case, the F-111As were going to reach the first squadrons before 1970. This left the RAF contribution to NATO's immediate tactical/medium strike force reliant upon the Canberra B(I)8 and B(I)6 squadrons of RAF Germany and nothing else. The reconnaissance and tanker squadrons were swiftly replaced, in all fairness, but at the expense of a sizeable chunk of the nuclear deterrent. Mk 2 Victors replaced the Valiants of No. 543 Squadron in the reconnaissance role, two Victor Mk 1A squadrons were re-roled as tanker units to replace the Valiants of No. 214 Squadron, the three bomber squadrons were not replaced and two further Victor squadrons, Nos 10 and 15, stood down.

The answer to the problem was also the ultimate cause of the TSR2's downfall – the F-111A option. The Wilson government had comprehensively reviewed the requirement, in depth, for the need to replace the now rather embarrassing-looking Canberras. This may be a subjective remark, but on a more objective level, the Canberra Mk 8 and 6 jets stood a very poor chance against the hailstorm of Soviet anti-aircraft weaponry that would be thrown against them. They would have stood a very slightly improved chance of survival if they had had TFR (terrain-following radar) and could have flown at Mach 1 at hedgerow height. This is exactly what the TSR2 had promised and what the American F-111 now offered as a cheaper alternative. A government report on the 1965/66 Defence Review claimed that the F-111 offered such a step up in performance that 'the existence of this capability could well enable us to avoid operations taking place at all'.

Shortly after taking office, the government of Harold Wilson was already looking at the viability of the TSR2. The previous Defence Secretary, Peter Thorneycroft, in his last statement on defence had described the TSR2 as promising to be one of the most potent and flexible instruments of military power yet devised and with a predicted long and effective life. Production contracts for fifty TSR2s were being negotiated, covering a number of development aircraft and the initial production order. Fast forward to January 1965, and the new government adjourned a decision on the future of the TSR2 until March. BAC was facing the closure of its Weybridge plant and redundancies in the company were expected. A newly set up ministry, the Department of Economic Affairs, along with the Treasury, suggested that the resources released from cancelling the TSR2 could be redeployed to earn or save substantial amounts of dollars to set against the cost of purchasing the F-111A. The information upon which a decision was to be reached was now available. The TSR2 project was costing the government £1 million a week in development costs. Denis Healey, the Defence Secretary, was in favour of cancelling and taking up the F-111.

Both aircraft had, by early 1965, reached the same stage of engine and airframe development. However, the TSR2 had been gestating for five years whereas the F-111 had taken only two years to get to the same stage. On the other hand, the TSR2 was now accruing considerable flying hours, having seen earlier engine problems ironed out, whilst the F-111 was at the time contending with serious problems concerning its engine. These, though, were expected to be resolved in a short space of time, as the Americans were allocating substantial resources to tackle the matter. Another benchmark consideration was that the TSR2 was designed from the outset as an advanced weapon system. Initially, the F-111A would be fitted with a current avionics and weapons system, the intention being to upgrade this in a Mk 2 version, bringing comparative performance with that of the initial TSR2s. To Healey, the merits of the two were finely balanced and either would satisfy the military requirement. Furthermore, costs as they stood suggested an overall purchase of 110 F-111 Mk 2 standard aircraft, but of course that was not necessarily the number which would eventually be bought. The ultimate price comparison put the F-111A at least £200 million cheaper than the TSR2 and perhaps as much as £280 million if the expected lower operating costs proved to be the case. These figures also took into account a cancellation fee of £70 million against the TSR2 and a further £70 million expected in interest payments against purchasing the F-111s on the credit terms being offered by the US government. What was odd about the financial arrangements on offer was the expectation that the cost advantage was expected to increase should the UK government buy fewer than 110 aircraft. Certainly a lower cost all round, but the unit cost was also expected to be less as a result. The maximum number of TSR2s which the government would have bought was expected to have been 158. However, doubtless due to the expectations with the AFVG project, the number of F-111As to be purchased was eventually settled at fifty, at a cost of $1.25 billion at 4¾ per cent interest, spread over a period up to 1977. This figure was a credit loan, the bulk of which did not need to be spent until after 1969/70. Further, the fifty aircraft would be delivered not later than January 1970. The report concluded that the military requirement for 'some' F-111As was proven. It was also envisaged that the F-111, being a swing-wing aircraft, would help the government with the development and eventual production of the Anglo-French variable-geometry aircraft project, considered vital to UK industry and future European co-operation. Just the same, there was a sense of ever-increasing doubt about the purchase of the F-111, despite recommendations following the Defence Review that the aircraft should be bought subject to successful negotiations.

If either aircraft was to take on commitments outside of the European theatre, which would in all probability be the case, then 110 airframes would be required. The next battle was to promote the F-111 over the Buccaneer. Much had been done by Mountbatten, more in determined defence of the Navy than by objective assessment, to promote the Buccaneer over both the TSR2 and the F-111. A simple yardstick comparison left performance considerations in no doubt whatsoever. The F-111, operating from any one of six strategically held bases from Gibraltar through to Darwin, showed that with a 10,000 lb bomb load it could provide seamless overlapping strike range. This was based on the aircraft's 1,500-mile radius of action. The Buccaneer, with the same bomb load, could not hope to produce anything anywhere near such a projection of force with a range of only 350 miles. Interestingly, other comparison reports of the Buccaneer and F-111 determined that the latter could operate from a shorter runway and was not dependent on concrete, and, very notably, the F-111 had the capability to reach supersonic speeds whereas the Buccaneer had been designed from the outset as a low-level subsonic aircraft. Payload comparisons were in the order of 34,000 lb for the F-111 to the Buccaneer's 10,000 lb. However, despite all this, in a set scenario it was shown that on the basis of cost-effectiveness both were roughly comparable, and that the decision as to which to go with should be made on other considerations:

1. The total inability of the Buccaneer Mk 2 to meet the reconnaissance requirement.
2. The greater flexibility of the F-111 to deal with a variety of operational
   circumstances arising from its superior performance.

3. The scope for development of the F-111 against the Buccaneer, which was described at the time as being stretched to the limit. (A note here regarding the more modern argument about Typhoons, Tornados and Harriers. The Typhoon has far and away the greatest potential for future development and its current performance in terms of sheer speed and agility already outstrips the other two.)

4. The points made at 2 and 3 are what made the F-111 a far more realistic and likely deterrent against possible aggression in the first place.

5. Commonality with the US and Australia.

6. The belief that every F-111 would be delivered before the first Buccaneer Mk 2.

7. The Buccaneer Mk 2 numbers would have to be restricted to sixty to leave room for the AFVG programme. (The buy of F-111s was already restricted to fifty aircraft because of this. One of the favourable arguments for Buccaneers was that more could be bought to make up for performance deficiencies). This would make the Buccaneer more expensive and less worthwhile industrially.

Mountbatten's assertion, when Chief of the Defence Staff, that cost value was to be found in the comparison of three or four Buccaneers to one TSR2 or, as was now the case, one F-111, was shown to be misleading as the operational value was that as many as four Buccaneers would be needed to achieve the same task compared to a single TSR2 or F-111, and even then some inflight refuelling would be necessary. Proponents of the Fleet Air Arm have recently criticised the RAF operation of using air-to-air refuelling to get a number of Tornado GR4s to Libya all the way from Norfolk and back, whereas a carrier capability would negate this. The number of carriers with Buccaneers required to provide the level of strike coverage provided by F-111s operating from Gibraltar, Akrotiri, Aldabra, Gan, the Cocos Islands and Darwin in 1970 would have been prohibitive. Other performance measurements were looked at, including the F-111's supersonic capability compared to the subsonic Buccaneer, all of which added to a clear and obvious choice. Furthermore, the F-111/ TSR2 design was to provide a reconnaissance capability for which the Buccaneer was not even considered suitable in light of the level of saturation defences which in 1966 were expected to be encountered in the 1970s due to limitations in speed, height and stand-off photographic capability.

Much store was set by adequate air strike and reconnaissance in the future, as much to deter emerging forces from Second and Third World countries (the African continent being given as an example by Denis Healey when reviewing the option for the F-111 in February 1966). The withdrawal from the Far East, however, and the change of Britain's military posture across the planet was what the cabinet of 1968 were thinking about. The F-111, and before it the TSR2, had been ordered primarily to support Britain's remaining presence and role in the Far East. The shift now towards Europe and a more substantial and realistic tactical reliance, its cornerstone being the AFVG, was part of Healey's defence economy proposals in order to save the F-111, which was placed outside of defence requirements as global reach was deemed no longer a British political aspiration. In the meantime, there were concerns about how the defence chiefs, who remained unanimous about the F-111, would react given the need now for a deeper and wider reappraisal of defence policy. A statement on the defence cuts would need to bear this in mind and effectively put a decision on the backburner for now as to whether Britain should retain a capability to develop and produce advanced combat aircraft in the future.

A year and a half after the government had abandoned the TSR2 and negotiated the purchase of the F-111 the die was cast, presaging the beginning of the end for the entire strike reconnaissance project. On 3 January 1967, a report on short-term economic forecasts indicated that further measures were called for in order to tackle the balance of payments, including the need to reduce the deficit and therefore public spending by £850 million to prevent a cumulative debt expansion. Civil expenditure reductions were applied at a much lower rate: £325 million in 1968/69, and a further £370 million in 1969/70. Exactly a year later, further 'substantial' reductions in defence expenditure were announced. Roy Jenkins, the new Chancellor, said that Britain's standing in the world depended on the soundness of its economy and not on a worldwide military presence. Shortly before this, on 18 November 1967, he had recommended devaluation of the pound sterling to take effect from 18 November. This is said to have ended the economic strategy and national plan the government had been pursuing hitherto, to which end the Treasury was to have its powers reduced to short-term financial management. The new Department of Economic Affairs was to be the new authority overseeing the longer-term management of industry and the economy. Although there were still considerable reserves of foreign exchange, and they were as yet not compelled to devalue the currency by sheer lack of liquid resources, there had been serious speculation against the pound which at times had reached grave proportions. Attempting to hold parity was about to exhaust reserves, therefore devaluation of the pound was unavoidable, the currency being devalued from $2.80 to $2.40. On 4 January, the cabinet now found favour with cancelling the F-111.

Just how desperate Denis Healey had been to get the F-111, especially following the TSR2 debacle, is a matter for endless political debate, but he was invited to make economies elsewhere if he wished to hang on to it. He proposed savings of £3.5 billion, to be spread over five years, much of which was to be absorbed by the withdrawal from the Middle and Far East that was well and truly in motion. Healey believed that the risks to service morale were acceptable with the expected rundown. The reductions in overseas commitments would mean that certain capabilities would be eliminated, while retaining those deemed necessary to meet the kind of warfare in which Britain would be likely to get involved in the future. If the cuts were to be based on the retention of the F-111, then to pay for it, the carrier force would have to go.

The preferred option was to cancel the order for F-4 Phantom fighters to replace both the Navy's Sea Vixens and the RAF's Hunters. The savings sought amounted to a serious compromise whichever way the cake was sliced. The order for the Navy Phantoms was considered not worthwhile cancelling at the stage reached, so reducing to a single carrier might have to happen instead. Of the four carriers the Royal Navy had in 1968, two were Audacious Class vessels, *Ark Royal* and *Eagle*. Only one was to be refitted to carry the F-4 Phantom; the other was for the chop. The Army was to lose 13,000 personnel, which translated into twenty-eight major major units. That the F-111's retention enjoyed support from all the Chiefs of Staff, must have involved something not short of a miracle to bring such bipartisan agreement, especially given that the other services were to have their own equipment programmes reduced to accommodate it, but the F-111 was seen as something of a panacea to the protection of servicemen's lives that we simply could not do without. Falling to the level of air contribution of Belgium and Holland was mooted as an example of what to avoid should the F-111 be cancelled. This would mean buying a further seventy-five Phantoms, which in turn would cut the savings from the F-111 programme down to £115 million.

When proposed, the cuts included the planned phasing out of the carrier force altogether by 1970/71, the abandonment of Polaris, the Army to lose specific vehicles and weapons etc, and the RAF to lose the Harrier and the AFVG in addition to the F-111A cancellation. The number of Phantoms for both the RAF and Navy were to be reduced and the Martel missile, which would eventually be carried by the Buccaneer and Jaguar, was to be cancelled. On 12 January 1968, the Foreign Secretary, George Brown, said in a cabinet meeting that he had had a disturbing and distasteful discussion with the US Secretary of State, Dean Rusk. He had also met Robert McNamara, the US Defense Secretary, and then had a telephone conversation with President Johnson. He had faithfully and forcefully presented the case for the cabinet's decision to withdraw from the Far East and from the Persian Gulf by the end of the financial year 1970/71 and to cancel the order for F-111 aircraft. Rusk's reaction had been, as always, kindly and courteous. But he had not concealed his shock and dismay. He had indeed used the phrase 'For God's sake, act like Britain' and had gone on to say he clearly felt that the British government was opting out of its world responsibilities. Rusk finished the conversation by saying that it was the end of an era. Brown took this to mean that Rusk was implying that it was the end of the age of co-operation between the US and the UK, and was sure that confidence in the UK had been terribly shaken. Another official at the meeting also noted that Rusk had asked what kind of role Britain thought it could play in future, if it planned to withdraw from both the Far and the Middle East and, as he understood the Prime Minister to have implied in a recent conversation with US Under Secretary Katzenbach, even from Europe, if Britain did not secure a 100 per cent offset for the

The General Dynamics F111, seen here at RAF Finningley at the Royal Silver Jubilee review of the RAF in 1977. This aircraft is owned by the Royal Australian Air Force; the British Government deemed that the advanced Tactical Strike Aircraft was beyond affordability and selected instead the home-designed Buccaneer. (*Tony McGhee*)

foreign exchange costs of stationing its forces in Germany. What Rusk had called a 'fait accompli' had hit them deeply and hard. The consequence of these decisions was described as potentially very grave and their cost in the short term could be greater than the savings they were meant to achieve. The decision by the British government to cancel the F-111 was taken on 13 January 1968.

By the end of the 1960s, the RAF had neither the TSR2 nor its cheaper and more reliable American alternative, and now the Defence Council needed to be engaged as a matter of urgency to decide what they were going to do. As a footnote, it is worth pointing out that the F-111 went into service with the USAF and the RAAF, serving both for many years. The Americans, once again as decisive as ever on defence matters, were able to replace their F-111s earlier with the F-15E Strike Eagle, while the RAAF soldiered on until getting its chosen replacement, the F-18F Super Hornet, at the end of 2010!

The loss of the carriers was seen as a further logical consequence of Britain's withdrawal from the Far East, but as events in the decades to come would prove, this was once again a short-sighted political decision based on a narrow remit. This produced some public comments by former senior military officers who were out to defend their respective service. On 4 March 1966, a letter appeared in *The Daily Telegraph*, written by Rear-Admiral Sir Alexander Bingley in response to one on 28 February by Air Marshal Sir Robert Saundby in which he accused the Navy of wanting to retain its carriers primarily to build up its empire or take over that of the RAF. Bingley asserted that over the previous twenty years carriers had been involved in providing close support for troops ashore, and fighter cover for them and for ships and aircraft on passage. They had, he claimed, had to do these things even within close range of British air bases ashore, this last point a nettled reaction to the boys in light blue. Many of his assertions could be taken straight out of letters written in more recent times regarding the SDSR and the reaction by some retired Army and Navy officers today. One of Bingley's claims was that a carrier could operate 100 to 200 miles off the scene of operations and each of its aircraft could do up to six sorties a day, compared to a shore-based aircraft being lucky to manage one.

A number of other scathing but vaguely substantiated claims were made in the same letter, prompting the Chief of the Air Staff to respond by having a draft letter prepared to be handed to *The Daily Telegraph* in order to rebut the claims made. However, Sir Ralph Cochrane, whom the CAS had hoped would write to *The Telegraph*, was not persuaded, but the prepared responses included a query from the CAS as to whether Bingley's assertion that a shore-based aircraft from Australia or Gan would be lucky to manage a single sortie could be substantiated. That even half the six sorties claimed by Bingley could be flown in practice is, in my view, improbable in the extreme. Even if this claim were to be true, the carrier would very soon use up its stock of bombs and aviation fuel, and would need to withdraw to a safe distance to replenish. A similar warning was made about not building the new CVA-01 carrier and that other projects for new aircraft, ships and missiles were likely to cost several times more than the saving from cancelling CVA-01. The rebuttal here was that three such carriers would be required to keep one on station, and the cost of such a force would be £1.4 billion over a ten-year period. Anyone who has followed recent press reports by similar people today will doubtless feel a touch of *déjà vu*. As late as 1969, attempts continued from the outside to lobby the Chiefs of Staff as well as the government over the foolhardiness of not maintaining the carriers until at least a mooted lightweight example could take over. No lesser individual than Mountbatten approached both Sir Michael Le Fanu and Sir John Grandy, respectively First Sea Lord and Chief of the Air Staff, with a plea to retain the carriers, suggesting that of course the aircraft would be flown by RAF pilots. To this, he was told that it was entirely against defence policy; the money now used for carriers could be spent more effectively elsewhere, and anyway, how would the Navy man them? Sir Michael Le Fanu was also described as being content with the government's plans. Mountbatten's approaching the two chiefs was described by Mr A. R. M. Jaffray, Healey's Private Secretary, as highly embarrassing and he warned the Prime Minister's Private Secretary that he might be heading in his direction next, and wanted the PM to know how to react.

Not long after, a report appeared in *The Times* on 30 October 1969, stating that the Defence Ministry had virtually decided that the Harrier vertical and short take-off jet aircraft would not be suitable for use at sea. This had been the proposed light carrier to replace the CVA-01 but which had now been cancelled due to Healey's 'nothing east of Suez' defence policy. The Harrier was by that time already operational with the RAF, and the idea had been to bridge the gap between the removal of other

ANNEX A TO
F540 FOR MAY 1969

Seen here in May 1969, aircrew of the first operational RAF Phantom Squadron, No. 54, pose for
a group shot at Coningsby. (*The National Archives*)

fixed-wing aircraft and the arrival of what would be the new Invincible Class carriers
by having Harriers operate from smaller ships. The article went on to mention that
'many naval officers feel that its development in a maritime role has always remained
low on the RAF's list of priorities'. This may well have been the case, and perhaps
because the RAF did, and usually does, have a set of priorities at variance with the
Navy and Army. In this case, the forming of three Harrier squadrons to replace some
of the Hunters based in West Germany was a more pressing requirement for the
Junior Service. This time the real villain of the piece was neither one service nor the
other; it was the elected 'great and good', Her Majesty's government, that had frankly
assigned the role of maritime air a much lower priority. The fact that Harriers were
being looked at to see if they could operate off the decks of cruisers converted to
through-decks, and the cost involved, was testimony to the typical compromise and
fudge that was just another step along the way towards disasters in the future which
were only narrowly averted thanks to the point in history at which they occurred and
the point in the process of 'restructuring' defence. But in a reaction similar to that
of recent events following the SDSR, the RAF was held responsible in the minds of
some for influencing government policy and its impact upon the Royal Navy. In any
case, the role of the Harrier afloat was not to make good the role of the Sea Vixen,
Phantom and Buccaneer which would eventually go with the older Audacious Class
vessels; it was described as being able to cope with reconnaissance and air defence

against a light threat and small-scale strike, but the eventual Sea Harrier FRS.1 was deployed operationally on the Invincible Class carriers as a carrier-borne interceptor and nothing more.

In due course, because the RAF did not actually have any tactical aircraft of the type it was looking for, it was now at last seeing its own Phantoms and the Harrier enter service, the Buccaneer, which the RAF had dismissed as unsuitable to besubstituted for the TSR2 and F-111, was now to enter service as the only other option. Truth be known, given the situation, a fair chunk of the RAF's Phantoms were to now be assigned to the strike role as well as tactical air support. It then came to light that the Phantom was not able to carry the WE177 nuclear bomb, so an American weapon had to be loaned to the three squadrons eventually equipped at Brüggen in Germany. Owing to American sensitivity, this also required the provision of USAF security and maintenance personnel to be based at Brüggen in order to provide the specialist handling and also to ensure that the level of security that they required for their nuclear bombs was not in question.

The RAF had faced something of an uphill struggle to justify the various tactical aircraft projects which it succeeded in doing. By making the case for one, it had to raise reservations on the suitability of another. The case for the development of the

F4 Phantom II became more heavily relied upon than originally intended following the cancellation of both TSR2 and the F111. This is a USAF example photographed three years before the first aircraft were received by the RAF and RN. (*John Wharam*)

Hunter low-level attack; by the time its successor, the Harrier and Phantom started to arrive, many of the airframes could not fire all the four cannons which they were armed with. (*Warwickshire County Records Office, Reference no.: P4 (N) 600/1674/34a*)

P1127 into the Harrier had been questioned amid the search for economies in the 1960s. The justification for its continued development and entry into service was made on the grounds that the Hawker Hunter, as of 1966, was already lagging behind other new fighters entering service. At this time, some Hunter airframes were restricted to firing only two of the available four 30-mm Aden cannons in the nose, such was the toll on the fatigue life. The Phantom, which had originally been mooted as the Hunter's replacement, was confusingly being described, in the face of Healey's Defence Review, as too heavy and therefore restricted to operation from certain airfields, which were described as being well known to the Soviets. The point was that as a battlefield support aircraft, it would be limited, particularly further east and south, if required to operate locally to provide immediate support for ground troops. The kind of situation envisaged would see Phantoms operating in this role forced to fly from as far afield as 200 nautical miles from the action. The Harrier of course would operate from just about anywhere: sports field, farmland, high street and rooftop. Some may regard this as contradictory to the recent SDSR decision to scrap the Harrier in favour of the equally big and heavy long-runway-reliant Tornado. However, as is explained later, the circumstances governing the 2010 comparisons were positively stark when compared to the luxury of detailing the finer points between the Harrier and Phantom in 1966. Alongside the development of the P1127/Harrier was the joint Anglo-French project, the Jaguar. This aircraft, at an earlier stage of development in 1966, was also dismissed against the VTOL design.

Nevertheless, the RAF was pushing for a force structure this far back, which envisaged V-bombers released from the nuclear deterrent role by Polaris, providing a stopgap until the arrival of the AFVG, anticipated in 1975. The F-111A was still expected to enter service in small numbers from 1969. Eventually, the AFVG and F-111A would comprise the RAF tactical strike and reconnaissance element.

Air defence and close support would be deployed as follows. The Phantom would largely carry out the air defence role, supported by the retention of a small number of Lightnings, while close support would be found by Harriers and Jaguars supported by a small number of Phantoms. This was expected to be the layout by 1976, following which the Lightnings would be removed and, from 1980, an air defence version of the AFVG would replace the Phantoms. The close support side was seen as giving the Army the best possible range of air options, with Phantoms providing the weightier punch in battlefield support when needed. Even if restricted to a certain number of airfields, this particular point seems to have caused far too much concern at the time as Phantom aircraft during their subsequent service managed to get on and off a hell of a lot of runways that could be considered very limiting. Ultimately, the Air Staff saw the P1127/Harrier and Jaguar as the two primary close support platforms to fulfil this requirement. The latter two options certainly represented how things largely materialised, if you substitute AFVG for MRCA and accommodate a time lapse of about seven years.

That said, Sir John Grandy was concerned about the loss of the carriers, long-range strike and reconnaissance aircraft and stockpiles of equipment in base installations in the Far East. All of which, given the situation with the Americans in South Vietnam, could easily escalate, and recent aggressive tendencies shown by North Korea made pulling out of the Far East an ill-advised decision and suggested that before planning for the withdrawal was further advanced, a study to determine just when the point of no return would be reached should be made, clearly with a view to providing an opportunity to halt the process. In a response to a letter of support in difficult times from Air Chief Marshal Sir Augustus Walker, Deputy C-in-C, Allied Forces Central Europe, Grandy said:

> We are going through an appalling time. Our aim is to ensure that the defence position of our country is safeguarded, and we are fighting hard. But as you will know there is a weight of opinion in high places which, through ignorance (one hopes?) is prepared to sacrifice what we regard as the foundation of a sound defence policy in the interests of short-term consumer benefits.

This message was sent out at the end of 1967, on the eve of the RAF's Golden Anniversary, the following 1 April.

Just how bad morale really was throughout the RAF, indeed the wider military establishment, with so many reductions on top of cancelled programmes, was about to be demonstrated by one particular flight lieutenant, Alan Pollock, at the time serving with No. 1 Squadron based at West Raynham. Sensing a lack of preparation to mark the service's birthday in 1968, or not happy with what was in the pipeline, he chose to mark the event in his own spectacular and career-dashing way. The event has for some reason generated a renewed interest in recent times, but for the uninitiated I will explain. Flt Lt Pollock had taken off on 5 April from RAF Tangmere, where he had been detached with four other aircraft, to return to the home base at West Raynham. Before departing, the Squadron Commander, Sqn Ldr G. Jones, had heard from the other pilots that Pollock had tried to encourage them to 'do Downing Street' on the way back. On hearing of this, Jones confronted Pollock, with another pilot, Flt Lt Webb, acting as witness, and clearly briefed Pollock on the conduct of the return flight to West Raynham. With Webb as flight leader, once airborne Pollock asked Webb for permission to break formation and return to base independently. This was heard over the R/T by Jones, as well as Webb's reply ordering Pollock to return to base in formation with the rest. Pollock is then said to have used his tone button to indicate speechless procedure for transmission failure.

The Station Medical Officer at West Raynham interviewed Pollock and concluded in his statement that:

He broke formation to bid farewell to Dunsfold, home of the Hawker Hunter, the aircraft he was flying.

Flying to a position a few miles south of London, so that he could study incoming traffic to Heathrow before returning to London and crossing underneath their approach or departure route, he made contact with several aircraft, in particular a Boeing 707 making its final approach in a westerly direction at a distance three or more miles away from Pollock.

He was purposely at a low level at which no airliners would have been flying.

His objective was to fly across the Richmond Park area, locate the Thames, and turn over the Houses of Parliament and Downing Street, without endangering Buckingham Palace.

He circled these objectives three times and then flew at low level eastwards down the Thames.

He had not intended to fly through Tower Bridge but, having then seen it (and that it was down), he flew through it. He mentioned the existence of traffic including a double-decker bus on the roadway of the bridge.

He then followed the Thames and turned north-east for Clacton in time to avoid Southend Airport and then flew past the southern dispersals at Wattisham.

He then turned north and overflew Honington's control zone, calling them on their frequency.

He then did a slow run over No. 492 Tactical Fighter Squadron dispersals at Lakenheath and headed for Marham. After some discourse with the Controller, whom Pollock states was hostile, he did a flypast over their northern dispersals despite the hostility.

He then executed an inverted flypast at RAF West Raynham, landed, telephoned his wife and mother to mention his activity, and asked for secrecy.

On 6 April, the Provost Officer, Sqn Ldr Walter Tomlinson was taking Pollock's own statement beginning at 09:00 hours and continuing until 12:30 hours, at which stage Pollock was asked by the Station Medical Officer how much longer he was going to be. He replied, 'About another eight hours. I want to get everything in, it's my statement.' At 14:10 hours, in a moment that smacked of farce, a Flt Lt MacLachlan continued taking down Pollock's statement, asking, 'Do you mind if I write for a while?; the squadron leader has writer's cramp.' The statement was completed at 14:50 hours; then Pollock took until 16:30 hours to go through it, make amendments and eventually signing it.

In his statement he made various comments that clearly indicated his disheartened state of mind with the modern RAF and the country more generally. One thing that had particularly dismayed him was the reaction from some airmen at Tangmere. When he had asked if they had had a party or dance or a holiday on 1 April 1968, the response had been unfortunately typical of the modern age – none seemed to be aware of the significance of this date with regard to the service they were in. Whether he was having his leg pulled or not, he found a similar degree of apathy when speaking later on to the AOC No. 38 Group, former Dambuster Air Vice-Marshal Mick Martin, and other senior officers, who seemed to be unaware of the significance of Pollock's squadron, No. 1, and Tangmere, its location at the outbreak of war. This was at a function the night before his renegade flight and seems to have helped make his mind up to celebrate the RAF's 50th birthday in his own dramatic style.

Pollock faced a total of eight charges, all of which were dropped, despite the RAF's own Provost and Security Branch recommendations that charges under sections 36,

51 and 54 of the Air Force Act 1955 be made against him. He was spared a court martial. It has been suggested that had this happened and Pollock's reasons for his actions been recorded, a court martial would have proved most embarrassing for the government. Instead Pollock was offered a medical discharge with a small pension and a place in RAF history. The public reaction was largely sympathetic, and many thought he possessed just the sort of spirit that makes a fighter pilot what he is. Indeed, he was suffering terrible sinus problems, not uncommon among air crew, and therefore the medication he was receiving may well have affected his judgement, this being the official verdict on the incident. Whichever way you look at it, the fact that any one officer felt this strongly was a symptom of the changing approach by the mainstream political establishment towards its first duty when in government – the defence of the country and its citizens, as the current Prime Minister maintains.

The 1970s began with all the various Defence Review changes under way. The Navy still had its two Audacious Class carriers operational, but only one, *Ark Royal*, was equipped with the McDonnell Douglas Phantom, a single squadron; the other, *Eagle*, was still putting to sea with Sea Vixens that were supposed to have been replaced, but with only two years of active service left. The two promised CVA-01 carriers were now gone for ever, along with the daily rum ration. The Army had been through the usual round of regimental mergers. The RAF had had to bite the bullet and accept the Buccaneer, its nuclear deterrent role had been passed to the Navy's new Polaris submarines, and the withdrawal of personnel and bases east of the Suez Canal was well under way. By 1978, not a single RAF operational squadron would be based outside of the UK and West Germany.

There was an up side, however. The first of the Harriers (P1127) and the American Phantoms were now being deployed, their General Electric J79 engines replaced by shorter and fatter Rolls-Royce Spey turbofans. The idea here was twofold; the Speys were more powerful, and were British built, therefore providing a small gesture of accommodation to what remained of the now largely nationalised British aircraft industry. The decision to put Spey engines in the UK Phantoms had the effect of rendering a comparatively more sluggish performance at higher altitudes. The expectation had been that as they were more powerful, they would render higher performance.

The RAF that saw out the end of the 1960s had been so far reduced that from 1967 a series of command amalgamations were brought into effect. The first such change represented merely a change in title, that of Transport into Air Support Command. In 1968, the first proper merger took effect when the two principal operational commands, Bomber and Fighter, merged into Strike Command. They were joined the following year by what was left of Coastal Command; thus the former big three were now represented respectively as Nos 1, 11 and 18 Groups. Flying and Technical Training Commands also merged and Signals Command was reduced to 90 Signals

Shackleton of 236 OCU landing with port props feathered. (*CAM 1041, IWM*)

Group, as it had been pre-1958, and subsumed into Strike Command. Far East Air Force remained for the time being, though its days were numbered and it would not survive beyond 1971. The Near East Command lasted a little longer, until the end of March 1976.

The RAF squadrons assigned to NATO's Second Allied Tactical Air Force were still flying Canberras and Hunters at the start of the 1970s, the far more capable Phantoms, Buccaneers and Harriers starting to replace these aircraft over the period 1970-72. Despite these changes taking hold at last, the longer term needed to be addressed. The RAF was not altogether ecstatic at settling for the Buccaneer and was now looking at what to do about replacing the remaining Vulcans, which despite having lost the primary deterrent role were still very much the backbone of its long-range strike force. In addition, other NATO air arms were looking for an all-round capable and versatile combat aircraft to replace the Lockheed F-104 Starfighter. This aircraft had been designed as a high-altitude interceptor with emphasis on very little else. Following the experiences of Korea, a greater emphasis was placed on the ability to climb faster, reach greater altitudes and greater speeds. The ability to turn tighter and out manoeuvre, was, for now, regarded as less important. The

F-104 met this requirement without any room to accommodate the other attributes. This in turn led to a reverse or rather additional emphasis of the requirement for manoeuvrability following air-to-air combat over Vietnam in the 1960s. This new requirement resulted in aircraft like the F-15 and F-16.

For now, since the beginning of the 1960s, the rocket-like F-104 equipped the bulk of European NATO air arms, not only as an air defence fighter but also as a tactical ground attack, strike and reconnaissance aircraft for which it was wholly unsuited. But this direction was followed in order to avoid cost in banknotes, instead transferring the cost, wholly unexpectedly, to that of airmen's lives, trying to fly the damned thing with too much ordnance too close to the ground and with a vicious stall threshold. Added to this was the greater fuel consumption at lower level over land. The whole concept was a recipe for disaster. Now at the end of a disastrous decade, for the Federal German Luftwaffe in particular, there was a demand to see a more suitable replacement for its specific requirements. At one time this could well have been met by the AFVG, but not now, so it was back to the drawing board and a requirement for funding to start all over again. What to do then? No F-111, no AFVG, and a return to square one.

The answer for those air arms particularly concerned – the RAF, Federal German air force, Italian air force and the *Marineflieger* (Federal German naval air arm) – was in effect to resurrect a version of the AFVG. The new project dubbed MRCA (Multi-Role Combat Aircraft) was born as a concept in December 1968, when the original requirements were approved by the respective air force Chiefs of Staff. The following month, and before a more definitive idea of what aircraft was being considered, a request by the Defence Review Working Party was made to the Chiefs of Staff Committee for an idea of what kind of numbers were being talked about. Sir Charles Elworthy, now Chief of the Defence Staff, told the Secretary of State for Defence on 21 January 1969 that 385 were needed for the British requirement. This number turned out to be the very number ordered by the British government for the RAF. This figure was based on a like-for-like replacement of the sum total of roles expected to be handed over to the MRCA, which included air defence as well as medium bomber and tactical roles. It is something of a minor miracle that this number was ordered, given that the Secretary of State was looking at a requirement for no more than 200 to 300. Indeed, Sir Charles was expecting a compromise whereby he would request a two for three replacement in the strike and reconnaissance roles, reducing the overall order to 315. In order to avoid fudging on numbers, he wanted to put forward the argument for the aircraft in purely military terms and avoid trying to take into account budgetary and political considerations and therefore present a case for a straightforward requirement for 385 aircraft. To ask for less would be to reduce the RAF's commitment to NATO. The First Sea Lord, Sir Michael Le Fanu, was more circumspect about this figure which was being advanced by the RAF Defence Chief and the Chief of the Air Staff, suggesting that ministers would already have a maximum figure of 300 in their heads and that it may not be in anyone's interests to pitch too high a figure for an aircraft that was merely a speculative project. The paper, titled 'Multi-Role Combat Aircraft – Examination of UK Numerical Requirements', was put forward to the Secretary of State for the Defence Review Working Party to consider, with an emphasis on the military requirement and a covering note regarding budgetary and industrial considerations and how these might affect the later development and total number of the aircraft ordered. A year later, with West Germany, Great Britain and Italy united to produce the MRCA, a Munich-based management agency had been stood up called NAMMA (NATO MRCA Management Agency). Conflicting interests emerged from the programme at this most embryonic stage. The original design concept was for a single-seat aircraft, something the Germans would have trouble with from the start and attempt to tweak in various directions. They were never happy with the proposed SEP (Specific Excess Power), take off and landing speeds, basic operating weight, wing loading and so on.

In January 1970, a report suggested the project had a doubtful outcome and criticised it on other levels, recommending that West Germany should withdraw from it. The report, from Lieutenant-Colonel Willi Klapper, who was a division leader in NAMMA, had been sent to the American company Lockheed and also to the Luftwaffe Chief of Staff, the wartime ace General Johannes Steinhoff. (The Luftwaffe 73rd Fighter Wing has since adopted Steinhoff's name as its identity in common with the practice of German Fighter Wings adopting the name of a former fighter ace such as Immelmann and Richthofen.) Klapper, who had spent two years on assignment at Lockheed, criticised the 'British brigadier' at NAMMA who, he claimed, was slow to take decisions and doubted, actually quite rightly, whether the project would come to fruition by its 1975 deadline. The brigadier was believed to be Air Commodore Ray Watts.

Klapper's recommendation was that Germany should withdraw from the MRCA and build a national combat aircraft. It later materialised that Klapper had been away sick at the time the report was issued. The RAF air attaché in Bonn had been in touch with the German officer heading NAMMA, General Krueger, who had told him he knew nothing of this report. Klapper, meantime, had returned from sick leave and was now asking for a 'long talk' with Krueger, who could not grant such an audience at the time but told the British air attaché that he felt Klapper was 'nervous and on edge' and suggested that he may well have written the report unilaterally whilst under strain. More was to be forthcoming once Krueger had returned to Munich. It turned out that the source of the story was a German aviation industrial agent known as Hauser. He had received his information from a local Lockheed agent, who had seen the report but, alas, did not have a copy to hand. Hauser was described as an unreliable individual in business dealings, but it was suggested that there was no reason why he should fabricate such a story. What was more reassuring, however, was that Steinhoff had stated, back in August 1969, that the MRCA was of the utmost importance and that he was determined that it should succeed. The story then seemed to disappear without surfacing in the national press at the time. Shortly after, a signal was sent out to the MoD in London from NAMMA HQ in Munich advising that Klapper would like to leave NAMMA and return to Luftwaffe duties on technical management as of 28 February 1970. The signal went on to request MoD approval for the appointment of a Lieutenant-Colonel Kahtz in his place. It also pointed out that Klapper had assumed his duties in July 1969 on the proviso that he would be there for only a year, and that he had certainly done a good job in filling a vacancy that otherwise could not have been filled, but that Klapper's interests, and probably his abilities, lay with logistics and management. He had been head of Administration and Personnel at NAMMA.

While the definitive airframe was being pursued, the Germans stipulated, among other things, a requirement for reducing touchdown speed to an incredible 104 knots without coming up with any suggestions as to how to achieve this. The only way was said to be reducing weight and/or increasing wing area, which of course would increase weight. The Germans were keen to reduce the weight of the aircraft, but again no suggestions were forthcoming as to what could be done to achieve this. In fact the degree to which the Germans wanted weight reduced would mean going it alone with a separate project, as the French would do over the EFA European Fighter Aircraft (Typhoon to Rafale) some years later.

The German position was blamed largely on their hitherto experience with the F-104G. In fact there were other individual specification priorities that only complicated matters and did not necessarily ally any two of the three partners against the other across the board. Some interests united the British and the Italians; others united the Germans and the Italians. The British and Italians were taking the MRCA down the path of a single-seater, the Germans together with the Italians were placing emphasis on air superiority, while the British were more concerned with the strike role. For the latter, a two-seat variant was being proposed. The Germans regarded the single-seater as a 'ruined design' and were naturally for a two-seater interdictor/strike (IDS) aircraft. But they remained sceptical over the level of manoeuvrability that either variant would have, as the design stood, both with variable-geometry wings and each already being seen as no match in the air for the MiG-21 Soviet fighter of the day. The Germans, once again, were doing nothing to rectify the lack of manoeuvrability and, to make matters worse, were continuing to pursue a higher wing loading and a reduced touchdown speed. The British side were hard-pressed to understand why the Germans were being so particular, as the projected manoeuvrability fell approximately within the confines of the originally proposed specification. With the wings of the aircraft at the proposed minimum sweep-angle of 25 degrees, the pilot/crew, it was agreed, would be in trouble should they encounter MiGs or other fighter aircraft. However, the setting in such a battle environment was more likely to be 45 degrees, which would give the MRCA a better turn performance than the F-111 and comparable to the Mirage G (competing in house design to rival AFVG French development, destined for cancellation). It later emerged that the German concerns, rather than being performance driven, were cost driven.

At the time, the Germans were in the process of buying the F-4 Phantom from the US, as Britain had earlier chosen to do. These would be entering service soon, but the F-104, which they would have liked to have gotten rid of sooner, would need to soldier on until about 1982, under the forecast of 1970. In the meantime, the requirement for an interceptor and a close support airframe would be met by increasing their purchase of F-4s. It also came to light that the Germans were secretly in discussion with the French government for a purchase of Mirage F1s to replace the F-104 in the air superiority role. These negotiations, as of the end of February 1970, had fallen through and they then went looking to the Americans for a suitable alternative. This became a further buy of 125 F-4s as a stopgap measure. The British for their part had no misgivings about the single-seat MRCA design, but were of course pursuing a different set of priorities. The Italians too were desperate to replace their F-104s and were now looking at an interim buy of American Phantoms. The British concern was having to extend the Vulcan and the Buccaneer, now the two principal strike aircraft on the RAF's inventory, as far as the late 1970s. This already envisaged an Operational Conversion Unit for MRCAs, somewhere in the UK by March 1976, and replacement of the Vulcans by March 1977.

By the end of March 1970, the Germans, who had originally said they would need 600 MRCAs, were now suggesting they would require a smaller figure with an additional purchase of a small Franco-German advanced trainer to be used as a close support fighter. This aircraft would become the Alpha Jet. The Germans and British, largely in agreement about the two-seat standard design, were now happy to go it alone, whereas the Italians, committed to the single-seater, were looking at dropping out altogether. Another matter undermining the project arose in a meeting between the Italian officer in charge, General Colagiovanni, and Air Vice-Marshal Giddings ACAS (Operational Requirements). Colagiovanni confided his belief that the Germans would stay with the project only as far as the end of the first phase, which was expected at the end of 1973. He also said that they had already scrapped their requirement for the single-seat aircraft and would have gleaned sufficient technological information from the project, after the end of 1973, in order to invest in their own aviation industry. The RAF officer dismissed this claim as a misinterpretation of a conversation with the German officer leading their end of the project, who in fact had been trying to persuade the Italians to stay on board.

Belgian Mirage V and Mirage F1 (F.A.F.); two diverse developments of the original Dassault Fighter. Britain's aircraft industry suffered such set back in the '60s that any such development of a similarly versatile aircraft for the RAF was not possible. (*Author's collection*)

Mirage F1 (reg no. 12Y1) nose and cockpit (F.A.F.) at Bitburg, 1981. (*Author's collection*)

As the project moved on, the Germans did firm up their intentions to stay with it, but their original requirements were changing largely due to political sensitivities. The government in Bonn was looking to make substantial defence cuts in order to reinvest in welfare programmes, and the idea of West Germany having a hand in the design and procurement of an aircraft with the capability for deep-penetration strike was an overtly aggressive aspiration under the circumstances. Nevertheless, the British understood the German air force to be thinking along the lines of being able to strike at targets either side of the FEBA (Forward Edge of the Battle Area) this being all-important to any notion of stopping a Soviet armoured thrust with overhead air cover into West Germany. By the end of April, the Italians were studying the effects on their operational requirements of changing to a two-seat aircraft.

The development of the MRCA as a variable-geometry winged design prompted some questions. The F-111 which the Americans now had in service had experienced not a few teething problems, and reassurance was required as the Americans were now developing another aircraft alongside the MRCA. The F-15, however, was a fixed-wing design, the explanation for this being that the USAF was looking for a pure interceptor, a single-purpose design, and therefore did not reflect USAF misgivings about the F-111. Furthermore, the US Navy was pressing ahead with the purchase of the F-14 as a multi-role platform. This was being looked at as early as May 1970 as a competing design against the MRCA, and threatened to take not just British but European military aircraft design technology back down the road of the TSR2. With the two-seat, twin-engine VG variant being seen now as the favoured design of the MRCA, its projected performance and handling were compared to the two aircraft just entering service with the RAF, the Phantom and Buccaneer. Projected performance already showed that the Phantom had the edge in terms of speed and manoeuvrability, from the air defence point of view, but lacked the MRCA's radius of action and supersonic acceleration at low level, the latter being a requirement for the reconnaissance role. The MRCA was also expected to have short-field performance which was non-existent in the Phantom. Because of the Phantom's large wing area, it was subject to significant turbulence conditions during high speed at low altitude, giving the crew a 'hard ride', which in turn was seen as a problem with regard to accuracy in weapon delivery. When comparing the Buccaneer, the reverse was the case. It had outstanding low-level high-speed handling and appeared to have an advantage over the MRCA in this regard. Then again, while it could cruise at a high Mach number, only marginally less than the MRCA, it had no reheat, no potential for the development of such and therefore no supersonic acceleration at low level at all. Further, the Buccaneer operated at the extent of its specific excess power and consequently did not possess the defensive manoeuvre and acceleration characteristics to ensure some chance of survival while flying the kind of deep-penetration missions envisaged for the MRCA.

The idea of selecting the F-14 ran into all kinds of problems. The aircraft would be heavier, with a degree of redundancy in capability that would have to be paid for, of course. With the TSR2 story influencing the RAF mindset, the idea of forsaking British industry for a more expensive beast with spiralling costs all going to Grumman in the US, and unit costs already expected to be much higher than for the MRCA programme, it was not a difficult decision to stick with essentially the home-grown effort this time. Consideration of the political and economic impact precluded any other aircraft from outside being considered.

The UK share of the development effort was to be 42.5 per cent, which the Treasury argued should be less, for the reason that the UK did not plan to procure as many as the Germans, who also took the same percentage share of the development, and of course that Britain would be paying a greater share of the initial outlay. Thirdly, the RAF had determined, as early as 1970, to develop 165 airframes as air defence fighters. As the Germans and Italians, who were originally looking for an air defence capability, were now happy to procure a single design for themselves, this being the strike aircraft, this of course placed the burden of further research work in developing an interceptor version on Britain alone. The RAF counter-argument was, to put it simply, the greater the share of the workload, the better for UK industry – probably one of the rare times that the military brass have given due consideration to the industrial impact of procuring new equipment. They also had doubts about the ability of the German aircraft industry at that time, having spent so long outside of military development, to do as well with a larger share of the burden. The Germans for their part were wholly in agreement that the division between the two should be equal, perhaps for the same reason.

By December 1974, the air defence variant (ADV) of the MRCA was being considered as the long-term answer to UK air defence; that said, no one seemed able to summon much faith in the aircraft for this role which was being looked at as far ahead as the 1990s under the Long Term Threat Assessment study and a further one looking at maritime air defence. The ADV was seen to have its advantages at an early stage, with its ability to intercept low-, medium- and high-altitude enemy bombers attacking the UK in all weathers and in a dense electronic countermeasures environment. However, it could not intercept very high altitude reconnaissance flights in peacetime or confront anything requiring a close combat capability. In addition, the Air Staff study determined that it lacked sufficient potential for future development. There was also the long-term suggestion that the future replacement for the Harrier and Jaguar, just entering service, should have an air combat capability. The RAF was also looking at approaching the USAF with a view to assigning some of its high-performance fighters to UK air defence. The F-15, still to enter service with the USAF, was an aircraft the RAF was keen to look more closely at.

Despite a definite enthusiasm for ditching the idea of a fighter version of the MRCA, there was a reluctance to do so due to the constant fear of the government taking an axe to the better part of the overall number of MRCAs to be built, in further defence spending cuts. For this reason, the RAF was prepared to shut up and press ahead with what was already seen from the outset as a less than adequate aircraft to meet the full spectrum of forecast air defence threats, lest the MRCA programme be seriously curtailed as a result. A key difference in respect of the fighter role was acknowledged by 1976, when the RAF was looking for an air defence interceptor while the Germans and Italians wanted a slightly different beast: an air superiority fighter.

The explanation for the different requirements was simple. Britain's priority was for something to counter the more strategic threat of the long-range bomber. The Germans and Italians, particularly the Germans, were right on the edge of the enormous tactical force which could sweep forward across the inner German border turning North West Europe into one great battlefield once again rather like it had been in 1944. Tangling with shorter-ranged but agile fighters escorting the tactical attack aircraft was the pre-eminent threat here.

It was accepted at this stage that the ADV would be a different aircraft to the standard MRCA, but the airframe would differ little and the plan was to have the same RB199 engine, emphasised for long range at low level rather than high altitude and high energy. The Labour government of Jim Callaghan published a paper by the Study Group on Defence Expenditure which criticised the fact that the RAF would have an aircraft assigned to a variety of operational roles with performance aspects that the study group considered unnecessary. They complained that the service would have a strike aircraft capable of high agility and cab-rank loiter capability, as well as a close support bomber capable of supersonic speeds and a reconnaissance aircraft with a fast climb rate. These attributes were not regarded as bonuses in the mindset of the study group, which described them as 'wasted characteristics'. The economic argument was to the fore again as the claims by Germany, Italy and Panavia that the costs of development were holding steady were believed to be wrong. The study group's conclusion was that the ADV would be cancelled due to pressing economic circumstances and, as they saw it, the limited progress made thus far.

In February 1976, the Chief of the Defence Staff, Field Marshal Sir Michael Carver, asked the Defence Secretary to consider replacing the ADV if not the entire MRCA programme with a buy of American F-16s, which were at a similar stage of development. However, the deficiencies in the F-16 regarding the all-weather strike role would be particularly marked. On the commercial side it would have a disastrous effect on the UK, German and Italian aircraft industries. It was also suggested to the Chief of the Air Staff, Sir Andrew Humphrey, that agreement of the Defence Secretary's colleagues to the full MRCA programme might be difficult to

An early Tornado lifting off Cottesmore's runway, *c.* 1979. (*The National Archives*)

Staff of the Tri-National Tornado Training Establishment (TTTE). (*The National Archives*)

obtain. Sir Andrew told the Defence Secretary that the number ordered was critical and that any attempt to reduce it might bring about the collapse of the programme, and that 165 was the absolute minimum number of the variant required in order to sustain a viable front line.

The two preferred options again were the American F-14 or F-15. The former was considered the closest in comparison but fell short on expense grounds, and its operating costs would be significantly higher, with its greater fuel consumption requiring 20-30 per cent greater tanker support. The F-15 was accepted to have a greater aerodynamic performance and greater stretch potential. It also possessed a higher operating ceiling. Its comparison with the kind of tactical high-performance Soviet aircraft over the Central Region (or North West Europe as it is better known outside of NATO) was outstanding. But because the primary concern was for an aircraft to confront long-range bomber and reconnaissance types, the F-15 was seen to offer little advantage. Again, the single-seat configuration of the F-15, despite a high degree of automation in the cockpit, which might be seen as an advantage, raised concerns over the aircraft's ability to survive in a heavy jamming environment against massed raids. In short, the airframe/engine performance gains offered by the F-15 were not enough to justify the budgetary and industrial penalties involved should it be bought in place of the ADV. A further interesting assessment was that keeping the IDS side of the MRCA programme alive would mean buying additional IDS airframes, which would be unacceptable largely because it would be at the expense of the planned Harrier/Jaguar replacement programmes. If a balanced force was to be maintained, then close support needed to be properly addressed, and while the MRCA was an outstanding strike/attack reconnaissance aircraft, it was not optimised for ground attack in terms of close support. Further it would not have the capability to engage attacking fighters, a key aspect of the Jaguar replacement.

The Navy briefly pursued a line of purchasing between thirty and thirty-five F-14s armed with Phoenix missiles, together with a buy of 120 ADVs for the RAF. This was expected to cost no more than 165 ADVs. However, the Navy soon lost interest for some reason. So, based on the fact that the F-15's high agility would have little value intercepting long-range Soviet bombers over the North Sea, and that additional IDS MRCAs in place of the projected Harrier/Jaguar replacement (expected to have a high agility capability) would actually place the RAF in Germany at an operational disadvantage in the future, the decision to go ahead with the ADV was made.

CHAPTER 7

The '70s and '80s: Strategic Air Force to Tactical Air Force

With the arrival of aircraft of the calibre of the Phantom, Buccaneer and Harrier, the RAF at last had a tactical air force in Germany that was now equal to the task. The Harrier GR1 was perhaps now the best possible close air support aircraft in theatre, the Buccaneer and Phantom providing a respectable and fair chance of delivering tactical nuclear weapons against heavy concentrations of Soviet armour and reaching the other side of the FEBA (Forward Edge of the Battle Area). That chance was as good as for air crew from other NATO air arms attempting to fly similar missions. The survival chances of RAF and other NATO air crew flying into the air-defence-saturated Soviet Bloc airspace was slender, to say the least, but there was a much more realistic chance of fulfilling their remit than before with Canberras. By the time the RAF was able to commence replacing the ageing Canberras and Hunters in RAF Germany, the commitment to other overseas bases was well and truly rolling up. From the start of the 1970s through to the 1980s, the RAF gradually relinquished its strategic element, which became wholly the responsibility of the Navy, and transitioned to an all tactical air force.

Of major concern outside the RAF's tactical ability was the Royal Navy's efforts to reverse the Wilson government's decision to rid it of its carriers on the grounds of cost and the much vaunted argument about ending Britain's commitments anywhere east of Cyprus. The carriers had become something of an election issue, just as the decision over whether to buy the TSR2 or TFX had been for the Australian government, albeit with hardly anything like the same public interest in the matter. Britain by the end of the 1960s was not a country particularly exercised by defence concerns. Indeed, worry about a nuclear war did not really impact upon the minds of the majority, who could only think of war in historic terms, represented largely by the many Second World War films being made at the time. Truth be known, veterans of that conflict during this era enjoyed nothing like the respect and interest that they receive from the media and younger generation today.

If there was any public reaction to Britain's military posture during the 1960s and 1970s, it came from politically motivated organisations such as CND and, later in the 1960s, all manner of left-leaning groups from hippies to Marxist elements. It was difficult to determine whether their ideal was the abolition of all manner of military means and posture, or was simply that they felt Britain and perhaps the rest of Europe should fall within the Soviet/Warsaw Pact defence sphere rather than be a satellite of the capitalist American dogs, with all that would entail. In 1968, a demonstration outside the US embassy in London against the Vietnam War, which to all intents and purposes Britain was not involved in, turned violent as the police found themselves doing all to prevent demonstrators coming into contact with the US Marine Guards on the inside of the embassy building. Had this happened, the outcome could have been deeply regrettable. But perhaps this would have been all the more ironic, given that 1968 has since gone down on record as the only calendar year in which not one single British serviceman or woman was on any kind of war footing.

Whatever the public mood, the country's defence chiefs still felt it their bounden duty to impress upon the government of the day the military threat possibilities faced by the nation in and out of NATO, and of course to advise on the range of recommended options to stand the best chance of none of them becoming frighteningly real. The Labour Party in 1970 were proudly claiming that the country was now spending more on education than defence, and would soon be spending more on the NHS as well. Accusing the Conservatives of wasting hundreds of millions of pounds on prestige defence projects, they gave themselves a pat on the back for getting it just right. The British taxpayer was getting better value for money as a result of fewer commitments, but of course it was the fewer assets and capabilities that were the principal achievement.

While the Labour Party were setting great store by working with other nations to reduce the threat of war, and therefore the need for military expenditure at all, the Conservatives, long since recognised as the mainstream party with the stronger defence and security policies and with the greater emphasis and priority on such requirements, were promising to stand by the country's allies and strengthen its defences. Their take on the reduced commitments of which Labour were proud was to claim that the withdrawal of British forces from the Middle and Far East was a betrayal of the peoples and governments of these regions. They further claimed that Britain's interests and its allies in the East were soon to be exposed to unacceptable risk.

On 18 February 1970, a Conservative MP, Patrick Wall, while attending a seminar on international air support at the Royal United Services Institute, quoted his leader, Edward Heath: 'While the Conservative concept of a five-power force for South East Asia does not depend upon aircraft carriers, a Conservative government would prolong the life of the existing carrier force and so get value from the large sums recently spent re-fitting.' There were more claims along similar lines from other Tories.

Circa 1971, official visitors including Naval and Army Officers receive a flypast by Phantoms of 43 Squadron at Leuchars. At the time the issue of the Carrier-borne fighter was still causing some controversy; some expected the RAF to accommodate by deploying RAF personnel to sea. (*The National Archives*)

It was 'manifestly absurd', said Geoffrey Rippon, the Tory defence spokesman, to spend £30 million refitting the *Ark Royal* and then to scrap it, and further, 'it would not be easy to undo the damage done by the stopping of the training of Fleet Air Arm pilots and the deliberate redundancies of trained personnel, but we must try'.

The Navy was not slow on the uptake here .The Navy Board produced a scenario that assumed three aircraft carriers; *Ark Royal*, *Eagle* and *Hermes* would be retained, and that *Eagle*, like *Ark Royal*, would be refitted after all, to take the F-4 Phantom. Current plans, which had emerged following the end of the F-111 saga, included the reassignment of about thirty Phantoms to the RAF, with about thirty-six Buccaneers to be land-based and declared to the Supreme Allied Commander Atlantic (SACLANT). Some Sea Vixens would also be retained and embarked for the specific purpose of providing fixed-wing air defence cover of the fleet and maritime air strike/attack reconnaissance. Under this scenario, the RAF would embark on retained carriers, the alternative being to retain a wholly fixed-wing naval force. What was being proposed was joint manning of RAF Buccaneer and Phantom squadrons by RAF and Navy personnel in order to ensure that the right balance of naval aviation expertise was to hand when embarked. This would impact on the numbers of RAF operational crews, as the Navy wanted all key posts to be manned by its personnel on the squadrons which would embark, and also that they should be predominantly Naval manned. Should this plan go ahead, the RAF could expect to lose some 52 out of 330 pilot posts to the Navy. These posts, as the Navy admitted, would be lost from among the RAF's Phantom and Buccaneer crews.

The thirty Phantoms were to be divided into three squadrons all based at Leuchars in Fife. As well as being assigned to the requirements of SACLANT, these units were also responsible for maintaining the Northern QRA. At the time, RAF interceptors at Leuchars were being scrambled at least once a day to intercept Soviet long-range reconnaissance bombers entering the northern reaches of the UK Air Defence Region. Two of the three squadrons were equipped with Lightnings at that time, and it was envisaged that more Lightnings would be used to supplant the Northern QRA in order to make more Phantoms deployable. This, due to the Lightnings' thirsty engines and not very realistic method of carrying extra fuel in overwing tanks, would inevitably mean a greater demand, yet again, on the existing inflight refuelling force. As things stood at the time, the remaining carriers were due to be paid off in 1972, including the *Ark Royal*. When this happened, the fleet's Phantoms and Buccaneers would transfer wholly to the RAF.

This was described as establishing red-carpet treatment for British military assistance and therefore removing the need for complex and expensive intervention forces or aircraft carriers. No one was thinking about the Falklands during this period, and quite understandably so, given the Euro-centric defence policy future envisaged by the government. As of July 1970, Sir John Grandy, still CAS, had as his major concern the now despairingly small size of the RAF front line. The Navy plan would now split this further. To justify refraining from any such split, he described the formation of Strike Command as a strategic move to bring the weight of air power to bear where it was most needed rapidly and at the right strength.

What it actually represented was the inevitable result of the further dilution of the RAF's post-cuts operational strength, which could now be comfortably condensed from three former commands into a single one, as that was all that could justify what was left. But of course avoiding any further split of RAF resources was the primary concern, and to thwart the idea of a sizeable chunk of Strike Command being assigned to the Royal Navy. One contention in favour of shore-basing was that extensive maintenance and modifications could not be carried out on carriers. In addition, a considerable amount of training, according to the CAS, would be necessary for the Phantom crews before the pilots would be *au fait* with land-based air defence flying. Thus the Navy's claim that the aircraft could be operated from ashore when the carrier was not at sea was not as straightforward as it seemed. But more precisely, the argument against the carriers was that they were, and are, far more vulnerable to enemy action. A single missile from a Soviet ship could disable a

A Phantom of 43 Squadron, the first dedicated air defence fighter unit to be equipped with this aircraft. (*Keith Butcher*)

carrier, but the same missile would not disable an air base and such a vessel would soon come under attack itself. A single available carrier, as was likely to be the case, could not serve the entire fleet, again as had been described as 'organic air' for the whole Royal Naval force, especially if the carrier was, for example, in the Indian Ocean. Where would the rest of the fleet be when assigned to Commander Strike Fleet Atlantic (COMSTRIKFLTLANT)?

On 12 October 1970, the incoming Conservative government announced that *Ark Royal* would continue beyond the planned phasing-out period and instead would remain operational until 1978. Sir John Grandy had been expecting the Navy's Phantoms and Buccaneers, but they were now to remain in Navy hands, although when ashore they would be based at RAF stations. The Phantoms' parent base was to move in 1972 from Yeovilton to Leuchars, and the Buccaneers would be based at Honington instead of Lossiemouth, which was about to be handed over to the RAF as the base for its Jaguar OCU.

The RAF was expected to provide the bulk of maintenance and administrative support for the aircraft on land. Increasingly, the aircraft would be flown by RAF crews, as the Navy would no longer be training ab-initio pilots and observer/navigators. As Grandy explained to his staff, elements of the RAF's air defence and strike forces would, until 1978, spend part of their time embarked on a carrier under Naval command. Those elements would get bigger towards the end as more Fleet Air Arm personnel retired or moved to other posts in the Navy.

Before the announcement was made, however, the Defence Secretary was concerned that those with more than a passing interest should understand that the previous government's decision to abandon the carrier fleet was in no way being reversed and was 'now regarded as settled policy for the future'. The First Sea Lord arranged an interview with the editor of *Navy News* and also planned to write to a number of senior retired naval officers in order to 'make sure that the right slant was put on the government's decision and prevent jubilation'. Just the same, this did not mean that the Heath government was fully in agreement with the decision of the Wilson government. It considered the earlier decision to phase out the aircraft carriers had been made without due regard to bringing into service effective weapons for their replacement. There were just two remaining carriers, *Eagle* and *Ark Royal*, which had been destined to go in early 1972 when the withdrawals from the Far East and Persian Gulf were complete. The new Defence Secretary had considered retaining both in order to ensure a fully operational carrier was available at all times. But this posed manpower problems which went beyond what was planned, meaning the loss of other ships if the two carriers were to be held onto. HMS *Eagle* required an upgrade to see it beyond 1972, and that would still be with Buccaneers and Sea Vixens. The Sea Vixen was considered inadequate for operations in the likely theatre of the Atlantic and Mediterranean, so *Eagle* would need some further capital outlay in order to ready it for Phantoms instead. The decision as to which to go with was therefore not a difficult one. It was stated that there were no plans for carriers beyond 1978. However, this did not refer to the VSTOL cruisers, as they were known at the time: the Invincible Class light carriers with ski-jumps for launching the Sea Harrier. These were still planned for the longer term and, furthermore, a new missile system was expected to be available to be fitted to them. The loss of *Eagle* meant that a carrier would be available for only two-thirds of the time.

In order to demonstrate the spirit of co-operation between the Navy and Air Force, the First Sea Lord told Grandy that when he next visited the *Ark Royal*, following the decision to run it on, he would like to be flown onto the deck in a Phantom by an RAF pilot. Only too eager to oblige, the CAS told Admiral Sir Peter Hill-Norton that, as he had rather suspected, up to that point the RAF had no carrier deck trained Phantom crews but could accommodate with a Buccaneer flown by an Air Force pilot. ...There still remained misgivings within the Air Staff about directing their ground crews to serve afloat. They even had concerns about recruitment literature which mentioned nothing about sea duty, and there was no desire to include such a feature with recruitment on a fine edge. There was no expectation that there would be too many volunteers from within the ranks to serve on the carrier, and the Air Staff believed that airmen could not be compulsorily ordered to serve unaccompanied tours at sea without leaving themselves open to the charge of omitting such detail when recruiting. As such, despite the Defence Secretary, Lord Carrington's announcement

Royal Navy Phantom of 892 Squadron taking off from *Ark Royal* in November 1978, marking the end of Royal Navy fixed wing operations before the Harrier. (*HU 109895, IWM*)

Phantoms of 892 Squadron on board *Ark Royal* with Sea Kings, arriving in Norway in 1970. (*HU73942, IWM*)

that the Fleet Air Arm would no longer be recruiting for *Ark Royal* in light of its numbered days, Grandy was unwilling to make a commitment of ground crew as yet. This was yet another good old-fashioned British fudge: one government, not at all unexpectedly, decided that carriers were no longer relevant because it was rolling up the British presence east of Suez, while another, which had been so critical of the carrier loss when in opposition, now did not quite know what to do about it other than reach some form of compromise.

Anyone who remembers the day in October 1977 when it was announce that the *Ark Royal* would be decommissioned at the end of the following year will recall much in the way of disparaging remarks about the Callaghan government of the day. But if truth be told, the decision to decommission it in 1978 had been made eight years earlier. The later decision to keep *Ark Royal* afloat was described by Grandy as being based on political and economic grounds rather than military ones, especially seeing as £31 million had just been spent on an extensive refit so that it could carry Phantoms.

In order to make good, the Navy was prepared to make sacrifices, if not quite hand over the family silver. Other ships were to go: *Lion* was to be converted from cruiser to Sea King ASW role, *Hampshire* was to go in 1976 instead of 1978, and *Intrepid* was placed in storage. On top of this, however, SACLANT did ask the government to maintain at least one carrier. Grandy was very disappointed at the decision, believing that the likely split of his air force would not serve national defence interests. That said, he was also determined to make the arrangement work. It was now incumbent on the RAF to prove its worth in deep maintenance, supply, administration and other facilities ashore. The First Sea Lord gave the CAS his assurance that the carrier would not exist beyond 1978, and that there would be no new carriers. He looked forward to 1978 as being the year that the RAF would assume total responsibility for all fixed-wing air requirements.

The RAF, now flying the Buccaneer as a 'stopgap' following the debacle over the TSR2/F-111/AFVG, had taken some press ribbing over getting a design which had first flown some fifteen years earlier, but the service had in fact taken to this aircraft. RAF crews who had volunteered to serve on the Buccaneer force, however, were now not sure where they were going to end up in a couple of years. On top of the carrier retention, albeit temporarily and with RAF co-operation, was another election promise made by the Conservatives in opposition to bolster the RAF in Germany. Something of a compromise seems to have been arrived at which allowed the Fleet Air Arm to wholly retain two operational squadrons to serve the one remaining carrier. The Navy gave up some more territory, with the handing over of the Royal Naval Air Station at Lossiemouth, from the end of 1972, to the RAF, which installed its newly formed Operational Conversion Unit for the new Jaguar aircraft. Further, the Phantom Headquarters Training Squadron, No. 767,

Royal Navy Phantom of 892 Squadron taking off from *Ark Royal* late in 1970, during what is probably the first deployment with Phantoms on board; onlookers appear to be a visiting party of families. (*HU 10989, IWM*)

stood down at Yeovilton and a Training Flight was stood up at RAF Leuchars, which was already operating the same version of the Phantom, the FG1 (F-4K in US parlance) and was therefore the most appropriate place to land-base the Navy's remaining F-4s. Its remaining Buccaneers, when not embarked on *Ark Royal*, were accommodated now at Honington, the RAF UK Buccaneer Base, in place of Lossiemouth.

While arrangements to run on one carrier were accepted, allowing the Navy to keep operational control of its Phantoms and Buccaneers, the RAF's third new front-line acquisition, the Harrier, was generating a separate concern. The aircraft was receiving upgrades to the existing Mk 1 variant, including an uprated engine, the Pegasus Mk 102. Problems here had caused some delays in delivery. By the autumn of 1970, deliveries of the Harrier were so far behind that the planned stand-up of four squadrons had to be redrawn completely and, by March the following year, a further slippage threatened to leave the RAF short of six aircraft by the coming autumn. The reason for the delay was that deliveries of Harriers to the US Marine Corps were now taking place simultaneously, the Marines having asked for the first three Harriers powered with the newest development stage engine, the Mk 102.

An example of the Hawker Siddeley Buccaneer seen here shortly after its entry into RAF service. (*Keith Butcher*)

Because the penalties of losing further contracts were considered too severe, Grandy, who was just coming to the end of his tenure as CAS, was facing a shortage of eight aircraft. It may seem a paltry number in the great scheme of things, but these aircraft represented the bulk of the already delayed fourth squadron. As a result, this would now have to wait until 1972. Rolls-Royce were largely being blamed for their failure to develop the Mk 102 engine on time, but there were also delays with the airframe for which Hawker Siddeley were accountable. Grandy was willing to accept the situation in the spirit of placing national interests at the fore, but was not happy about the RAF again taking on the burden of accommodating commercial industry. The delay would of course need to be explained to SACEUR, to whom the entire RAF Harrier force was primarily being committed. A feasibility study was carried out with a view to giving the Harriers a nuclear strike capability, which was seen as a practical proposition, but again it was purely cost versus priority of other projects that went against it. If it was to happen, more Harriers would have been needed as the numbers assigned to close air support were not to be reduced in order to provide a further contribution to the nuclear strike force. Among the arguments in favour was the Harrier's greater chance of survival when dispersed in the event of

Harrier GR3 of 233 Operational Conversion Unit, an outstanding close air support aircraft. Consideration was given in the early 1970s to the idea of arming the Harrier with nuclear weapons. (*Michael Brazier*)

hostilities; the safety considerations were expected to be little different from those in place regarding the Army's Honest John missiles.

With a change in government again in 1974, the new administration was looking to realign public expenditure. Harold Wilson's second term in office supported by the Liberals brought another look at defence spending, with a similar view to that taken ten years earlier. The new Chancellor, Denis Healey, who had been Defence Secretary in 1964, was proposing an average annual increase in public expenditure of 2.75 per cent as against 1.3 per cent for defence. This information was made available to the US government in consultation about the new government's Defence Review. The American reaction was described as strongly deprecative. The Prime Minister also admitted that he could not see how what amounted to a cut in defence spending could be achieved without assuming some reduction in defence capability.

By December, a statement on the review was released. Reaction within the remaining RAF commands was sought by the CAS and, not unexpectedly, the response was dismay at the level of cuts in manpower that the RAF was facing, particularly as there had been a series of economic reviews resulting in piecemeal cuts to personnel over the past few years. That they should now be facing the greatest reduction in manpower of the three services was having a bad effect on morale. A

The Vickers VC10, seen here, became the mainstay of RAF Strategic Transport in the 1970s and '80s. (*Keith Butcher*)

further rub was that civilian staff reductions across the board were less than that of the RAF personnel cuts alone. Various questions were raised about the logic of the new cuts in respect of the remaining eastern hemisphere bases, especially given recent concerns about increased Soviet influence in the Indian Ocean region.

The aim of the 1974 review was to protect the front line and concentrate on reductions in support, research and civilian staff. The latter has proved to be the one growth sector in the MoD. The need to concentrate the defence and military effort on NATO meant there would be some wastage somewhere, but this time overseas commitments even within NATO requirements were to be withdrawn. The Navy would no longer patrol the Mediterranean in support of CENTO, the Royal Marines 41 Commando Group would disband, and the RAF would withdraw its remaining Vulcan, Lightning and Canberra squadrons from this theatre. The first level of expenditure was, in all, expected to leave the RAF with twenty-eight aircraft fewer than what was described as the critical level from the strike/attack/reconnaissance role, nineteen fewer strategic transport aircraft, thirty-two fewer helicopters, thirteen fewer search and rescue (SAR) aircraft and 3,000 fewer serving RAF personnel. The review was announced in October, and by December each of the services was preparing to make formal presentations of its plans. The Navy and Air Force departments were told that the new Secretary of State for Defence did not require to see these. He did, however, wish to be kept abreast of developments following upon the Defence Review, and he was ready to chair meetings of the Defence Council in order to review plans for urgent matters such as redundancy, the closing of RAF stations and organisational adjustments.

It had been decided that the RAF was to lose 17,000 personnel. This time the axe would fall on the RAF's transport and logistics end. Twelve RAF stations, and debatably more, were to close. The RAF's Strategic Transport Group was going to lose the Short Belfast, de Havilland Comet and the Bristol Britannia; the Tactical Group would lose the not very old Hawker Siddeley Andover. It was proposed that the stations that were to go by January 1977 would be Abingdon, Benson, Bicester, Chessington, Church Fenton, Colerne, Cottesmore, Finningley, Hullavington, Leconfield, Thorney Island and West Raynham. Because none of these possible closures was announced, there was an increased sense of apprehension among both military and civilian personnel alike. As a definite figure of twelve stations was bandied about publicly, those in the firing line of closures were convinced that the twelve were long since confirmed and that the government was simply refusing to say in order to keep everyone guessing, rather than making plans which would not necessarily be convenient to the smooth running of the said twelve in the present. Of all that was considered for cutting from the defence budget as a whole, one thing was deemed sacrosanct, the Royal Yacht *Britannia*, which Harold Wilson had no intention of dismissing.

On the up side, the MRCA project continued apace with the first prototype flight being made from Manching in West Germany in 1974. The RAF also began to receive the first SEPECAT Jaguar aircraft. In due course, the Jaguars were issued to all squadrons hitherto operating the Phantom FGR2 on a like-for-like basis, and one Harrier squadron, No. 20, was stood down as a close air support unit then re-equipped with the Jaguar and assigned to the strike role, joining the wing at Brüggen on the Dutch border. The Phantoms in turn were used to replace all the remaining Lightning squadrons save two, which remained at Binbrook in Lincolnshire. The transfer of the Phantoms to the air defence role represented an increase in capability in terms of range and firepower and thus an improvement to the overall air defence fighter coverage of the UK. This was long overdue. The Sandys review had inflicted some severe damage in regard to the new trend toward 'flexible response', the promised missile defence shield to replace the fighter had never fully materialised before it was rapidly run down to a single UK-based squadron of Bloodhound missiles by 1968, along with five squadrons of Lightnings to confront a strike force of Soviet long-range high- and low-altitude bombers which stood nearer to Luftwaffe proportions during the Battle of Britain. The remaining operational squadrons from the Mediterranean were all to return home by the end of 1976. These included the

Near East bomb wing which was incorporated into the Vulcan wings at Scampton and Waddington, and a single squadron of Lightnings, which returned to Wattisham in Norfolk before re-equipping with Phantoms. Two Canberra reconnaissance squadrons returned as well, but a single squadron of Nimrods, No. 203, did not survive beyond 1977.

The greatest impact of the 1974/75 review was to be brought to bear on the RAF's strategic transport element. Fixed-wing transport aircraft were to be reduced to fifty-eight from a total of 157. The transport fleet by 1977 would be a tactical force of four squadrons of Hercules and a strategic element of a single squadron of VC10s. The loss of the Belfast was particularly hard to understand as it beat allcomers in carrying the heaviest cargo over the greatest distance, a point recognised by civilian air haulage operators. The company Heavy Lift bought them all and then charged the MoD for their services some years later when the aircraft's ability in this very arena was desperately needed to support the Falklands campaign.

With a concentration on front-line assets being the priority, the wisdom of allocating so many front-line airframes to the role of operational training and evaluation was raised by the newly appointed Chief of the Air Staff, Sir Andrew Humphrey, who, clearly trying to put together a rational presentation to the Defence Review, was now questioning just why quite so many front-line aircraft were effectively lost to the front line in order to provide training. His concern was with the seemingly high number of such aircraft available which were not actually serving with assigned front-line squadrons and thus perceived as out of step with the general policy of giving top priority to maintain front-line strength. 'That is, after all, what we bought the aircraft for in the first place,' he reasoned. Figures as of March 1975 showed that of 141 Phantoms purchased in total; forty-seven were not actually assigned to the operational squadrons, not counting thirteen write-offs. This left a shortfall on front-line establishment of 6 per cent, after other matters such as maintenance were considered. The situation was far worse for the Jaguar, Harrier, Buccaneer and Nimrod establishment, which varied between 11 and 17 per cent short of unit establishment figures. One suggestion, that training tasks should be carried out by the squadrons, was considered undesirable, as the same number of aircraft would be involved with training new crews and providing refresher training for others. Furthermore, to move first tourist air crew straight into the environment of an operational unit when they had, to all intents and purposes, to sit in the cockpit for the first time, might have proved somewhat stressful to trainees who would fare better with the continuous attention of an assigned instructor, and of course make for a safer transition towards such complex and demanding high performance aircraft as those in question. In addition would be the constant short-notice prioritisation of operational crews for any aircraft tasked for a training sortie.

Along with the Comet, Bristol Britannia made up the bulk of the RAF's Strategic Long-Range Transport capability from the end of the 1950s until the great transport cull of 1974. (*Warwickshire County Records Office, Reference no.: P4 (N) 600/1674/9a*)

Improvements in the UK air defence system, however, were still to be properly addressed. The most pressing need concerned a proposed interceptor replacement for the Lightning and, in time, the Phantom. This required further study but was expected to be the air defence variant of the MRCA. Other areas of priority remained the provision of strike/attack aircraft in NATO's Central Region and the RAF contribution to airborne early warning operations. The US AWACS E-3A aircraft was already the favoured option for replacing the Shackleton AEW aircraft. Among the economic measures then favoured by Humphrey was merging the RAF's own infantry force, the RAF Regiment, with the RAF Police. Again, the eternal air of optimism in official language, even from senior officers, was present in order to mask what was a loss of means, of assets and of personnel. Humphrey described the process as laying down a blueprint for a more operationally effective air force of the future. The commanders-in-chief wanted any surplus funds to be diverted, as a matter of first priority, to updating weapons stocks, both quality and quantity. Recent NATO exercises had demonstrated a particular need for increased numbers of air-to-air missiles but funds for such were, unsurprisingly, unlikely. Other money-saving measures were to be introduced; training courses were to have anywhere from a couple of weeks shaved off a 36-week course to being cut in half. Basic pilot flying training was to be reduced from 52 to 33 weeks. Admittedly, Britain was spending a larger proportion of GDP on defence; 5.8 per cent compared to 3.8 per cent for France and about 4.9 per cent for West Germany, but it was Britain which agonised over its ability to meet such obligations, despite the massive reductions and withdrawals from across the former Empire. The saving of £300 million from running down the transport squadrons as soon as possible was regarded as the best way to absorb the up and coming redundancies and also to protect the remaining front line and new aircraft such as the MRCA. The defence budget overall had to find £4.4 billion of savings over eight years, £1.4 billion of which was to come from the RAF budget. There followed the largest equipment disposal programme that the RAF had been through since the ill-advised Sandys paper on the future of manned aircraft. The race was on to clear those stations slated for closure of their 'junk' as soon as possible in order to avoid forestalling the closure of these bases.

The twelve RAF stations to be vacated were confirmed. For now, Abingdon and Finningley were to survive, the former having lost its Andovers was looking forward to a future as the deep maintenance centre for the growing number of the new Jaguars, and in all likelihood nowhere else could realistically take on the already centralised rear-seat air crew and multi-engine pilot training carried out by No. 6 Flying Training School at Finningley. The other stations on the chop list were offered to the other two services. Thorney Island was looked at by the Navy as an alternative to a planned rebuild of Lee-on-Solent, and the RAF's loss offered a great deal to the Army which was still billeting a lot of soldiers in wooden and corrugated iron Nissen hut camps. Many famous RAF airfields were destined for the Army, including Bassingbourn, Colerne, Debden, Driffield, Hullavington, Leconfield, Little Rissington, Oakington, Spitalgate and Tern Hill.

This was manna from heaven to the Army, especially the junior ranks, who, truth be known, have never enjoyed the same conditions of service as the RAF. Indeed, the Navy have also never held a candle to the Junior Service when the life of a rating was compared to that of the average erk. Apart from somewhere nicer to live, the average ranking airman, certainly of the Cold War era, was kept firmly in one location. Not for him or her the prospect of being deployed (save for the RAF Regiment and those who clamoured to get on the Harrier and tactical helicopter squadrons) into a frozen potato field or forest on the North German Plain and told to dig in. They did not face the likelihood of routine stretches at sea, sharing sleeping quarters on the mess deck. Even in bases in Germany prone to NATO exercises, the hardships of being woken up at three o' clock in the morning by either a piercing tannoy, heavy banging on the door or megaphoned instructions to report for duty immediately by the RAF Police or Orderly Corporal driving round the station in order get everyone up and out of a deep sleep and running around ready for yet another Taceval/Mineval, or even war, did not compare. The station exercise would last about three or four days at most, and those not settling into round-the-clock twelve-hour shifts at their designated place of work on the station would report to the makeshift Guard Quarters, usually an otherwise unused building like a store, workshop, air-raid shelter or billet set aside for the task. Comparatively, this was still a breeze, and hot food, tea and coffee were never far away. Those on sentry posts would be relieved regularly throughout the exercise every two hours then head off back to the Guard Quarters to play cards, listen to the radio, watch TV and drink coffee or, indeed, sleep. Those who served in the RAF during the Cold War have much to thank the Warsaw Pact for. Indeed, the RAF of the latter half of the Second World War had developed an entirely tactical command in the form of the 2nd Tactical Air Force, whose ground crew could expect to fight through the fields of Normandy as infantry. Elsewhere, the Second World War air force, in particular in North Africa and Burma, developed along the lines of a tactical field force.

After the war things had gradually moved back to how they had been, and having fewer overseas locations may, among other factors, have contributed to a growing culture among RAF enlisted personnel in particular of regarding themselves unofficially as civilians in uniform, a mindset that particularly affected the 1960s and 1970s. This was the time when the RAF had again become a predominantly strategic bombing and static defence force. There were of course large, if decreasing, elements deployed abroad outside of Germany, where a more realistic attitude towards local defence arrangements could not quite so easily be ignored but, again, these were largely static and strategically relevant while they remained. This was the nature of the Cold War philosophy. The early warning radar stations were not mobile; they were rooted into the land at permanent locations. Air defence fighter squadrons had one overriding concern – the defence of UK airspace against Soviet air strikes, however overwhelmed they would be in the event – and, furthermore, the defence of the V-force which would carry Britain's retaliation. Deployment for them meant being shuffled around other home air bases or occasionally a similarly well-provided-for NATO air base overseas.

This seemed, over time, to generate a sense of resentment among many airmen in ground trades at the notion of carrying a rifle at all. Not that this attitude was all-pervasive; it varied according to who you spoke to. Often, comments that sounded quite scandalous were nothing more than flippant humour. But many enlisted airmen in the RAF of the 1970s regarded traditional military customs and training to defend their own airfield, missile base, radar station or supply depot with arms as anachronistic and futile nonsense and, in some cases, felt that they were above it all, being men with a trade, and that sort of buggering about was for the Army. One airman serving as a driver in Germany, who could well have found himself driving in a convoy of vehicles under threat of air or ground attack should the much-feared

Soviet intervention have happened, told the author that he was off to Canada should that happen, and that if he had wanted to get himself killed fighting the bloody Russians he would have joined the Army. That is not to say that he honestly meant this, but his flippant take on his role as a serving member of HM Forces was thoroughly disappointing. There was no trace of irony or cheek when he said it. On another occasion, a US military evaluation team monitoring the ground defences under exercise conditions at one RAF station in Germany in the 1970s noted the professionalism of the likes of the RAF Police and Regiment units, but were not quite so satisfied with the average airman on guard duty who for all the world gave the impression that he had just been press-ganged. This was the big problem; the erks, while professional enough at their designated task, whether radar operator, store clerk, ATC assistant or airframe technician, had by and large fallen into a belief that this was all anyone had a right to expect of them. In some cases, the attitude was more obnoxious, some believing that if the RAF wanted to retain their exceptional talents and not lose them to lucrative tax-free contracts in Saudi Arabia, then its senior management ought to jolly well ease up on the military bull once and for all. Furthermore, the senior management seemed happy to oblige. I can appreciate that this all sounds highly disparaging, but much of this is a reflection of the times, and if their airships carry any responsibility at all for the problem child among the ranks, it is that they too felt less of a need for a skilled avionics technician to let out a blood-curdling scream while charging down a hessian sack of straw in the rough shape of a human body, armed with a rifle and bayonet.

This culture that had developed from the National Service era and through the overseas contraction of the post-war years and into the 1970s was not passing without notice. The author came across something more than an urban myth that seemed to reflect the change of heart experienced by some of the more senior officers. In an instance that all too closely mirrored one played out in the film *Strategic Air Command*, an Air Vice-Marshal, when due to carry out the annual formal inspection at one RAF station, arrived at the airfield just as a helicopter pilot requested permission to make an emergency landing. As the chopper touched down, the inspecting senior officer's car arrived to be greeted by the Station Commander in front of the formed ranks of station personnel and the Guard of Honour. No sooner had the visiting officer stepped from his vehicle than armed individuals emerged from the helicopter and charged toward the assembled parade, firing blank rounds and throwing thunderflash grenades. The mortified Station Commander was immediately put on the spot by the Air Vice-Marshal, who seemed quite comfortable with the situation, by asking just what the Station Commander planned to do about the unexpected interruption to the proceedings. A more serious and realistic attitude toward tactical preparedness was at hand. The old RAF did not see the point in providing DPM (Disruptive Pattern Military) clothing on general issue outside of the aforementioned RAF Regiment, Helicopter and Harrier units. The new RAF did. Furthermore, the RAF of the 1980s was going to ensure that a minimum degree of physical fitness was maintained. By the latter end of the decade, all personnel were obliged to pass an annual basic fitness test, which meant running a mile-and-a-half in about twelve minutes. Still not quite as extensive as that for the Army, but all the armed services were by 1988 required to complete the test. Failure to do so could see booked annual leave cancelled until any shortcomings had been remedied. The same applied to personal weapon testing, in the form of the annual range qualification, which included rudimentary firearms maintenance. It was not much in the great scheme of things, but the message was getting through, especially when a growing number of RAF stations started forming things like the Station Guard (or Reaction) Force. This newfangled outfit had the very duty that many both in and out of the RAF thought the RAF Regiment and perhaps the RAF Police were meant to be doing. The Station Reaction Force was an innovation originating from the RAF in Germany, the intention being to have a trained core of station personnel ready to deploy as an armed sentry and air base defence unit should the need arise. This was often put to the test during the years of Baader-Meinhof and IRA terrorism.

Towards the end 1976, the idea of amalgamating the armed forces into a single uniform was raised above the parapet to gauge reaction. The bean counters got a quite single-minded reaction. Otherwise, while no one would have believed it, the RAF was about to embark upon a period not only of stability but of actual growth in operational strength through to 1991. There would be changes here and there to the squadron line-up, and aircraft would be replaced with new ones, seemingly without too much bother. The future hinged on the arrival in service of the Panavia Tornado. The aircraft, once known to one and all as the MRCA, was very much seen by the three NATO countries responsible for its development and entry into service with their respective air arms as nothing short of a panacea to meet every conceivable tactical role together with deep-penetration strike and, once all competitors had been firmly dismissed for whatever reason, as a very much needed long-range all-weather interceptor for the RAF alone. The other two partner nations, West Germany and Italy, were not keen on the Tornado as an air defence fighter and preferred to stay with the F-4 Phantom in the German case, and the even older albeit final version of the Lockheed F-104 Starfighter in the case of the Italians.

Despite the early emphasis on Interdiction Strike, the Tornado was more than equal to the demands of all-weather strike, reconnaissance and close air support. Maritime anti-shipping and suppression of enemy air defences were also more specialised roles within the frame of low-level attack which this aircraft was comfortably able to carry out. The suggestion of a specific version as an air defence fighter was not entirely unworthy, as constant press reports (ill-informed as often as not) were keen to point out, provided that the air defence demands were strictly limited to the unique requirements of flying several hundred miles from base over the North Sea up towards Iceland and the Faroe Islands in order to intercept and, if need be, engage and destroy Soviet long-range strategic bomber reconnaissance aircraft, and nothing more. The Tornado ADV promised to be an ideal aircraft for this, as anything requiring the need to close with an aircraft of a higher level of performance would realistically be better served by something else. For this reason, the UK air defence commitment over the north of West Germany would continue be met by the now venerable Phantom fighters. This was a far from ideal solution, as the Phantom was honestly no more a dog fighter than the Tornado. However, it was all there was. The notion was that of the two, the older aircraft was by a margin better suited in this regard. Some may consider the decision to leave the Phantoms in service in Germany as testimony to its greater effect as a tactical fighter, meaning it could turn its hand to ground attack and reconnaissance more easily than the Tornado ADV. Here the Tornado variants were definitely different aircraft to one another. The long-range interceptor was no more an interdictor strike aircraft than that particular variant was a search and rescue mount.

The longer range of the Phantom over its predecessor the Lightning, together with the growing likelihood of Soviet aircraft able to carry out air strikes from the west, prompted a review of fighter bases further south. RAF Cottesmore in Rutland was considered as the third base for the Phantom interceptors rather than Wattisham, the latter having been home to air defence units throughout the better part of the post-war years owing to its proximity to the east coast. The assessment had decided that threats against Scotland and northern and central England could best be met by fighters operating from Leuchars, Binbrook and Coningsby. Binbrook was to be retained only for as long as any number of Lightnings remained. However, the most important targets in the south of England, despite being of primary concern, were to be covered by a single base. Wattisham was chosen to continue rather than move the fighters to Cottesmore, owing to the threat of attacks against the east coast remaining of paramount concern. Wattisham lay in the threat line here; in other words, in the most likely path of a raid. Considerable and concerted air attacks against major population centres and other strategic targets across the UK were a cause of much concern in 1974. From Wattisham, raids could be intercepted some seven minutes earlier than from Cottesmore, this being particularly important in relation to the high speed of the Soviet Tu-22 Backfire bomber and the short warning times likely to be available. Further, the recovery time to Wattisham would be shorter, and time spent actually engaging raids would be longer. In Cottesmore's favour, it would be further from harm's way in either direction, but the Bloodhound missile defences around Wattisham addressed this. As for the air defence Tornados, given their range and again the greater likelihood of air attacks, any direction prompted a further

Dramatic shot of the Lightning. (*Author's collection*)

review of future fighter bases with a view to moving away from the east coast, putting bases more closely associated with the V-force into consideration including Scampton, Waddington and Honington.

By the start of 1976, the Soviet Union was deploying new types of intercontinental ballistic missiles and increasing its inventory of ballistic missile-armed nuclear submarines. Eleven Delta Class vessels were in use and threatening North West Europe and North America. In his statement on the defence estimates for 1976, Defence Secretary Roy Mason noted that the USSR was also soon likely to deploy a new medium-range ballistic missile capable of hitting all major cities in Western Europe. In addition to this, steady improvements in Soviet conventional weapons were noted. The balance all across the board showed a numerical superiority of the Warsaw Pact over NATO. On top of this, the substantial level of Soviet forces in the western USSR was capable of rapidly reinforcing those based in the European Central Region, whereas the West would be slower in reacting due to the need first to get substantial US forces across the Atlantic.

The Labour government was concerned not so much by the prospect of a military assault by the Soviet Union than by its use of military muscle to lever and influence events in the West. Mason's statement also made the point that theatre nuclear forces were indispensable to NATO for two reasons. First, they deterred the Warsaw Pact from using its own theatre nuclear weapons, and second, they represented a link between NATO's conventional and strategic nuclear forces, thus increasing the range of options open to the alliance should its conventional forces fail. Without such weapons NATO might be forced to accept either the annexation of part of its territory or initiate a strategic nuclear war. The Defence Secretary went on to say that it was not sufficient simply to possess nuclear weapons to ensure deterrence but was also necessary to make it evident to a potential enemy that Britain would be prepared to use them if it had to.

In view of the situation, almost all of UK forces were now devoted to supporting NATO strategy. At the time over 70 per cent of the alliance's immediate maritime capability was provided by the Royal Navy, and a force of 55,000 made up the British Army of the Rhine which was now receiving the Lance tactical nuclear missile. The RAF, for its part, was now streamlined into four commands: Strike, Training, Support and RAF Germany. All remaining overseas units outside of North West Europe fell under the umbrella of Strike Command which was headed by a four-star officer (Air Chief Marshal), while the other three were each headed by a three-star officer (Air Marshal).

In spite of everything, the review of 1974/75 was going ahead and this meant that the Navy would face the Soviet threat with fewer than the hitherto planned number of frigates, destroyers and minesweepers. The Navy's last serving Audacious Class aircraft carrier *Ark Royal* had another three years. It was announced after the review, in October 1977, that it too would be heading for the breakers' yard. The Army was to face a reduction in its planned number of armoured reconnaissance vehicles and helicopters, while further savings were being sought by reducing or deferring in the short term a list of over forty types of equipment described as relatively low priced. The introduction of an anti-armour guided weapon to be fired from helicopters was also deferred.

The RAF had of course lost essentially its strategic transport arm, a list of bases and a reduction in the number of its Nimrod anti-submarine force by a single operational squadron. Further to this, a cut of up to one-third in the planned delivery rate of the MRCA was being negotiated with the governments in Bonn and Rome. So the Comets, Belfasts and Britannia long-range transports were no more and the RAF support helicopter numbers were further reduced following the government's intention to rid itself of its NATO commitment in the Mediterranean. By the time of the Queen's Silver Jubilee in 1977, the RAF had just completed re-equipping and restructuring in order to concentrate all operational assets within the European theatre. The Jaguar was fully deployed at a strength of eight squadrons, and the Phantoms had all been reassigned to air defence. The Navy was about to lose its last bona fide carrier and the Air Force was to inherit its Phantoms and Buccaneers. The

A Vulcan scrambles from Finningley in the Silver Jubilee rehearsals in 1977. ((C) MOD *Crown Copyright 1977, reproduced under the terms of the Open Government Licence*)

Silver Jubilee review of the RAF took place on 29 July at Finningley, near Doncaster, with the official air show the following day. Present were representative aircraft from a number of countries pledging allegiance to the British Monarch including Australia, whose air force sent an example of the General Dynamics F-111 to take part in the flying along with an American one. The Tornado pre-production model was also on show, courtesy of BAC.

Towards the end of the Callaghan government, efforts were already being made within the Air Staff to find a replacement aircraft specifically aimed at the Jaguar and Harrier, and with those deployed on the Continent in particular. The project, nothing more than an Air Staff Target (AST), as of 1979 had yet to become publicly acknowledged. One of the key requirements of AST 403 was that it would need to be supremely agile. Like the Canberra some twenty years earlier, the Air Staff were concerned at the vulnerability of the current crop of tactical aircraft available to launch from the North German Plain and how they would fare against the opposition. As before, the key worry was shear airframe and engine performance. This might be an appropriate juncture to point out that the Harrier, for all its popularity and public perception, was never much more than a short-range battlefield attack aircraft. It performed well, but its overriding saving grace, the ability to take off and land

The RAF's latest front-line manned combat type, the much troubled Eurofighter Typhoon. (*Trevor Thornton*)

vertically, was not a very good idea if range and weapons needed to be brought to bear. The amount of fuel and the limit on armament prevent this from being of any use other than in the most dire and near-irretrievable of circumstances. Once up, in conventional flight, the Harrier was left way behind by many of the recent Soviet types which it would have to try and avoid. There have always been interesting claims about Harrier successes in mock air-to-air engagements with other fighter types from across NATO, and, indeed, genuine ones during the Falklands conflict when Blue Fox intercept radar equipped Royal Navy Sea Harriers enjoyed an outstanding degree of success against Argentinian Mirages, but these are remarkable for the very reason that they were somewhat unexpected. The Harrier was a success, but it would be a gross mistake to rely too heavily upon it, certainly in its air defence role. The need to replace it with a 'Super' variant or something with a much greater range of performance and greater agility was evident even in the 1970s, and the same applied to the under-powered Jaguar. Again, while this aircraft has met with some success sticking to the close air support role, it has not really had to operate in a particularly challenging environment. In the first Gulf War, what the Iraqi air force had to attack other aircraft with was very much held off by the other Allied air forces' F-15s, F-16s and the like.

The Anglo-French Jaguar was originally intended as a High Performance Trainer but outgrew this requirement and was ultimately deployed as a Nuclear-Armed Strike Aircraft to replace the Phantom, which was needed as a stop-gap Lightning replacement. (*Keith Butcher*)

The proposed replacement, as of 1979, was soon being referred to as the ECA (European Combat Aircraft). As the name suggests, this was a European collaborative project and once again a specifications headache. Early on, the other principal partner, West Germany, was at odds with the British over what the requirements of the design actually needed to be. The early projections on cost and the likely in-service date put the ECA back from 1987 to 1990, and quite soon this prompted concern that the Jaguars in service by then would be due for replacement and a front-line deficit would have to be faced. By the 1980s and 1990s, the expectation was that the Jaguar would no longer be a viable close support aircraft given the kind of hostile airspace anticipated over the Central Region. A further project being pursued as an interim was ASR 409, which crystallised into the Harrier GR5 and later GR7 and GR9 variants. By no means intended as a competitor to the ECA, the ASR 409 was regarded more as a means of maintaining numbers in anticipation of airframe fatigue loss among earlier aircraft while introducing some improvements, but the problem of the Jaguar's survivability into the 1980s and beyond was still going to require costly improvements in order to bridge the gap between about 1987 and the ECA's initial entry into service. This was the plan before the in-service date for the ECA/AST 403 slipped again to 1995.

Preparing for the imminent arrival of the Panavia Tornado, the Cottesmore Station Commander and his good lady officially open the 'Swingers Club', the new junior ranks watering hole. (*The National Archives*)

Two early production Tornados (MRCAs) fly over Cottesmore on 8 May 1979 to mark the occasion of the signing of the Memorandum of Understanding between the partner nations to co-operate on introducing aircraft into service with the formation of the Tri-national Tornado Training Establishment. (*The National Archives*)

In the event, the improvements to the Jaguar were considered essential but not financially viable, so instead the decision was taken to deploy the Tornado GR1 in Germany, and this was the state of play by 1980. Five options were being considered to ensure that the RAF front-line operational air support in West Germany could best meet the projected Warsaw Pact air threat by 1995:

A. a straightforward purchase of AST 403/ECAs or a little-known purely British project by the name of P96F,

B. abandonment of AST 403 and an increase in the number of Tornados and ASR 409/Advanced Harriers,

C. purchase of a home-built lightweight version of AST 403,

D. replacement of AST 403 with an STOVL version, and

E. purchase of a comparable aircraft to AST 403 off the shelf.

The first option was considered far too expensive; the second would render no long-term improvement; the third would not be much cheaper or the best operational solution; and the fourth would take too long, even though it was otherwise seen as the best option. The expected delay in getting it into service would necessitate the continuation of Jaguars and, interestingly, Buccaneers. The fifth option, the off-the-shelf choice, would best meet the requirement, would be cheapest and would be in time to prevent any extensions of the Buccaneers and Jaguars. If that course was followed, there would still be a later development of an advanced supersonic STOVL technology demonstrator as a future replacement for Harriers, Sea Harriers and perhaps even Tornados. This was seen as a necessary consolation to British industry for buying an off-the-shelf aircraft from abroad.

To further demonstrate the problems with vectored-thrust designs in relation to performance in the air, studies showed that while the Air Staff remained keen on an STOVL Fighter, a vectored-thrust design would meet this requirement together with the necessary performance required of an aircraft capable of fully meeting the demands of air-to-air combat. While the Germans were looking for a pure fighter to replace their F-4 Phantoms, the British were looking for something more: a strike aircraft capable of defending itself in the kind of dense hostile air environment which future Warsaw Pact designs were expected to bring. A study of performance comparisons between that projected for AST 403 and ASR 409 against the known limits of the Tornado, F-15, F-16, Jaguar and Harrier further confirmed the need for a more agile and robust design to replace the latter two. Specific excess thrust at sea level comparisons put the predicted performance of the Harrier GR3, Jaguar GR1 and ASR 409 all near the bottom rung, with the Tornado GR1 holding a respectable midway comparison just above that of the MiG-21 and 23 Soviet fighters but below the F-18 and significantly below the AST 403 prediction and F-16. Further comparisons with a slightly altered line-up looked at sustained turns with typical combat configuration at sea level, and this time the results were little different:

Jaguar GR1:   carrying 6 x 500 lb CBUs = 3.3g at Mach 0.96

Harrier GR3:   carrying 4 x 500 lb CBUs = 4.49g at Mach 0.86

ASR 409:   carrying 6 x 500 lb CBUs = 3.9g at Mach 0.81

Tornado GR1:   carrying 5 x 600 lb CBUs = 4.8g at Mach 1.1

F-15:   carrying 11 x Rockeyes = 8.3g at above Mach 1.2

                 (Rockeye is a cluster bomb weighing about 490 lb)

AST 403:   carrying 6 x 500 lb CBUs = 8.9g at above Mach 1.1

These comparison figures were drawn up between December 1980 and March 1981. Furthermore, the projected structural limit of AST 403 was placed at around 10g+, whereas it was around 9g for the F-15 and F-18.

Clearly the Jaguar and Harrier lacked the degree of performance needed, but funding for what was to replace them would certainly mean another collaborative venture and the problem here, apart from variance between partner nations on the finer details of specification, was the ability to convince the electorate in some cases that such an endeavour was neither a waste of money nor an escalation of the arms race but a much needed improvement in air crew survivability. In 1981, the West German Defence Minister, Hans Apel, risked public wrath in his country by silencing critics of the ECA/AST 403. In order to reach a satisfactory compromise with the electorate, the West German government was considering buying off-the-shelf F-18s. Fearing this would happen, the British even approached the Saudi royal family with a view to financial support to continue the project. The idea of Britain going down the off-the-shelf route was opposed by British Aerospace and risking any industrial problems here was the British government's more pressing concern.

When the 1970s ended, the last pre-Blair Labour government left office and with it went the last Labour administration which was lead by a statesmanlike leader. The arrival at No. 10 Downing Street of Margaret Thatcher brought a degree of misplaced expectation and, yet to gain the nickname 'The Iron Lady', was already filling the hearts of many, not just among the unions, with trepidation. There was perhaps an expectation that a more robust approach to defence than previously was on the cards. Whatever the expectations and whatever the long-term strategy, within two years of taking office, Thatcher was on her second Defence Secretary and he, John Nott, was, as expected, looking to save money from the defence budget. The RAF was going to see a reduction in some operational support units, including the loss of one of two Canberra-equipped target facilities squadrons and, from the front line, one of two reconnaissance Canberra squadrons. The counter to this was going to be that they would each stand up again over the next decade without any further

Harrier T2 landing on the deck of a ship during carrier trials for the development of the Sea Harrier, *c.* 1976-78. (*HU 109896, IWM*)

reductions elsewhere, one with the new (to the RAF) Chinook, and the other returning to the reconnaissance role with the Panavia Tornado. The biggest blow was about to be inflicted upon the Navy, which had only recently lost *Ark Royal*, although it was now bringing into service the Sea Harrier and the first of three Invincible Class light ski-jump carriers. In the meantime an old vessel, HMS *Hermes*, had been converted for this role and in 1982 would be the flagship of the South Atlantic Task Force. A year earlier, the Navy was about to go through a round of surgery similar to that which it had endured scarcely ten years before that.

The Argentinian invasion of the Falkland Islands put the British government on the spot, and it is widely accepted that had the cuts to the sea-going fleet taken place prior to the Argentinian invasion, not a great deal could have been done about retrieving the Islands. The RAF, along with the Army for once, were at a severe disadvantage, and when the RAF demonstrated its reach by launching Vulcans, on the point of retirement, and Victors, to mount what was at the time the longest round-trip bombing sortie in history, the point was not missed that this was indeed a task requiring a carrier more along the lines of the old Audacious Class rather than those of the small ski-jump Invincible Class. Again, HM Forces through their excellent resolve and by proving their ability to adapt and overcome, at least in short spurts, convinced the bloody-minded politicians that they had done nothing wrong in removing quite substantial assets.

However, where the direct defence of UK airspace was concerned, the sense of urgency and the need to upgrade and even expand was firmly on the agenda. By August 1979, the Air Force Board confidently proposed a fighter requirement over and above what existed. To attempt to achieve this, three timescales were considered. The short term looked ahead to 1985, when it was expected that the now confirmed new air defence interceptor/fighter, the Tornado ADV, would become operational, at the time still expected to be identified as the F2. Inside this period, the shortfall was expected to be partially met by the standing up of a third squadron of Lightnings, even though this aircraft by rights should have been withdrawn and replaced. In the medium term, three squadrons of Phantoms would be retained in addition to the Tornado F2 force, and in the long term, the Phantoms would need to be replaced by the purchase of new fighters, not necessarily Tornados.

To meet this, the AFB were looking at two further proposals, described as likely to affect all three timescales, one being the increased number of F2s and another being an offer by Grumman of fourteen ex-Iranian F-14s, at a reasonable cost. The option to increase the production of F2s considered increasing the expected production run from four to five aircraft per month from April 1986. This could be further accommodated by reducing the production run on the strike version, GR1, after 1985, by which time the number of GR1s delivered was expected to be 200, nearly all on order, to support a front-line strength of 170. This in turn would allow the build-up of air defence Tornados to achieve a front-line strength of nine squadrons with a unit establishment of fifteen aircraft each by mid-1988. The original plan was to achieve the same by the end of 1989.

The early 1980s had already been identified as a period of significantly increased risk and had seen a wide range of upgrades to new aircraft. During the same period, other NATO air forces were acquiring the first of their F-16s, and the Americans in addition were building up their F-15 squadrons in Germany and Holland. As a further priority, the RAF also expected to have replaced the ageing Vulcans well before the middle of the decade. Should matters need to move at an increased tempo, and additional/replacement air defence fighters were needed urgently, then four American aircraft types were in the running as the prime candidate for an off-the-shelf realistic enough front-line interceptor. These were either one of two naval variants of the F-4 Phantom, the J or S model, the F-14 or the F-15. Two other likely contenders, the F-16 and F-18 were not deemed far enough into development or sufficiently advanced in the production stage to see them available in significant numbers soon. The F-16 was also criticised as falling short of the mark because it

From 1981 the F16 entered the service of smaller NATO air forces; the RAF lacked a highly manoeuvrable fighter of this calibre until the arrival of the Eurofighter Typhoon. (*Author's collection*)

did not possess a true all-weather look-down/shoot-down radar. The expansion of manpower to accommodate a surge in capability also posed something of headache, with all the available personnel expected to be drawn from fast jet squadrons in other operational roles. Even if the Lightning squadrons were to be replaced by any one of the American fighters on a like-for-like basis there would still be a need for extra manpower, as the Lightnings would yield only about two-thirds of the requirement needed for even the least manpower-intensive of any of the replacement types. This did not even take into consideration the prospect of additional navigators/weapon systems officers. Binbrook, the last home of the RAF's Lightning fleet, was expected to continue as the home for any US aircraft, including a small OCU. If this had been done, in addition to the expected delivery of Tornado F2s, the RAF would also have been able to give early retirement to its own Phantoms, originally used to fly low-level strike, attack and reconnaissance roles and therefore with some considerable fatigue life used up already.

After reviewing the costs, however, two conclusions were arrived at. One was to build up to nine F-2 squadrons, all based in the UK and run on the existing strength of Phantoms based in Germany at Wildenrath. This would mean an increased purchase, however, of thirty more F-2s. The second option considered an emergency situation in which the three US fighter squadrons would be bought to replace the Lightnings

Public demonstration of a high-energy climb by a Phantom over Finningley in 1990. (*Author's collection*)

early on. This would also mean relying on US support and training and the adoption of US procedures and would create an undesirable effect on other fast jet squadrons outside the air defence role. The decision, taken in July 1979, was to stand up an additional Lightning squadron and, in addition, to arm with AIM-9L Sidewinder missiles the BAE Hawk advanced trainers which were at the time replacing the Gnats and Hunters in both advanced flying training and initial tactical training roles. A memorandum of understanding was also signed with the governments of France and West Germany to carry out collaborative studies into a future surface-to-air missile system to replace the Bloodhound.

No sooner had the step to create a third squadron out of the remaining pool of Lightnings been made than a question arose regarding the Fatigue Index for all the remaining airframes. At the current use of twenty-four out of seventy aircraft on the front line, together with about eight more for operational training/conversion, the fatigue life of the total banked hours of 2,690 would be exhausted by early 1986. If the third Lightning squadron was formed when expected, around 1981, this expiry date would be brought forward to late 1984. Conversely, BAE assured the RAF that the initial operating capability date for the first Tornado F2s could not be brought further forward to compensate. Even before this, the RAF had had misgivings about forming an additional Lightning squadron at all, despite the demands of the new government to improve the UK air defences. Should the plan have gone ahead, postings from the Lightning force would have been partially frozen, while additional pilots from a small surplus in the pool of Jaguar ground attack/strike pilots would have been utilised together with pilots now serving on ground tours who were already Lightning qualified.

The biggest programme embarked upon at the start of the 1980s was the introduction of the Tornado. No other front-line aircraft since the Javelin and Hunter had been introduced into service in quite so many numbers. By the time the strike version, GR1 being the UK designation, was fully deployed, it equipped eleven operational squadrons, two conversion units and an evaluation unit. Throughout the decade governments on both sides of the Iron Curtain were busy introducing the next generation of aircraft to form the backbone of their respective air arms. By the end of 1989, the RAF re-equipment programme was almost complete. As well as the expanding Tornado force, tactically deployable radar heads were now available. Correspondingly, the air defence version of this aircraft was fully deployed by 1990, allowing an increase in the number of interceptor squadrons to nine in the UK and two in Germany. In a final repudiation of the Sandys theory about missile defence, one of the two remaining Bloodhound squadrons was stood down to stand up once again as a manned fighter unit, with the Tornado F3, this being the definitive air defence Tornado variant.

A note on the Tornado F3: never has an aircraft (apart from the Eurofighter Typhoon) been more contemptuously treated by the popular press. Much of the criticism centred on the fact that the ADV Tornado, originally billed as the F2, was (not at all surprisingly) delayed in entering service. The delay was due largely to the trouble developing the Fox Hunter radar, the problems proving so difficult to iron out that the first eighteen aircraft were delivered to the RAF in an effectively unusable state. The first three arrived at RAF Coningsby in October 1984, each fitted with a lump of concrete in the nose cone on account of the Fox Hunter not being ready. This resulted in the nickname Blue Circle radar.

Furthermore, because the airframe engine performance was not up to expectations, an uprated version was to be used in the definitive version. The Mk 104 Turbo-Union RB199 engine produced about a further 10 per cent thrust in reheat through the extension of the jet-pipe by some 18 inches.

There remained one aspect about this aircraft that seemed impossible to impress upon many commentators then and since: that the Tornado F3 was not expected to dog fight in the way the F-15 or F-16 do. It was a long-range bomber destroyer, expected to hunt down the low, fast-moving strategic strike aircraft of the Soviet air force attempting to reach UK airspace in the middle of the night on Christmas Eve.

Panavia Tornado ADV prototype. Delays in getting this aircraft into service prompted the air staff to look at an interim replacement for the Lightning and Phantom, including more up to date ex-US Navy F4 Phantoms. (*Jeremy Hughes*)

So to criticise the lack of high energy of the Tornado is certainly to miss the point. Well almost. It is clear that long before the end of the Cold War, indeed long before the definitive Tornado F3s were being issued to RAF squadrons, there was a need for a more agile fighter. It could be argued that the emphasis on an air superiority fighter was an attempt to redress the expected degree of shortcomings of the F3. For all that, those who flew the F3, like that other 'plain-Jane', the Buccaneer, became particularly attached to it and would swear by it.

But whatever the inability of any in-service aircraft to tight turn up its own fundament, the RAF of 1990 was readier to respond than it had been since the move from trip-wire to flexible-response NATO policy on reacting to Eastern Bloc aggression. Just before the Berlin Wall came down, the British government had approved the order of a further forty Tornado aircraft. The number of the new EFA expected to enter service was 250, and the RAF had a strength of about 90,000 personnel operating and maintaining some thirty front-line operational squadrons with six fast jet types as well as four maritime patrol squadrons equipped with the Nimrod MR2P, a high-altitude reconnaissance unit equipped with the Canberra PR9, and a tactical transport force with four squadrons of Hercules and five variously equipped with Puma, Wessex and Chinook transport helicopters, not counting the various Operational Conversion Units (OCUs). Together with all this, the RAF Regiment was now armed with Scorpion light tanks as well as Rapier missile anti-aircraft fire units and the service could now deploy several mobile tactical radars. It is almost a shame that at this juncture the Cold War began to thaw at all too fast a rate.

CHAPTER 8
The '90s: Cold War Fading

The collapse of the Berlin Wall took many people by surprise, even considering the thaw in East-West relations since Mikhail Gorbachev replaced Konstantin Chernenko as Soviet President in 1985. No one had seriously entertained the idea of the Cold War ending on good terms. That it did, despite the unpleasantness over President Ceausescu of Romania, left everyone wishing to do the right thing in order to assure the West's new-found friends in the USSR that we held nothing but the best of intentions toward them. There was no clear way forward, no contingency as to what to do next, but a compelling need to do something. Everyone was in the same situation and of course the prospect of substantial disarmament seemed most attractive to all governments. There was a fly in the ointment, as some will recall, in 1990, this being the Iraqi invasion of Kuwait in July.

The conventional armed forces of all NATO countries, with the exception of the US, and speaking proportionately, did not really exist as forces with any kind of in-depth capability to fight a protracted war, certainly not against anything that could be described as a heavily armed aggressive state. The military arrangements of the North West European countries were aimed at fighting such a war against the Soviet Union no longer than beyond about three days. This was deemed sufficient for the much greater and more definitive American ready-to-go weight of force to arrive in theatre in order to take up the cudgels. The hope was that the American reinforcements would arrive in sufficient numbers well before anyone felt it necessary to (in the spirit of 'flexible response') to move matters to the next step and start launching battlefield nuclear weapons at the enemy. Now that nightmare was receding fast, but despite already developing concerns about the stability of an unbridled Eastern Europe all going their separate ways and the ever-present concerns of the flashpoint that was the Middle East, with various unsympathetic countries at least as far as the West was concerned, no one was prepared to give up the opportunity to reinvest taxpayers' money in a more enlightened fashion and also, of course, convince the Russians that we were all friends now. Indeed, they for their part, and not a just a smidgen to do with the

Three VC10s and two Tornados (B.O.B. 50th Anniversary Flypast over Abingdon). (*Author's collection*)

communist state's crumbling economic circumstances, were looking to dismantle much of their gargantuan military complex.

The problem now facing the Thatcher government, as others, was exactly what could be dispensed with from the Order of Battle which would serve to show we were doing our bit and also ensure that the standing military force that remained was not just a token. As with the USSR and US, the retention of the British nuclear deterrent was non-negotiable. The cuts would fall on the very elements that would be needed in the future and in the coming months with the formation of a coalition of US-led armed forces to liberate Kuwait from Iraqi occupation. But something had to go. The Army was to lose eighteen infantry battalions, later revised to sixteen. The armoured regiments were to be reduced from nineteen to thirteen, to allow one of the three divisions resident in Germany to disband. The RAF was to see its own tactical fixed-wing element bear the brunt, but the axe would fall essentially on the older airframes. Before the Berlin Wall came down and the British government put together the subsequent Defence Review under the title 'Options for Change', the Phantom and Buccaneer aircraft were due to be retained up until 2003; now they were going once and for all. In addition, the agreeably large Tornado strike force was to be trimmed by three squadrons, with two more to be returned home from

Five of eight diamond sixteen fighter formations over Abingdon in the B.O.B. Flypast, 15 September 1990. It is hard to imagine the RAF staging such a spectacle ever again. (*Author's collection*)

Germany. A further two would be reassigned to the maritime strike role in order to replace the outgoing Buccaneers, as this was their unique contribution hitherto. The anti-submarine Nimrod force was to be reduced by 25 per cent. An odd development was the creation of a further support command while RAF Germany was reduced to group status and brought under the umbrella of Strike Command. The last of the Bloodhound missiles were withdrawn and the early warning Control and Reporting post at Bishops Court in Northern Ireland was stood down. The new personnel figure for the RAF was to be 75,000. Redundancy packages were offered to those for the chop, which was not seen as too much of a problem because the economy, on the edge of a new recession, was going to receive a boost from the peace dividend, thanks to all the money saved by not employing quite so many people in the forces or operating as many tanks, planes and ships, at least after we had helped drive Saddam Hussein out of Kuwait.

Phantom Diamond sixteen segment of B.O.B. 50th Anniversary Flypast over Abingdon, 1990. (*Author's collection*)

It appeared that, like everywhere else, the MoD had bitten the bullet, so to speak, and rebalanced the armed forces with any unnecessary flab trimmed off to leave them lean, mean and fighting fit. In the intervening years to 1997, Thatcher had been replaced by John Major. He had faced the concerns of the much expected break-up of Eastern Europe and the Balkan genocide, over which the United Nations had presided in predictable style, with fine words and inaction. The financial difficulties affecting not just the UK but other western countries did not appear to be going away, and even more determined to get a return from the end of the Cold War, the German Defence Minister, Volker Rühe, threw the still alive EFA programme into a flat spin by calling for the aircraft in its existing form to be cancelled and the technology used to develop a new aircraft. This would be based on a single-engine design and was dubbed 'EFA Light' by the press. Rühe also suggested that Britain might want to do the same by claiming that the streets of Britain were not paved with gold. A further alternative considered by the Germans was the development of the MiG-29 with the new Russian Federation. Fortunately, some may think, the programme had to press ahead with the Germans on board. The contractual agreements which

Rühe's predecessors had entered into were very similar to those which the British government entered into regarding the Queen Elizabeth Class carriers, and there was nothing to be gained through withdrawal or returning to the drawing board and starting again with a scaled down, less able design. The end of the Cold War had brought an expected reduction in order numbers. The German order fell from 250 to 140 aircraft, and the UK order had also been reduced slightly from 250 to 232. By 1996, the Germans had revised their order again, this time increasing it to 180, with an idea for replacing a chunk of their Tornado fleet.

By 1994, a further reduction in the RAF was sought following another review, this time carrying the title 'Front Line First'. The front line, it seemed, were to benefit from this exercise, but reading between the lines what was pursued was cuts elsewhere – the RAF was to lose some more runways and infrastructure. In addition, a further squadron of Tornado interceptors were stood down just before this review was made public. The new review found that two air bases were surplus to requirements: Scampton, of Dambusters fame, and Finningley. Scampton was at that time the home of the RAF aerobatics team, while Finningley had received some infrastructure upgrades and additional units just prior to the review. No. 100 squadron had moved in following its re-equipment with the BAE Hawk to operate in the target facilities role. Now that the station was to close, the various elements of No. 6 Flying Training School were to be dispersed to other stations. This was all rather piecemeal and seemed to follow on not from any kind of assessment to determine what could be needed but rather what could be dispensed with. The plan was that the team would be based at Cranwell and rehearse over Scampton. Six years later, the station was opened again and the team returned as no other suitable arrangement could be made. Doubtless this exercise did not result in any recognisable savings, with the closing down shortly followed by the reopening of an air base.

Much can be said for the prevailing mindset of the political establishment and the direction in which they had set defence arrangements and were determined for them to continue. The 1990s saw the first deployment by NATO armed forces, under that banner, in anger. From the first Gulf War, through the enforcement of the northern and southern no-fly zones over Iraq, to long-range bombing missions flown from bases in Germany over Kosovo, the RAF, as well as other NATO air arms, had seen more demand for its services than at any time since the end of the Second World War. Certainly the operational tempo in relation to the ever-contracting size of the Air Force raises some serious questions about the mainstream political establishment in Britain and their comparative inability to avoid overseas trouble spots while continuing to fund defence in a manner which suggests a completely different set of priorities and challenges.

While defence spending cuts continued, unlikely criticism of them was being voiced from the opposition benches. This was the new-look Labour Party. Remember, this

The Red Arrows, seen here in their debut display season in 1965, were equipped with the light advanced trainer, the Folland Gnat. The idea was to continue to maintain aerobatics teams, but with fewer and less costly front-line fighters. (*John Wharam*)

The Red Arrows at their best. (*(C) MOD Crown Copyright 1973, reproduced under the terms of the Open Government Licence*)

was the party which in 1980 lurched toward a radical left position on defence once Michael Foot replaced Jim Callaghan as leader on 4 November that year. In 1981, Labour officially shifted to a much more radical position on Britain's relations with NATO, and more so with the American position within the organisation. They were going to fight the 1983 election committed to establishing a non-nuclear defence policy. This was to include those operated by US forces. So far to the left was Foot's defence policy that, had Labour managed to sink the Conservatives at the 1983 general election, the most serious post-war crisis could only have followed, with Britain's new Defence Secretary tasked with explaining to Washington that Britain was not only abandoning its independent nuclear deterrent, indeed its entire nuclear military arsenal, and implementing a far-reaching defence spending review which would lead to deep cuts in the remaining conventional capability, but was also requesting that US nuclear armed forces, if not the entire US military deployment, in Britain be withdrawn. Conventional forces would have been reduced to a level described in the 1983 Labour manifesto as adequate.

If the unilateralist position on nuclear weapons had been pursued as advertised, the government of Michael Foot would almost certainly have found itself facing very severe cuts in military resources with a conventional capability as well as a nuclear strike one. This would be because ensuring that nuclear weapons were placed outside of use by any US forces, welcome to remain in situ in order to meet conventional defence requirements, would mean removing aircraft, for example, capable of delivering nuclear weapons and certainly those tasked primarily to do so. This would result in the removal of the two USAF F-111 wings based at Lakenheath and Upper Heyford, and the closure of the Holy Loch submarine base. As far as UK nuclear capable forces were concerned, it would mean closure of Faslane on Gare Loch, and in all likelihood the loss or at least severe reduction of the Tornado force, already two squadrons into the build-up in 1983, the disbandment of the Buccaneer force and possible withdrawal of the Phantoms which had all since been reassigned to air defence. Also affected would be the Nimrod maritime force, because these aircraft were equipped to carry nuclear depth charges and torpedoes. These far-reaching measures would probably have been necessary in order to convince those outside of Britain's trust, like the Kremlin leadership, that the UK was prepared to honour such an offer with complete sincerity, if the unilateral path was to have any kind of value at all. It is difficult to see what else could be managed. The entire western defence apparatus would have been seriously impaired and weakened to a position that may well have invited a more aggressive drive for yet more concessions, military and otherwise, later on.

Labour, in 1983, were also committing themselves to reducing the proportion of the nation's resources devoted to defence spending. They also claimed they would bring UK defence spending into line with other major European NATO countries. Exactly what they meant by this is not very clear given the variations in comparative GDPs, emphasis in the military capabilities and, of course, conditions of service of other European countries. Whatever the anticipated outcome of such radical changes, the party expected to have to plan to ensure that savings in military expenditure would not lead to unemployment for those working in defence industries, and plan for industrial conversion of valuable resources in the defence industries to what could be used for the production of what the party described as useful goods. Whether those actually serving in the armed forces of 1983 could expect to be counted among those saved from unemployment was perhaps something else which would need clarification. But that a serious political party was prepared to be anywhere near as frank about such radical ambitions as this in its published manifesto would, even fourteen years later on, give cause for concern, regardless of the policy changes of the intervening years.

Foot's leadership was the writing on the wall for some MPs within his own party. Early in 1981, the party was split, with four senior members – the Defence Spokesman and former Home, Foreign and Education Secretaries – leaving to form their own breakaway Social Democratic Party. The 'Gang of Four', Roy Jenkins, Bill Rodgers, David Owen and Shirley Williams, were welcomed into a new political alliance with the Liberal Party led by David Steel. Three general elections later, they had merged into a single party, the Liberal Democrats, but throughout the intervening years failed to achieve their aim of replacing the Labour Party as Her Majesty's Loyal Opposition, much less the aim of government. So it was that the Labour Party under the leadership of Michael Foot, and then Neil Kinnock following Labour's dismal performance at the 1983 election, remained firmly to the left of centre. Both Foot and Kinnock had taken Labour to the polls at each general election on a unilateralist ticket, but despite attempts to try and reassure the electorate that the party was not weak on defence and security, such a reckless policy, certainly outside of conventional defence arrangements, was clearly off-putting.

Two young men sought election to Parliament as Labour candidates in the 1983 general election: Tony Blair and Gordon Brown. These same two in 1997 were now respectively Prime Minister and Chancellor of the Exchequer. By this time Labour's, or rather New Labour's, defence policy had been reconstructed completely. The intervening years, since Thatcher's initial poll victory in 1979, had doubtless caused the party to review its student politics style of defence policy, resulting in the Labour government that was elected in 1997 being committed to retaining Trident, and also being openly aware that the country took pride in the professionalism and courage of its armed forces and, furthermore, that the new government would ensure that they remained strong to defend Britain.

CHAPTER 9
New Labour, New Wars and the RAF

When the Labour Party, led by Tony Blair, won their landslide victory in May 1997, there would have been many a senior military officer and conservative-leaning commentator who would have wondered just how things were going to materialise in the future. Indeed, the national security considerations of 1983 and 1987 were radically different to those of 1997; the justification for retaining an independent nuclear deterrent and the threat of a pre-emptive intercontinental nuclear strike were in remission.

At the time of New Labour's victory, 'Options for Change' and 'Front Line First' conclusions had been applied. The RAF in May 1997 had retained very much the same operational support elements which it had in October 1989 when the Berlin Wall ceased to have any relevance. The strength and number of tactical and strategic transport and tanker squadrons were unchanged. The front-line element had shed approximately a third of its strength over the same period, whereas the Fleet Air Arm had remained largely unscathed, retaining its small force of Sea Harriers which had just received an upgrade from the Mk 1 to Mk 2. Essentially this was a new Blue Vixen intercept radar (from which the Typhoon CAPTOR is derived) and the ability to carry the AIM-120 AMRAAM collision-course missile. The Navy's Sea Harriers specifically served as the principal air defence fighter of the fleet. Whatever the concerns of the past, Tony Blair, and John Smith before him, had manoeuvred the Labour Party back to the centre ground. The unilateralist policy had been abandoned, not because Labour's ruling executive believed nuclear weapons were now, after the Cold War, a defence asset to be retained just in case but because it was a disastrous election loser. This did not alter the socialist ingrained attitude towards the old establishment though, as was soon to be discovered. The truly moderate Harold Wilson had, as mentioned earlier, refused to consider decommissioning the Royal Yacht *Britannia*. Blair and Co. had no compunction at all. Before the end of 1997, the Royal Yacht was headed for the breakers' yard, or would have been had it not been saved by the idea of turning it into a floating museum alongside the docks at Leith in Edinburgh.

The first move New Labour made after the 1997 election was to instigate the Strategic Defence Review. This was, yet again, to determine what level and emphasis of military capability would be required for the foreseeable future. At the time, the most pressing problem was the Balkans conflict and the task of maintaining no-fly zones there and over northern and southern Iraq. RAF Jaguars and, later, Harriers were operating from Incirlik in Turkey as part of the British contribution to enforcing UN resolution 688 over northern Iraq. Harriers of the RAF later flew off the carrier HMS *Invincible* in 1998, the same year the SDR was revealed, in order to participate in the enforcement of the southern no-fly zone over Iraq. The result of the SDR was the announcement of the further shutting down of existing assets despite an earlier claim that the review was not going to be a cost-cutting adventure just like the ones the Conservatives had carried out. Broadly speaking, the SDR was received by the defence establishment without too much contention but was criticised by those who wished to see a more radical departure from 'traditional defence strategy'. In other words, the now well-embedded hostility towards the Eurofighter Typhoon came to the fore.

The RAF has been routinely criticised for pursuing what is indeed perhaps the most versatile and able front-line high-performance combat aircraft of the current generation. The theory often advanced is that Britain's military planners are always fighting the wars of the past and never planning for the wars of tomorrow, but the wars of tomorrow are not so easy to determine, try as many might, and the preparation for them often seems to be overtaken by unexpected events. The conflicts which the post-Cold War world has seen have all been fought as effectively as we could hope with weapons often dismissed as Cold War relics. From the first Gulf War to the most recent no-fly zone enforcement over Libya, the response of high-performance aircraft and the selective strikes on targets well beyond enemy lines have constantly demonstrated the value of such Cold War relevance. If there are any shortcomings, the Achilles' heel has been overstretch rather than equipment unreliability. The 1998 SDR was intended, just as Liam Fox's SDSR had been, to wave goodbye to the Cold War once and for all and focus more realistically on future threats, which were going to need a radical approach. So, what then? Just what did government ministers think was going to happen that represented such a departure from the expected, and just what did they think was going to be needed to deal with it?

One idea was that the UK would need more in the way of rapidly deployable forces, the thinking being along the lines of an expanded Special Forces element and a move toward more light infantry. So having lost sixteen infantry battalions since 1990, one would imagine that a small increase here with the emphasis on light assault focused units would be the upshot. Think again. The decision was taken simply to trim more off the front line all round, albeit heavier units were to take the brunt. A couple of heavy armoured regiments were converted to armoured reconnaissance, and the RAF lost a couple more Tornado squadrons, one each from the strike and air defence roles. So all it amounted to was a defence cut again, and this at a time when Tornado squadrons, along with Harrier and Jaguar squadrons, had been routinely deployed enforcing no-fly zones over Iraq and in support of UNPROFOR policies in the Balkans. When the Kosovo conflict began in earnest in 1999, RAF Tornado GR1 squadrons were in action, again well before the ground offensive, in order to ensure that the enemy ground and air forces would pose the least possible threat. Other NATO air forces were similarly involved. Indeed, a hell of a lot of the weapons used in attacking this particular rogue state were all very much of the 'Cold War' variety, and I defy anyone to suggest a more efficient way of doing it. Light assault infantry alone would have been costly in human terms, think Churchill and the Second World War again, and the means of delivering firepower for the greater part, at the outset, were aircraft operating from land bases and carriers, and Tomahawk missiles launched from surface ships and submarines. This lasted from 24 March to 11 June, after which the land forces started to move in following the ratification of the international peace plan on 10 June.

A number of heavy price-tagged long-term defence projects were indeed commenced during the early Blair years. These included many that eventually became what the coalition government described in 2010 as the procurement black hole, the ones which spiralled out of control (the Eurofighter Typhoon not among them) and had to be begrudgingly maintained or cancelled to avoid further financial loss by the time of the SDSR. Otherwise, with regard to maintaining existing commitments, the 1998 SDR promised one thing for sure: less funding to do more with. Arguably, the loss of existing units and personnel this time round were to help fund recent overseas commitments and new future projects, two new aircraft carriers and the replacement for the Nimrod maritime patrol – anti-submarine warfare aircraft among them.

Another aim of the 1998 SDR was to restructure the process for buying equipment in order to avoid the runaway costs and compromises that had occurred previously, an aim which of course was not achieved. Co-operation between the services such as JFH (Joint Force Harrier) and the Joint Helicopter Command sprang from this review in order to reduce costs and better co-ordinate operations as well. The upshot of this was that any imbalance was revised up the scale, not down, resulting in unintended escalating costs, overdue equipment, reduced orders and reductions in existing assets and personnel. The MoD struggled to pay the increased unit costs and apparently failed to impose any kind of adequate penalty clauses for breach of contract where such increases were the responsibility of the manufacturer, which, as we all know, has continued despite the best of intentions. The pleasure is all the taxpayers'. Just why the MoD has failed, with all the legal services at its disposal, to ensure that agreed contracts are honoured and, if breached, that the penalty is the burden of the contractor is beyond any obvious answer. But we are assured that following the SDSR, the enormous £38 billion deficit accrued through years of mismanaged equipment procurement will be avoided in future.

It has to be remembered that all this was taking place against a vibrant economy. Unemployment in Britain was tumbling, yet Gordon Brown still felt the need to sell off gold reserves at whatever price he could get, at a time when it was openly advisable to wait. On top of this, private pension funds were picked clean by the Treasury, again to fill the coffers to overflowing. Through Blair's first term in office, British forces had been in action in Bosnia and Kosovo in the former Yugoslavia, and had mounted a precarious operation (Operation Barras) to free soldiers of the Royal Irish Regiment who had been ambushed by a notorious and brutally insane warlord-led gang in Sierra Leone, called the West Side Boys. The rescue operation authorised by Blair involved the SAS, the SBS, paratroopers and RAF Chinook and Army Lynx helicopters to air land and then airlift all concerned. The operation was a success, but at the cost of the life of one SAS soldier, Corporal Brad Tinnion. Twelve other commandos were wounded in the operation. Once again, British forces had lived up to their hard-won reputation. Yet no one felt it justified to at least consolidate numbers. The RAF, shortly after the Kosovo conflict during which sorties had been flown directly from Brüggen, abandoned this and the base at Laarbruch, thus departing Germany and the post-war legacy which continues to see an entire armoured division remain. Nowhere was any kind of retrenchment in evidence, yet Blair was about to call even more so on the diminishing military base.

It has been claimed by those who know Blair, and knew him at the time, that he held genuine and deep concerns about Saddam Hussein and Iraq's alleged weapons programmes. UN weapons inspectors had supposedly been thrown out of Iraq by Saddam in 1998. Although they were being thwarted by Iraq's security forces in their endeavours to find conclusive evidence of WMDs (weapons of mass destruction) they had actually left on advice from the US Ambassador, the reason being to avoid forthcoming US and British air strikes. Air strikes took place, but relatively few were targeted against anything that could be described as having to do with strategic weapons, or WMD, as was the preferred term. This is believed to be because so few locations fell into a specified category for sites with a 'high degree of certainty'. Just what intelligence knew about Iraqi strategic weapons development and the ability to deploy them operationally at the time does not seem at all conclusive. As was later found to be the case, any such programmes had been destroyed during the air raids of the 1991 war. The target was Saddam and his Ba'ath regime, and herein lies the real motive behind the invasion of Iraq in 2003. Before this, of course, public support had to be ratcheted up to a degree whereby any actual full-scale military assault would be acceptable. The opportunity to make the link with something which would afford an excuse came on 11 September 2001. Of course, 9/11 is the subject of many conspiracy theories but, nonsensical as they may be, no one can deny just how convenient this tragic earth-shattering event was to the new Bush administration and its obsession with regime change in the Middle East.

Blair was eager to participate actively in whatever operations the US government was to undertake. The earliest response was the identification of Al-Qaeda training camps in Afghanistan. Initially, Afghanistan could not be accessed by ground troops. The Americans, however, were not out of reach, having brought an aircraft carrier to the Indian Ocean. Heavy air strikes were carried out. Because Britain no longer had an aircraft carrier capable of launching aircraft with the required range, the UK contribution to operations at this stage was submarine-launched cruise missiles. Lots of Cold War technology to the fore again in another conflict with another rogue state. Somehow, the subject of Iraq cropped up again in the midst of operations to put Al-Qaeda out of action and out of Afghanistan. The heavy use of American air power here assisted internal war between the hitherto ruling Taliban and their chief rivals, the Northern Alliance. Not that one crowd were any more or less moderate or westernised than the other; they were both equally bad. But it was convenient for the forces for good to have one on side against the other.

Meanwhile, with Iraq inexplicably back on the cards, attention was being drawn to the idea of weapons of mass destruction yet again. As 2002 moved towards 2003, Blair was already consigning Britain's armed forces to a planned invasion of the country. Against these preparations, the RAF lost a further Tornado interceptor squadron in a piecemeal cut, not something which would have been able to contribute much to the planned invasion, but to be looking for any kind of material loss anywhere on the front line, and certainly without reassignment to another operational role (i.e. close air support), was hardly the kind of development one would expect of a country on the point of launching a military invasion – even on the coat-tails of a senior partner. Meanwhile it was said that if Saddam complied with US demands to allow weapons inspectors back in to Iraq, he would have nothing to worry about.

As the time grew nearer and Blair was getting round to a parliamentary vote on whether to commit HM Forces to action, the demands on Saddam changed again. Now he would have nothing to worry about if he packed his bags and fled. What made the Prime Minister's position on Iraq suspicious after the event was the purported evidence placed in the public domain about weapons. Supposedly, this was meant to be read as missiles being deployed with a 45-minute warning. Many who later criticised the invasion were quite prepared to accept at the time that the Prime Minister was genuine enough. He had to be. Surely something quite so exact must be evidence in itself that, if anything, the situation was far more serious than the elected authorities were prepared to let on. What made the claims suspicious before the event was the exposure of an apparently secret dossier based on a student thesis. Still the country was divided along the usual lines. The Conservatives, while not responsible for this conflict, were happy to lend it their support. Blair's own party were far less convinced. The late Robin Cook, Foreign Secretary at the time, having been made privy to the existing intelligence, claimed that he saw little evidence to justify any military action. This could have been Cook behaving in accordance with his left-wing credentials but, again, perhaps not. The Commons vote was held off until such a point that to vote against would have required utter indifference toward Britain's standing on the world stage. The entire UK military contribution was in place in theatre. With no more than two or three days to go until the start of hostilities, to stand down and start withdrawing some 44,000 British military personnel from the centre of attention would have so damaged the country's credibility and reliability that this can be regarded as political engineering at its most obvious.

The RAF contribution this time round was as significant as the first in 1991. Now, the Tornado GR4 as opposed to the GR1 was at the centre of the RAF deployment. Harriers were heavily involved this time, whereas in the first Gulf war the new mark of Harrier had not been cleared to carry ordnance and so was not involved. The Jaguar, which had been extensively used in 1991, was conspicuous by its absence in 2003. The Tornado F3s were deployed again, but as before, the reluctance of the air planners to use them in anything but immediate defence of Allied airspace told a story all of its own. The Tornado F3, for all its range, radar and missile armament, was not an agile fighter. It lacked the high energy performance at higher ceilings to give it a true chance against, say, any Iraqi MiG-29s, which in any case were withheld in the first war and flown out of the way to Iran in the second one, such was the reputation and expectation of Allied air power. As for the F3, the present-day Typhoon would have made a far more realistic contribution.

The cost of placing troops on a war footing is supposed to be borne directly by the Treasury as a capital cost, not from the defence budget, and surely this is what happened. But the Treasury was determined to reimburse itself for this ill-advised military blunder by clawing back funds from the defence budget somehow. In the summer of 2004, a further Defence Review was unveiled to the public with the awkward title 'Delivering Security in a Changing World'. It would appear the author was trying to find a title suggestive of being constantly caught out by unfolding events and forever trying to catch up. The previous reviews since 'Options for Change' had further reduced the level of serving personnel set as the determined requirement. So with just a hint of irony, while the demand on British forces placed on a war footing had accelerated, the level of personnel serving in the armed forces had further decreased, perhaps because the government, like other western governments, could not get used to the idea or refused to accept that the peace dividend never arrived. But everyone was determined that it would happen regardless. The new review, while described yet again as an opportunity to restructure defence for the greater good, was nothing other than a straightforward asset-stripping exercise. It could easily be argued that this was in order to make good the Treasury losses from the invasion of Iraq and the deployment of troops to Afghanistan in order to defend its population from a resurgent Taliban. Brown's own opposition to the invasion of Iraq has been widely publicised and it is all too likely that he won the argument to reimburse the Treasury from the defence budget. This should not have happened.

The RAF was now increasingly in the frame in the minds of politicians and the popular press as the villain of the piece. This was because the infantry, plain and simple, were, in terms of people, making the bulk of the contribution to the peace-keeping (for now) in Afghanistan and overseeing the maintenance of good order and conduct among the people of southern Iraq, and in particular the single largest population centre in the British-controlled zone, Basra. This was the image of modern war: soldiers in Kevlar, carrying assault rifles and of course sustaining casualties. Something of an irrational reaction to the other two services, the RAF in particular, was now starting to develop.

The 2004 review, however, impacted surprisingly heavily on the Army as well. The RAF was to lose the entire Jaguar wing at Coltishall, which would close as a result, and another Nimrod squadron would be disbanded. The Army, most surprisingly given the perceived logic of the time, was to lose four infantry battalions. The Navy was forced to abandon its primary fleet air defence asset, the Sea Harrier, yet this review and the previous one were described as representing a return to a maritime strategy from a continental one. The personnel number for the RAF at the time of the review stood at 52,000 and was now going to shrink by a further 4,000 at least. The Army was heading towards the 100,000 mark, which would leave it at its smallest since the Battle of Waterloo.

Increasingly, since the end of the Cold War, government defence policy decisions have been difficult to rationalise in terms of strategy and capability. Regarding actual combat assets, air power was the most heavily affected overall by the post-Cold War cuts, with the Navy losing its carrier-borne defence fighter and the RAF now down from thirty strike and defence squadrons in 1990 to fourteen by 2007. Two of the latter were by now equipped with the Eurofighter Typhoon. At the time, seven squadrons were expected to stand up altogether, but this was to be reduced to five and then further delays would see the deployment of Typhoons stagnate at three squadrons by 2010. Much is said about the technical complexities of the Typhoon, but the leaden-handed progress in fully deploying this aircraft has far more to do with recent economic uncertainties and a lack of political willpower to do anything.

Another serious development for the new rapidly deployable force for good revolved around eight new Mk 3 Chinook helicopters for the RAF. Ordered in 1995 and delivered in 2001, they remained in storage at RAF Odiham as the software program intended for them could not be used because the access code from Boeing did not form part of the contract. The Treasury is reported to have had a hand in this as well, looking to install cheaper UK software. This never worked, as Boeing had predicted, and the aircraft were reduced to Mk 2 standard and brought to airworthiness in 2010. It all makes for very poor reading, and rarely did the stated intent marry up with what happened in practice. By 2006, and outside of any of the economic difficulties which have surfaced since 2008 and the tightening of defence spending coupled with the growing level of procurement contracts which seemed to hand the customer (the MoD) the contaminated end of the stick each time, concerns were clearly evident among serving and retired officers of middle and senior rank that it was high time to start making the case for just how important their respective service was. Here the RAF was definitely slow on the uptake.

So far, ex-Army officers, usually of the Major to Brigadier variety, have formed the bulk of the Air Force's critics. In an article published in *The First Post* on 12 May 2006, Colonel Tim Collins called for the abolition of the RAF. He used the analogy: 'Like a ship in a storm we have to consider chopping down a mast if we are not all to capsize. We can't function without an Army or Navy, but we can manage without the RAF.' Collins is a professional soldier who rightly attracted a great deal of respect following his eve-of-battle speech in Kuwait as he and his men prepared to play their part in the invasion/liberation of Iraq. However, that he among others has fallen into the mindset, which he himself refers to in his own article, of infighting between the services, certainly between former service officers, seems to be the only plausible explanation for such a sweeping assessment of his country's military air capability. His article at the time was prompted not by the recent economic downturn and alarming deficit but by the conflicts in which the government of the day had engaged British forces. He went on to say:

> ... with wars running out of control in Iraq and Afghanistan, not to mention the pressure on forces elsewhere from Africa to the Balkans to who knows where next, we have to take drastic action. A conventional attack on UK Homeland is no longer conceivable because our enemies just do not have the reach. There is no prospect of any significant increase in the share of public money for defence, so we have to come up with a radical way for the armed forces to do what we ask of them within the budget available.

These comments were of course made in 2006, against the backdrop of what was understood at the time to be a strong economy. It was a reckless defence policy rather than a wrecked economy that prompted such a radical suggestion. Reckless, because the government sought, rightly or wrongly, to engage a substantial chunk of the armed forces, admittedly mainly the Army, in conflicts which were arguably selective, discriminatory and not altogether imperative in order to secure the national integrity and safety of UK citizens at home and abroad. Now this is not to say that British involvement in Iraq and Afghanistan was wholly unjustified. But it was not a case, as

Blair would put it, of having no other option, except perhaps for his own standing in the eyes of a US administration which at the time seemed determined to lash out at anyone who could even just wish them harm. That Blair was keen to play the part of right-hand man, First Lieutenant to George Bush Junior, seems quite evident. I have always been puzzled by this unexpected shoulder-to-shoulder approach by a British Labour MP who first sought election to Parliament as a member of a political party committed to unilateral nuclear disarmament and the expulsion of what would have been effectively all US military assets and personnel from the UK at a time when many, including within that party, considered the military threat to ourselves to be comparatively obvious, apparent and formidable. For his part, Bush Junior was somewhere to the right of Ronald Reagan and Margaret Thatcher. Blair could not wait to jump into this president's pocket and ride into battle from this vantage point. It was a baffling union indeed.

Nevertheless, in times of trouble party differences and political allegiances have to be set aside. There is no starker example of this than the alliance between Britain, the US and the USSR during the Second World War. However, it is difficult to understand the eagerness in Blair to have Bush effectively deputise him on the world stage following 11 September 2001 and willingly accept a military strategy targeting a country and a leader which, while not on the best of diplomatic terms with either Britain or the US, were not involved with the 9/11 terrorist operation either. Admittedly, Iraq and Saddam were not singled out for any such reason but because, according to the British government, they actively worked day and night to procure 'weapons of mass destruction', a term I have always found to be rather poor and unministerial for the world's leaders and the media to be comfortable using quite so routinely.

The phrase has been around for quite some years. WMD can be used to cover a variety of possibilities, including a homemade nuclear device transported in a suitcase or briefcase on the streets of London or New York. Just how possible it is that such an incident could happen in the future is clearly something that will cause premature grey hairs and baldness among those responsible for internal security. However, the 'Cool Britannia' government, I imagine, was more than happy for the general public to think of ballistic missiles in underground silos or on camouflaged launch trailers, ready to be deployed into firing positions within 45 minutes of the order from the Iraqi president. The 45-minute claim alone suggests a missile threat rather than some affiliated terrorist gang trying to scratch together rudimentary component parts from any source that they could afford, in order to put together some highly unstable device in a parcel or backpack and then somehow smuggle it into London or Washington DC. And if this was what Blair was more specifically concerned with, he might have clarified the understanding of the situation if the makeshift scenario was the case.

The policy of engaging the Taliban in a shoot-out in Afghanistan is all to do with preventing this happening again, at least up until 2014. This is the date slated for withdrawal of all coalition forces, come what may. What happens after 2014, if the circumstances are not quite what today's leaders are banking on, will be interesting to see. It scarcely seems possible that Blair had simply been wrong-footed by the intelligence. He promoted John Scarlett to head the Joint Intelligence Committee, and it has been reported, to use another cringing expression favoured by the press, that the intelligence was 'sexed up', meaning that it was not objectively clinical– not something a dispassionate and factual intelligence report should stand accused of. Further, there was the embarrassment of the out-of-date student thesis publicly presented as serious and convincing evidence to support the charge against Saddam. All this was exposed for what it was and yet, probably because the juggernaut of the military build-up was too far developed to reverse, no one seemed to be able to properly challenge just what it was Blair was playing at. However, the events which have unfolded since then have now seriously damaged Britain's credibility for intelligence gathering, not to mention the damage done to the defence structure.

If the cost of military action in Iraq and Afghanistan has been paid for out of the existing defence budget, this has not been publicly announced as policy, but the subsequent piecemeal loss of assets, people and infrastructure cannot really be explained any other way. The period hereafter to 2006 involved searches by land forces to find Osama Bin Laden and supporting the newly installed Karzai government along with investment in building and the introduction of more accommodating social policies.

Initially, it seemed the general understanding was that the Taliban regime had been beaten, and Al-Qaeda along with them. Rumour surfaced from time to time that Bin Laden had died, had been murdered in his bed or was seriously ill and had not long to go anyway. Subsequent video messages were constructed from old footage, it was suggested. As was later to be proved, all speculation was wrong. A build-up of Taliban and Al-Qaeda forces in the Paktia province of Afghanistan was confronted in March 2002 by US and Afghan troops. The tactics of the insurgent forces were to carry out hit-and-run raids on coalition positions and operate also from a number of bases established by Al-Qaeda across the border in Pakistan. The strength of the resurgent Mujahideen force of Taliban and Al-Qaeda volunteers had been underestimated by US commanders. Operation Anaconda referred to the coalition efforts from 2002 to 2003 to redress the situation and involved largely Special Forces operations, including the SAS and SBS from the UK. In 2002, the Royal Marines carried out a number of search and destroy missions at the request of the US government, due to their specialisation in mountain warfare. Again, the ultimate aim of the Royal Marines Commando deployment was to find Bin Laden. By 5 July, this and other operations involving the SAS were reported to have killed scores of insurgents. In one example during a firefight between an SAS unit and insurgents, four SAS soldiers were wounded while eighteen insurgents were killed. One reliable report, however, described the well-armed insurgents as being high on drugs.

Until the end of the year, the Taliban operations remained of a hit-and-run nature. The insurgents largely avoided more direct confrontation with coalition forces, retreating each time into the mountains to the east of the country and in some cases across the border into Pakistan. In January 2003, signs that the Taliban were recovering from the rout of 2001 were showing in earnest. Further engagements between US forces and the Taliban during Operation Mongoose inflicted further casualties on the Taliban while no US casualties were recorded. Far from discouraged by this, the Taliban continued to gather strength from new recruits through newly established training camps in the Pakistan border region. In August 2005, a week-long offensive mounted by US and Afghan forces killed a number of insurgents, with varying reports on casualty figures. While no major success against the insurgents could be claimed, the Americans carried out a number of engagements in the east and south-east of the country up until the end of the year, sustaining very few casualties of their own. From January 2006, ISAF (International Security Assistance Force) took over from the Americans, who were then more preoccupied with operations in Iraq. ISAF was a NATO land force, the nucleus of which was the British Army's 16th Air Assault Brigade but which included smaller forces from the Netherlands, Norway, Denmark, France, Estonia and Australia. The Australian SAS had been involved in earlier, post-2001, operations in the country.

As 2006 began, the successor to Geoff Hoon as Defence Secretary, Dr John Reid, announced the deployment of British troops into the Sangin area of Helmand province. Prior to this, hostilities towards ISAF forces had been relatively light, American forces having sustained the bulk. The first-line British infantry deployed had not found themselves engaged in earnest at all. Iraq was where heavier casualties were being sustained during the period from 2003 to 2006, prior to the premature pull-out of British forces from Basra in September 2007. This had come about as a result of insufficient troops and equipment, and a refusal by the government to accept any kind of surge, let alone expansion, to deal with the problem, leading to control of the city being ceded to Shi'ite militias fighting amongst themselves for ultimate dominance. The troops going into Sangin were not on a war footing, according to Reid; they were going to oversee construction work, rather like the US Peace Corps. So certain was he that hostilities would not be encountered that he staked his reputation on it by saying something he would have been wisely counselled to refrain from. Reid said that he would be perfectly happy if UK troops left Helmand in three years without firing a shot.

Now British forces and the rest of ISAF were about to find themselves on a war footing clearly not envisaged by Reid, and one which the Chancellor was clearly not prepared to fund with any additional resources. Furthermore, the very outfit in possession of the suitcase anthrax bomb or homemade nuclear device threat to our High Streets had been driven from Afghanistan into neighbouring Pakistan and also turned up in Iraq following the coalition invasion. The toppling of Saddam Hussein had made that possible. It took about three months for British ground troops to be engaged with the Taliban, in the most intensive campaign since the Falklands, and one which continues at the time of writing.

The Taliban had ruled Afghanistan at the time of 9/11, but while responsible for allowing Al-Qaeda to set up HQ and training camps, they are not likely to fit the bill of international terrorist network themselves. What they will do, of course, is turn the clock all the way back to the Dark Ages, presenting an awful prospect for Afghan women in particular and human rights in general. Part of the western coalition remit has been to move the hand forward as far as it will go.

The last three years of the New Labour government, with Brown having replaced Blair, saw further cuts in order to prop up the Afghan deployment. Some 430 British fatalities have been recorded as of September 2012, most having been sustained since January 2006. While the Army has been stretched to provide a rotation of a force of some 10,000, 10 per cent of its overall strength, in Afghanistan the RAF has been the next most heavily engaged of the three services, originally providing various transport, tanker and reconnaissance aircraft: C-17s, C-130s, Chinooks, Merlins, TriStars, Sentinel R1s, VC10s and Nimrods. A Nimrod was lost on 2 September 2006, XV230, coincidentally the first such aircraft to be delivered to the RAF back on 2 October 1969. It was a curious development that the vast range of types operated by the RAF should now comprise operational support aircraft.

The first combat types sent to Kandahar were a small number of Harriers in 2004. Just as for the ground forces, the Harriers did not begin to operate truly in anger until May 2006 when pilots of No. 4 Squadron began carrying Paveway II bombs, AGM-65G2 Maverick air-to-surface missiles and CRV7 air-to-surface rockets. The Harriers were withdrawn in 2009, by which time most had been upgraded to either GR9 or GR9A standard, the latter including the uprated Rolls-Royce Pegasus Mk 107 turbofan engine rated at about 25,000 lb thrust. The new engine provided a significant boost to performance, but only about half of both Mk 7 and 9 Harriers were refitted with it.

The withdrawal prompted the suggestion that the RAF was desperate to give the Tornado something to do in order to avoid having it looked at more closely by the Treasury in this new nonsensical era of demanding proof from the military that they have recently been in action killing people in order to avoid the chop. It had also been circulated publicly that at the time of the decision to withdraw the Harriers, the CAS had offered them up as a sacrificial lamb to the Treasury. Sir Glenn Torpy is widely reported as attempting to wreck fixed-wing aviation in the Navy in order to preserve as much as possible for his own service. Under the slogan 'one nation, one air force', the CAS had the opportunity to do this because since the Sea Harriers had been withdrawn at the end of 2005, the Fleet Air Arm was back in the same situation as it had been in the 1970s, relying on the RAF for its jets. From 2006, the RAF was to share its GR7s and GR9s with the Fleet Air Arm. As Torpy's predecessor some forty years earlier had said when the Navy were fighting to retain the *Ark Royal* and *Eagle* carriers, this represented a further reduction in the RAF's own capabilities and operational effectiveness.

Whatever the truth about disagreements at such a high level, that such stories are reaching the public domain with greater frequency is wholly the result of government lack of any sense of priority, despite placing a high demand on the armed forces and their resources. The more this happens, the greater the risk of the government being forced to confront a developing situation that will demand a military solution in which allies cannot be relied upon where shared interests are not equally paramount. This is different to a straightforward increase in defence spending. What needs to be preserved are the means, the experience and continuity, and prepare as best as possible against the risk, to put it bluntly, of the unthinkable – a decisive military defeat. The decision to remove the Sea Harrier was influenced by the cost of a further planned upgrade. Further justification for this was the expected anti-aircraft capabilities of the future T45 Destroyer. Of course, the T45 would not provide the same air defence reliability that a carrier with reasonably up-to-date fighters. Yet again, the government found it too easy to opt for the 'capability gap' rather than maintain the Sea Harrier through to its eventual replacement by the F35. The plan, assigned to Torpy, to abandon the remaining ground attack Harrier GR7s and GR9s was supposed to have taken effect from 2013, but even if it had been accepted in 2008, it would in the course of time have been overtaken by events.

In the same year that the government decided the Sea Harrier was not worth the cost of an upgrade it did agree to an upgrade for the Tornado F3. Bearing in mind that these decisions were taken prior to the invasion of Iraq, it is interesting to note the rapid rundown of the Tornado F3 fleet without any adequate operational replacement following the invasion. With five squadrons left operational since the reviews of the 1990s, another three squadrons were stood down between 2003 and 2008. Indeed, the first two Typhoons squadrons were to stand up in 2005 and 2006, but neither was in a position to take over from the F3s until at least 2007. Considering that the Typhoon squadrons were equally required to develop their proficiency in the ground attack role, some might say the removal of all but a single squadron of Tornado F3s by July 2009 created a particularly foolhardy capability gap. Furthermore, the premature retirement of the Sea Harrier further weakened the argument for retaining the Invincible Class carriers; *Ark Royal* and *Illustrious*, further down the line when the SDSR was born, by removing the carrier-launched

The American-designed Boeing Vertol CH47 Chinook, the most outstanding Battlefield Transport Helicopter ever to equip HM Forces. What contrasts starkly is that this amazing aircraft served US Forces as far back as 1967 during the Vietnam War, but it only started operational service with the RAF in 1982. (*Lloyd Horgan*)

fleet air defence force. Sea Harriers would have provided a stronger argument for a carrier capability at the time of Operation Ellamy in Libya. But without an actual air defence fighter to bring to bear, the carrier versus land based argument rather tipped the scales. The frustration was that to be arguing for the one over the other presented a very bad state of affairs indeed.

The ground attack Harriers operating from carriers could be rationalised for now, but the earlier suggestion of losing them as well became a matter for considering resignation for the First Sea Lord, Admiral Sir Jonathon Band. The more likely reason for replacing the Harriers in Afghanistan would be fewer available airframes, on top of which employing another equally if not more capable airframe would help spread the airframe hours further. Just the same, there should be no circumstances under which such arguments are able to develop. It would also appear to have been a long-term decision as the Tornado deployment was to commence following the extension of the runway at Kandahar airport. This is another open wound as far as the Harrier lobby are concerned, as the Harrier could operate from the airfield without any such provision; just someone to sweep the runway occasionally would suffice.

Even before the forthcoming SDSR, the last Labour Defence Secretary was having to announce the closure of RAF Cottesmore anyway, in order to pay for an additional order of twenty-two Chinooks. Liam Fox, the Shadow Defence Secretary, described this as economic mismanagement. A further charge of economic incompetence was to be laid at the feet of Blair and Brown in respect of how the RAF had been managed. Politicians like nothing better than putting off paying today what they can pay tomorrow, at three times the cost. Shortly before the FAA/RAF argument over Harriers, a report appeared in *The Sunday Times* concerning the purchase of the Boeing C-17A Globemaster III strategic transport aircraft. The MoD had wanted to buy four of them for £520 million, but Gordon Brown, still Chancellor at the time, refused, telling the MoD to lease them as it would be cheaper, provided of course none were lost to enemy action or any other unexpected problems arose. In the end, the C-17s had to be bought, but for £989 million, nearly double the original cost. The unit cost of a further two aircraft was £130 million. A total of almost £1.25 billion of taxpayers' money had been spent, whereas originally £780 million would have bought six!

Labour's legacy on defence and security, the first priority of government (and I have tried to be as impartial as possible in this chapter), has been an utter shambolic disgrace. Not that their Tory opponents are much different. However, if anyone harbours any doubt at all about the difficulty of the progressive left in affording even due regard for the first duty of government, let me remind the reader that it was Brown who decided that the defence portfolio commanded such prominence that it could be lumped together with the Scottish Office under a single cabinet minister, at the time Des Browne, he who once explained that the reason why the average British soldier on the front line in Afghanistan was paid less than the average provincial traffic warden was because they were otherwise unemployable. To his credit for quick thinking, he realised his mask had slipped and quickly readjusted it by pointing out that they were 'more employable' after a stint in the Army. When the decision to merge Defence with the Scottish Office was announced in November 2007, Browne claimed that this made no difference to his effectiveness, saying 'Tell me what it is that a Secretary of State for Defence should be doing that I'm not doing.' *The Guardian* described this as a robust defence of the government's record. And without a trace of irony.

CHAPTER 10
Strategic Defence and Security Review – Cause and Effect

By the time the New Labour government came to a close on 6 May 2010, the RAF had lost nearly half its remaining front-line squadrons since Blair's first election victory thirteen years earlier, and personnel strength had likewise taken a drubbing, having been reduced from 56,862 to less than 40,000. There had been cuts to the other two services naturally, but no actual shift in emphasis, no reinforcement of those aspects of the defence spectrum which were more likely to be in demand. Bearing in mind that what they inherited was what was left of the two previous post-Cold War reviews, further cuts could not really be justified on the grounds of excess. The new government had, of course, criticised the earlier cuts on the grounds of cutting for cutting's sake. Quite what the Conservatives would have done markedly different would be interesting to know, but once returned to office, cuts were again on the agenda. What was not obvious was that Labour's cuts were meant to have been thought out and applied to ensure an emphasis in the right areas and a reduction where redundancy could be identified; it just seemed like cutting for cutting's sake once again.

Part of the problem, and this has been the culture of most western governments, is the absolute refusal by successive post Cold-War governments to let go of their faith that the much heralded peace dividend has since remained intact. During the 1998 SDR, the government claimed it was going to reduce the defence budget by 4 per cent in real terms through smarter procurement. What is quite interesting here is that the defence budget actually never altered much as a percentage of GDP. In 1998, it was 2.78 per cent and in 2009, 2.99 per cent, and yet there has been nothing but loss of personnel and material assets and quite deep-reaching at that. All three services have been affected but, and I make no apologies for making this well worn observation again, the RAF, once more, suffered the greatest loss to its own front line pre-SDSR. There was of course a procurement deficit of £38 billion and the conflicts of Iraq and Afghanistan to consider, and it would seem very much that these conflicts explain the quite steady defence spending level. Instead of bearing the capital cost of Iraq and Afghanistan, the Treasury seems to have continued to quietly passed the burden on to the defence budget itself. This explains why, at the Chilcot Inquiry into Iraq, Gordon Brown having felt confident in defending his record on defence, saying that spending on it had gone up throughout his time as both Chancellor and as Prime Minister, felt compelled to return to the Inquiry to explain away the times that it had been reduced. When claiming that the service chiefs wanted for nothing, he was referring to the demands for less expensive but badly needed personal kit for soldiers fighting on the front line in Iraq and Afghanistan. This is exactly what should have been covered by capital spending, but it would appear not to be the case, given the attrition rate among various other military units. But the real problem bequeathed to the new coalition government was the amount of new hardware ordered by the previous administration that was still being developed but was a long way from being delivered, shrinking orders and expanding costs. This was back to TSR2 territory, but on a much grander scale. Brown was so sure of himself that he wanted to postpone giving his evidence to the Inquiry until after the then forthcoming general election.

It had been made quite clear long before the 2010 election that the MoD ledgers were in a parlous state and now that the national deficit and overall national debt were likewise critical, the future for whoever won the race to No. 10 Downing Street was, according to informed opinion, likely to end up in the most unpopular government in modern history. This assumption was due to the unavoidable and unpopular decisions that would have to be taken in order to put the country's economy back on the rails. This time, every government office would have to plan for brutal spending cuts. Trying to make the case for the defence budget not having enjoyed quite the same largess from the Treasury as other government departments, despite the unprecedented post cold-war operational demands, would just not wash, no matter what the defence and security concerns were.

Brown had been determined not to sacrifice or moderate any other government projects, which in many cases were in the pipeline before the protracted engagements in Iraq and Afghanistan, in order to support military deployments ordered by Blair. Indeed, it can be argued that he had no intention of shelving further planned defence cuts, meaning the cost of even the most minimal support of operations in overseas theatres would have to be met by losing something else. That something else was, through simple logic, those elements of HM Forces not directly or strictly involved in these two campaigns. Army officers and informed commentators made the case for the Army to be supported, even expanded significantly, at the expense especially of the RAF front line, in order to make anything like the kind of inroads in both theatres which were placing an admittedly heavy demand on land forces and the RAF's transport squadrons.

The incoming coalition government was expected to make the case that further, steep cuts would be inevitable and that the defence procurement deficit of £38 billion was not going to be treated sympathetically by the new Chancellor, George

Osborne, Tory or not. There simply was not going to be any more funding. Instead, particularly heavy cuts to the one department which had had to get used to them since 1991 were deemed unavoidable in the country's economic interests. But this time, other government departments would have to share some of the pain as the coalition grappled with the most appalling debt and deficit crisis since the late 1940s. Britain's total standing military payroll, save Territorials and Reservists, at the time of the SDSR stood at 174,690, of whom 100,290 were in the Army, 39,750 in the RAF and 34,650 in the Navy and Marines. In order to eradicate the financial black hole, this figure is to be boiled down to 147,000 by the end of the decade. There have been some unfavourable comparisons made with the armed forces of similar countries. France, in particular, is reported to have a standing military force total of 374,000, and Germany's *Bundeswehr* has a payroll of over a quarter of a million. This is quite some size when one compares the demands expected of Britain's military personnel with those of other European countries.

The RAF, which twenty years ago fielded the largest inventory of front-line combat aircraft in the western hemisphere outside of the US, now deploys a smaller force than either France or Germany and stands a not too dissimilar comparison with the air arms of Belgium and Holland. The deployment of new aircraft, specifically the Typhoon, has been especially leaden in progress and seems to have almost dried up completely, only three squadrons having re-equipped in the period from 2005 to Two more squadrons due to form, but not expected to stand up until 2014 and 2016, have more recently reversed the trend since this book was being finalised and become the subject of renewed interest. A fourth squadron has since formed, two years early, which I'll deal with further on. Otherwise, the previous plan amounted to one hell of a gestation period. The Tornado, an aircraft of a not much less complexity and at the cutting edge when entering service, formed new squadrons to the tune of eleven over a similar period during the 1980s. The availability of greater resources and funding is often cited as the reason, but in the normal process of events the situation should be no different proportionately today. However, a lack of any sense of haste means aircraft are on order but not being delivered. The possibility is that funds are so desperately affected that the run-of-the-mill process of introducing a new aircraft into front-line service has, in this case, come up against yet further attempts to slow production in order to avoid costs. So now, when financing a further two squadrons would present an unwelcome additional overhead, it can be further objected that as the Typhoon is not quite ready to assume the full range of ground attack duties, losing two more Tornado squadrons and replacing them with Typhoons would not be a good idea. At the time I started writing, it seemed almost certain that the next two Typhoon squadrons would replace two of the Tornado units, but this is unlikely to happen while the Typhoon's ground attack capabilities are yet to be fully developed. Until that time, the older airframes will continue to be relied upon as the preferred attack mount. As it was, the three current Typhoon units were delayed in standing up, due to the diversion of seventy-two aircraft by BAE Systems to the Royal Saudi air force. More are likely to head to both Saudi Arabia and Oman. This is good news, but of course in the 1980s, under the Al Yamamah project, Tornados were sold to Saudi Arabia, but with no similar disruption to the flow of aircraft to the RAF.

Much press speculation preceded the SDSR and, not at all surprisingly, it was wilfully alarmist. A good deal of it came from the broadsheets as well. When the Navy accused the Army of capitalising on the Afghanistan deployment, the media latched onto this and there were demands to know why there was insufficient body armour and not enough heavy-lift helicopters to ferry the troops around in theatre out of landmine harm's way. Interestingly, the left-leaning broadsheets *The Guardian* and *Independent* took a particularly sympathetic line on the Army's position. The villains of the piece were, of course, the Navy and the Air Force. These may well have been serious points to address, but the media selectiveness and, quite frankly, ignorance here, meant that in time there were questions being asked not by newspapers but by some well-respected military historians.

Of course, this chronic state of affairs will have played its part in the renewed fashion for traditionalists and modernists alike to suggest that the time was right to ditch the RAF. Of the three services, we were told, this was the one we could do without. And again, the knockers were not all from the radical left, as might ordinarily have been expected. They were, if they could be described in political terms, typically from the right of the middle ground. Four years after Colonel Collins' questioning of the continued viability of the Junior Service, the isolated comments were now about to become an opinion lobby and, like all such things, the aim was rather more subjective and intended to support the case for the increased prominence of the other services. The traditionalist view has a lot to do with this. It follows for such people that the older and more historic two services should definitely survive, and it suits such thinking to see the Johnny-come-lately Junior Service and its newfangled infernal flying machines disappear as a costly experiment that has finally run its course. But, without exception, no one could bring themselves to say that military aviation for the UK was surplus to requirements, simply that maintaining the status quo was more wasteful than a radical retro-shift back to the past, so the alternative was for the Army and Navy to provide the required air power. Hence there was quite a degree of media buzz throughout the summer of 2010 about the UK getting to the stage of fielding just two principal armed services rather than three.

Some made the case with an enthusiasm that made one wonder why they thought Britain, given its position, economic problems notwithstanding, was in a position to consider such a radical rebalance of its military structure and, in fact, downgrading of such. Letters appearing in one right-leaning broadsheet included a claim that the RAF had had its day and that military flying should return to its roots in the other two services. Another blamed the existence of an independent air force for the loss of air power elsewhere, suggesting that losses in the Falklands were due to the existence of the RAF because this meant no aircraft carriers were available to retake the Islands. Clearly, some people believe that the term 'carrier' can be applied only to vessels above a certain size and equipped with a complement of aircraft also of a certain size and performance. I dare say this particular contributor never held the Harrier in quite as high a regard as the anti-RAF lobby, who, in light of recent events, have been driven to incandescent rage at the absence of the Navy's ski-jump carriers and Joint Force Harrier. Another letters page contributor blamed the RAF for hoodwinking the politicians back in the 1960s, by presenting its case for how it could operate around the globe using overseas bases, a scheme in which it presented the global map with alterations to suit itself and convince the politicians of its importance. The strategic deterrence chestnut has also been raised as the point at which the RAF lost its entire reason for existence, when this role was transferred to the Navy. All these contributors have a common theme: none seem willing to apportion any blame to successive governments which have continually failed to match operational commitments with operational strength. Of all the industrialised nations, only the UK appears to have ex-military people and other respected individuals publicly advising the government to dismiss the nation's air force.

If the present roles and responsibilities of the RAF are to be retained and its functions maintained at a minimum level to be of effective use, then the suggestion of splitting it into elements of the other two services would not make any sense. The only justification put forward with any logic, in terms of economy, is that money could be saved on uniforms. Or would it? Money would be spent on providing new uniforms for those hitherto in Air Force service – no great expenditure, but an expenditure just the same. The amount of money spent on new unit identities, new aircraft markings (the Navy and Army would be bound to want to apply their respective brands to the aircraft they would each inherit), moving headquarters and ensuring that the nuances of Navy law and Army law were applied in place of Air Force law, would be unlikely to render any kind of advantage to the taxpayer. Everything to do with service customs, however petty and insignificant it might seem to the onlooker, right down to the correct manner in which to salute, would need to be addressed. This minutiae would have to be ironed out over a long period, testing the morale of all those who would end up crewing the new extensions to the Fleet Air Arm and the Army Air Corps, or Royal Flying Corps, should the General Staff feel a retro-image might be called for.

The argument that this is the right and rational thing to do, because of economic circumstances, is further supported on the grounds that air power has always been nothing more than a mere support function, and that each role can be assigned according to the overriding and wider demands of maritime and land operations. How this would be worked out is simple enough in some regards and far from obvious in others. Should the decision to dissolve the RAF be taken, the obvious allocation of assets, infrastructure and roles would see the rotary wing element split in two. The Chinook heavy-lift helicopters would be snapped up by the Army (the Army Air Corps) and the Merlin utility transport choppers would doubtless go to replace the Fleet Air Arm's geriatric Sea King Commando assault force. As for the *raison d'être* for an independent air arm in the first place, the fighter, strike and tactical reconnaissance element, the Tornados and Typhoons would naturally pass to the Fleet Air Arm. All fixed wing training would most suitably become the First Sea Lord's responsibility as well.

The elements which are more difficult to find a natural bidder for are the big planes. Strategic/medium transports, tankers and airborne warning and control would all pose something of an innovation to the other services. Today, these represent an inverse level of commitment for the Air Force. Currently the RAF is looking to take on twenty-two of the new Airbus A400M Atlas (Future Large Aircraft as it was known in the 1990s), the result of another European joint venture. Elsewhere there are the Boeing C-17 Globemaster III and E-3D AWACS aircraft, the remaining C-130Js and the yet-to-arrive RC-135 Rivet Joint. The last of these are Boeing 707 converts to replace those Nimrods prevented from standing down in accordance with SDSR planning to provide their much needed ELINT services for Cameron's unexpected no-fly zone over Libya. They have gone now, though.

However small and limited the RAF has become, it would still present the other two services with a mammoth additional responsibility (and budget) outside their usual remit. The Navy, with such a grossly expanded air arm, would definitely be looking to divert resources yet again from within. So the Tornado or even the Typhoon would almost certainly be looked at as candidates for a capability gap until the F-35s arrived at some time in the distant future. It would be frustrated by having such jets unable to operate off carriers – not that it has carriers to deploy them on in the first place. The Army, probably the least likely to find applications for aircraft, would just the same find its share of the Air Force most useful for serving its own requirements. It is also certain that on top of all their new-found commitments, neither service would be keen to take on the very specific role of managing UK air defence (to them, quite a distraction and a low priority outside their core responsibilities), a particularly vital component part of the defence of the realm that in its current elaborate form would not be particularly relevant to either the Army or the Navy. The Army might feel that missile defences, should Britain return to them, would suit it better. The air defence fighter element would be best assigned to the Navy.

However, the most awkward element to find a home for would be the early warning Control and Reporting system. This is absolutely paramount and could not be managed as a subordinate priority to policing the sea lanes and training the Afghan army and police, but it is certain that the Navy and the Army would not expect anyone to see it that way. The manning of early warning radar stations, whether static or mobile, is way outside the core responsibility of all but the Air Force. The air defence fighter force that operates hand in glove with the early warning system could not logically then be assigned to the Navy. This is no more relevant to it than assigning control of the hunter-killer submarine fleet to the Air Staff would be, and it could not fall to the Army, which seeks only those air capabilities that will support its land warfare effort, increasingly seen as an essentially expeditionary counter-insurgent force.

The government, of course, would want savings from any kind of radical restructure. If it worked, without the country facing serious problems as a result, then the next step would be further reductions as long as nothing came round the corner to test the situation. If nothing else, so long as everyone was prepared to accept that the defence and security of UK airspace remain matters for concern, then any idea of breaking up the RAF on this premise alone would be invalid. One of the media commentators to enter the fray on behalf of the other services, but stopping short of joining the abolition lobby, was the *Daily Telegraph* columnist, Simon Heffer. He stated that while Britain still needs an RAF or an air capacity to defend its shores against anything like a 9/11 attack, and a core service to deal with other threats to its security abroad and retain continuity of British expertise in aerial warfare, the RAF needed to be cut in these stringent times. Yet Heffer still thinks that cuts to the Navy and Army are anathema, and again the Afghanistan problem is cited to make the case: '... as for the Army, how can it be cut while we are in Afghanistan?'

Just how imperative the presence of coalition forces in Afghanistan is to western national security has divided opinion, but not, for once, over any questions of moral rectitude. Since the end of the Second World War, military action involving large western countries has often drawn accusations of imperialist aggression or greed over oil. In just about every case, it is the ones involving oil which may be guilty as charged. But I would not for a second find it immoral if, for example, the US government intervened with force to prevent a regional despot from using military force or the threat of same to increase his own proportion of oilfields. It is now routine to accuse those western nations that support such interventions of some kind of ulterior motive if oil can be linked to the situation at all. 'It's all abaat the oil, innit!' Well if it is, it is probably the most justifiable and vital reason to intervene that there is, unless of course people are prepared to pay over £3 for a litre of unleaded. But it would not stop there should the day ever come when all the oilfields of the Middle East were under the control of a wholly hostile regime. Oil and the security of its production, refinement and distribution is not so much the object of the greed of western governments as it is driven by the demands of western populations, among them those who find Anglo-American action to safeguard the security of it reprehensible. Put bluntly, the security of oil production in the Middle East is a vital part of the strategy to ensure that all the world's economies have reasonable access to it through a stable market. But it remains a mystery why so many people whose lives depend upon it feel that their elected leaders are behaving in a criminally self-serving manner simply by trying to avoid the worst-case scenario.

Much suspicion towards western foreign and defence policy stems back to the war in Vietnam. This conflict fell into the imperialist category, as did the Falklands conflict, although the latter had much unexpected support at home, doubtless due to the clearly understood position of the Falkland Islanders themselves. The Falklands, however, now looks like becoming the subject of a fresh dispute with Argentina, but this time oil is also on the agenda following recent explorations in the South Atlantic. However, the most prominent and long-running conflict where British and other western interests are at stake is Afghanistan.

The Afghanistan campaign is a curious one and, of all post-war military expeditions involving British forces, the most inconsistent with regard to objectives. The initial interest in Afghanistan is firmly linked to the terrorist assault on American landmark buildings on 11 September 2001, Afghanistan having been identified as the location of the alleged perpetrators, Al-Qaeda and Osama Bin Laden. The success of the initial campaign was essentially due to the predominance of American air power which, save for a number of cruise missiles launched by US and British ships and submarines, was followed by a lull which quite possibly encouraged the US government to forge ahead with plans to deal next with Saddam Hussein (no friend of Al-Qaeda). British ground forces did not appear in Afghanistan until the campaign to clear the Taliban out was effectively over. The intended role of the ground troops hereafter was to support the reconstruction work.

The initial campaign of 2001 appeared to have succeeded in securing the aim of denying the use of the country by Al-Qaeda as a training ground and base for launching terrorist operations against other nations. Western military involvement had transitioned from air strikes to destroy Al-Qaeda, followed by the establishment of land forces, the next step being to turn Afghan society around with a transitional government. Then came attempts to convince Afghan poppy farmers to grow something else, together with reconstruction of both infrastructure and mindsets, but the next thing we knew, British, American and other coalition forces were engaged in a predominantly land-based campaign which General Sir David Richards, then Chief of the General Staff, claimed could carry on for another twenty years, and other assertions were made that if British troops were not there, Al-Qaeda would be in Britain. Soon, providing security for building reconstruction and development became a war for the west's survival. The timing of the withdrawal of coalition troops depends on the training of the Afghan Army and Police to take over from those forces or ISAF, but various assessments indicate that achieving this is light years away; at the other end of the spectrum, the most optimistic claims are that significant progress in training the Afghan national force is being made.

The only reason left for staying in Afghanistan is to secure a respectable conclusion and make a seemly exit, hopefully avoiding embarrassment to the coalition partners, including the UK. To achieve something in Britain's favour would be great, but an outright victory seems not at all realistic, as has been conceded by the greatest western power. If the US President can set a date for withdrawal, with no clear decisive defeat of the Taliban in sight or an end to Al-Qaeda's aspirations to use the country as a training ground and bomb factory, then setting a definite date for withdrawal can only mean that no one is prepared to expend blood and treasure on a campaign which not even the US is prepared to risk a significant expansion to deal with. Even the most optimistic cannot be certain that the Afghan security forces will be reassuringly placed to carry the torch forward from 2015. They can only hope, and of course if Uncle Sam is determined to bring his forces home by then, it follows as night does day that Britain and all other contributors will do likewise, if not earlier, regardless of the various governments' publicly stated reasons for being involved.

In March 2012, a damaging event from a public relations point of view took place involving the shooting of sixteen Afghan civilians by a US Army sergeant. So fragile is the coalition position in Afghanistan that an accelerated withdrawal has now been announced by the US and France. When the Labour leader, Ed Miliband, questioned David Cameron about the British position in light of recent events, he was told that the UK was still working toward its planned withdrawal of combat troops by 2014, and that an appropriate operational profile would be maintained up to that point. This is a not a very clever way of disguising the answer 'We are going to do whatever the US government decides; when they leave, we leave.' To compound matters, the British Prime Minister also said that it was possible British forces could leave Afghanistan with or without a political settlement – again, an obvious indication that the UK will withdraw, come what may, by the date set, or sooner, as the case may be. The clear impression that this has been a military debacle, ill-advised from the outset and ignorant of history, is unavoidable. Yet the Army or anyone with an Army background seems to be convinced of an endless campaign which is necessary in order to defeat fundamentalist Islamic terrorism once and for all.

In fact, we may as well cut our losses and shift our efforts to the more direct defence of our territorial waters, land and airspace sooner, rather than keeping the campaign running in the hope of a far from guaranteed successful outcome. When asked about the long-term future of Afghanistan, Air Chief Marshal Sir Stephen Dalton said it was not impossible for it to descend into civil war once foreign arms left the country in 2014, but also maintained it would be another five to ten years before an accurate assessment could be made of whether western intervention had been worthwhile. For his part, Chief of the Defence Staff Sir David Richards claimed in 2011 that in ten years' time the fighting now taking place would be justified and it would be understood why it had been the right thing to do. He was also unsure of the outcome, believing that the immediate years following the withdrawal of the bulk of coalition combat troops in 2014 will be the period when the success or otherwise of the campaign would be determined.

Afghanistan is a conflict which, while dependent on the substantial use of air power, is centred on the land fighting effort. If you understand what I mean when I say this, it is no surprise that Richards had earlier spoken publicly about seeing British soldiers still fighting in Afghanistan some twenty years on. A cynic would accuse the good General of trying to make the case for a substantially increased budget for the Army, but today such cases can only be made while accepting the risk that this would be at the expense of the other two services, of course.

That the bulk of resources should be channelled into an emphasis on ground troops in light assault roles with more in the way of rough terrain vehicles capable of sustaining direct blasts from landmines indeed suits the current demands of Afghanistan, but if this cannot be done without further damaging erosion of the air naval and armoured forces, then it should not be, especially if the UK is going to follow, or rather precede, as in Iraq, the US military withdrawal. The argument for Britain's armed forces to become lighter and more mobile looks all the more like a desire to reshape everything into a niche counter-insurgent force, but, whatever the present climate, this would be a mistake. Denouncing as costly and outdated many heavier and more complex systems such as ships, tanks and high-performance aircraft which, ironically enough, have been very much relied upon in order to keep the Taliban at bay and were instrumental in ensuring a swift and relatively bloodless end to the two Gulf Wars has been argued to support the idea of an essentially light anti-guerrilla force. Anyone who thinks this is nonsense might like to ponder how the land warfare effort would have progressed without the intensity of air strikes and the devastation brought to bear on Saddam Hussein's army and command and control structure, not to mention just what made getting boots on the ground in Afghanistan at all possible in the first place and which end of these operations can, so far, justifiably claim any degree of success.

During the last Labour government's time, a report appeared in the *Daily Mail* on 12 July 2008, claiming that the then three individual service chiefs were not to be considered to replace the incumbent Chief of the Defence Staff, Air Chief Marshal Sir Jock Stirrup. The reason the paper gave for this was because the head of the Army, Sir Richard Dannatt, had been critically outspoken over government policy in Iraq. The First Sea Lord and Chief of the Air Staff respectively; Sir Jonathon Band and Sir Glenn Torpy, were being tarred with the same brush on the suggestion that they had closed ranks with the General. As a result, Sir Jock was asked to stay on beyond his expected retirement around July 2009. Dannatt had been expected to replace him, but now the RAF chief was to remain until about 2012. As this could not be the official government line, the assumption remains that for the first time in history there was no single senior British officer capable of filling the shoes of the head of HM Forces. Of all the nonsense that Britain's elected leaders expect the public to swallow, this has to be among the more outrageous.

When the coalition began sorting out the predicaments at the MoD, they decided early on that the Air Chief Marshal was to go before the end of the extension to his appointment. His replacement was not announced immediately, as the new Prime Minister was to interview likely candidates for the job, but it is most unusual for something like this to be played out in public. Anyway, the clear choice that everyone was banking on was Dannatt's replacement as Chief of the General Staff, Sir David Richards. A couple of years ago, shortly after being appointed to head the Army, Richards gave a speech at Chatham House in which he said the armed forces needed to be equipped with smarter weapons rather than relying on traditional ones. His view was that while, and he stressed the point, the more recognisable conventional and heavier arms needed to be retained as a safeguard against a state-on-state conflict developing, such conflicts were increasingly less likely and that the conflict in Afghanistan was a 'signpost to the future'. He has listed the very assets which, it can be argued, are used in the absence of anything more suitable but have been relied upon most effectively in such signpost conflicts: fast jets, tanks and ships. But unmistakably at the centre of all these arguments is a sense of resignation to an ever-decreasing defence budget, further hampered by the hitherto procurement waste, which the Treasury wants to pay off by dismantling as much of the operational military structure and capability as possible. So in respect of what to do with what is left, Richards believes that an awful lot of unmanned aerial vehicles (UAVs) of the current type, and Tucanos (basic turboprop trainer aircraft utilised for the light support role), can be bought for the price of just a few F-35s and tanks. At the time he said this, the RAF and Navy were expecting to share between them 138 F-35s of the more expensive and far less capable F-35B VSTOL model. Since the SDSR, this has been reduced to about forty or possibly fifty of the less expensive but far more capable F-35C carrier version. This is a very far from set figure however, but for the time being it is as good as it gets, especially as a unit cost for the aircraft has yet to be agreed. Not that Richards has been able to bring any influence to bear on this decision, but he is regarded as having influenced the SDSR early on and following a conclusion that had placed less of a burden upon the Air Force and Navy, with the result that the emphasis of cuts shifted back again. That said, cuts to the Army are yet to take hold, and in line with the culture of 'if you are not using it, you can afford to lose it', severe cuts to the Army are expected after Afghanistan.

Richards' appointment was confirmed a short while after the decision to appoint a new Chief of the Defence Staff. The only other candidate seen as a likely contender was the Vice Chief of Defence, Sir Nicholas Houghton. The reason for the clear preference for an Army CDS, despite three out of the previous five defence chief appointments going to the Army, was explained as being due to the heavy emphasis on the land-based operations in Afghanistan. It was further argued by senior Army figures that Stirrup had been neglectful in pressing the case for greater resources for the front line in Afghanistan. It is difficult, on the face of it, to imagine what the Defence Chief could possibly misunderstand about the situation in Afghanistan, but it is also understood that Gordon Brown when Chancellor and Prime Minister had a reputation for being unable to summon sufficient concern over the conduct of military operations anywhere. When the Libyan situation, very much an air campaign, took centre stage in the spring of 2011, I am sure that the new Army-background defence chief managed to convince his political superiors of the necessity to provide sufficient fuel, weapons and aircraft, without falling short in any detail. If the overall head of the armed forces cannot convince the politicians of the need for resources during a high-profile military campaign without recourse to pleading then it is probably not going to make much of a difference which service he hails from. I am further convinced that the Air Staff would have been advising accordingly at all times, as would the General Staff over the land war conduct in Afghanistan.

It is hardly likely that Stirrup would have been slow in coming forward over equipment for troops on the ground. When he gave evidence to the Chilcot Inquiry, he pointed out problems with the supply of body armour and other infantry equipment. Again, the fault with provision appears to lie with the government of the day and Treasury reluctance to accept the situation and make any additional provision, at least not without sacrificing something somewhere else. Furthermore, Stirrup drew attention to the lack of time given for preparation for the invasion of Iraq in 2003. However, not having been quite so openly critical of the Blair government as some of his Army contemporaries seems to have brought about the impression that he was not as robust as someone with a land warfare background might be in demanding more body armour and assault rifles for the infantry in one of the most intense and protracted field campaigns since the Second World War.

Five years ago, when an Iranian patrol boat intercepted and detained a Royal Navy and Marine reconnaissance patrol in the Gulf, Sir Max Hastings, one of the strongest pro-Army critics of the Air Force, having more recently suggested that the only reason the RAF continues to exist is because of a government lack of political courage to disband it, wrote that as the Army was the only one of the services properly engaged in operations, the CDS appointment should be permanently assigned to an Army officer: 'The British Army is thoroughly attuned to operating in an operational environment,' adding, '… in the nature of its role, most sailors – like the RAF – work not uncomfortable routines and scarcely suffer a casualty from one year to the next. They belong to the armed forces but have little experience of fighting anybody. This is why there is a strong case for ensuring that the Chief of the Defence Staff is always a soldier.' Such a sweeping commentary comes as a surprise, even a shock, from someone like Max Hastings. But whatever ascendancy the Army can claim on the back of Afghanistan, it is already a concluded campaign. Regardless of the outcome, given the logic of the pundits fighting the Army corner it may well be that there will be no need for an army either. Sir Max may be right about the Army being more attuned to operational environments but to assume that to defend its interests at home and abroad, Britain should or could now rely on only a small assault infantry-based army with a transport air arm and coastguard-based navy, albeit with four strategic nuclear submarines tacked on, suggests that its true standing in the world has slipped a good deal further than present political rhetoric indicates

It may well suit recent interventions in which the enemy can be expected to be relatively lightly armed and land-borne only, whereby British forces can up sticks and leave the foreign field of battle when they feel like it, as appears to be the case in Iraq and Afghanistan, but Britain can play this game only so long as it can rely on a larger ally like the US to act firmly on its behalf where vital strategic interests are concerned. No British politician would ever admit to anything of the kind, of course. It is just not the kind of image to project, however true in recent times.

The growing competition across the globe for vital resources such as oil, gas and food, and the means of producing them cheaply, are taking the modern world in a very precarious direction indeed. Added to these is the emergence of Chinese hegemony, for want of a more diplomatic term, and increasing despair over Iranian nuclear ambitions. But whatever the military concerns facing the UK today, following the election of May 2010 and given the desperate state of the economy, regardless of who was to blame, the Strategic Defence and Security Review was put into preparation as soon as David Cameron moved into No. 10 Downing Street. Sorting out the MoD was a priority for whoever found themselves confronting it. It would certainly have been the same if Gordon Brown had found himself surprisingly still in residence at No.10.

There had been recklessness by the banks but there was also runaway spending, often on government programmes with little public support but driven forward with political enthusiasm. Some were doubtful in the extreme. One of Blair's most incredible ventures was the idea of super casinos in some of the most deprived parts of the country, a scheme with potentially tragic outcomes. However, one can only assume that Blair and the minister directly responsible, Tessa Jowell, could see some overriding benefit not immediately obvious to Gordon Brown, who, if he can otherwise be criticised for any number of decisions, doubtless made the right one when he abandoned this particular scheme, or scam, depending on your view. But anyway, as of May 2010, the SDSR appeared on the horizon and its outcome would not be far off. Dr Liam Fox wanted to make it clear that for a Conservative Defence Secretary to be considering such cuts went against the grain. Many accused the government of putting forward a Defence Review while dishonestly applying only cuts. The government made it quite clear that, whatever the title of the review, cuts and severe ones were unavoidable, the lucky elements would be those escaping serious reductions or any reduction at all.

Aside from economic difficulties and financial mismanagement elsewhere, the MoD budget has been especially dragged down by its own procurement division, but not as much blame seems to attach to those responsible for how so much money, £38 billion, could go astray. Aside from contractual bungling, blame has very much been assigned to the process of ordering weapons and equipment. Supposedly, the case was very well made when such things as the Nimrod MRA4 were ordered. It may have cost a lot, but it was because it was so far from operational readiness that it could be dismissed so easily. At times like this, the government always resorts to describing what remains as leaner and meaner, and both descriptions are meant to be regarded as a positive outcome. The lean, mean fighting machine that our admirable armed forces are becoming can be relied upon to make do with less. We are simply invited to believe that every defence cut cloud has a silver lining.

So much is blamed on recent new weapons and systems and the inevitable runaway costs that it would be a grand thing if the equipment, once it arrived, could do what was originally expected of it. If there is a single success story, in terms of capability, of which BAE Systems can feel a degree of pride, despite everything else, it is the Eurofighter Typhoon. However, if I were to suggest such a thing in front of any random gathering of commentators on defence issues, I would first need to remember to place a tin helmet on my head and be on my guard for flying objects, because this very aircraft is despised by just about any UK defence commentator who does not or has not worn a light blue uniform. Much of the trouble here goes back to the collapse of the Soviet Union, and also to the Army's attempt to portray anything which is not ground-borne, with the selective exemption of transports and rotors, as a Cold War relic. Because the Typhoon was originally conceived in the early 1980s and had yet to fly as a prototype at the end of the Cold War (the technology demonstrator had already taken to the skies as early as 1986), the expectation of many seems to have been that the project should have been dead and buried. Few such detractors can pause for breath long enough to explain in even the briefest detail just what Britain, as a sovereign nation with so many interests and citizens overseas, alliance commitments and the responsibility for defending its own airspace as well as its own shores, is meant to carry on with, if not a realistic fighter.

The knockers are never full of ideas and suggestions other than 'the Cold War is over etc.' and the country must adapt to meet the future challenges of defence. Well that is exactly what this aircraft represents. As for the overall cost, the lynch mob need to go and gather outside someone else's door, as cost has once again been piled on to the Eurofighter project courtesy of every attempt to avoid it. There was a cheaper alternative suggested very early on, right in the wake of German reunification. Few were convinced it had merit despite attempts by the German Defence Minister, Volker Rühe, back in 1992, to make the case for it. He was deeply concerned about the cost to the German defence budget at a time when West German resources were fast being hoovered up by bringing the former East Germany into economic and industrial alignment with the West. Cost concerns gave rise to radical solutions such as continuing the project with a much reduced design, even redesigning the aircraft as a single-engine type. As mentioned in chapter 8, the Ruhe was warming to the idea of a development of the MiG-29, at the time recently inherited from the former East German air force. This would happen jointly with Russia, thus abandoning the other nations to continue with a much increased share of the burden, or seeking to go down the old buy-American route of signing up to one of their deals instead.

To suggest this uncomfortable period conjured up the ghost of the TSR2 would be a hell of an understatement. The project survived with the usual attempts to look at what features of the aircraft could be done without in order to make it cheaper. Fast forward to 1997, and both Rühe and the then British Defence Secretary, George Robertson, were toasting the success of the Eurofighter as an 'important day for Europe and the North Atlantic alliance. Robertson, for his part, described the Eurofighter as the best aircraft at the best price that was currently available. Together with their Italian and Spanish partners in the project, they had just signed their respective government agreements on the production of 620 Eurofighter Typhoons. An important point to remember here is that the success of military preparedness is not measured, as many alarmingly seem to imagine, by its extensive use in anger but by the fact that it never has to be called upon at all. The troubled psychology of this logic is like private medical insurance: the more you pay and the longer you go on without resort to it, you may even get to the stage of contemplating breaking your leg deliberately in order to get your money's worth. The project was saved in much the same way as the two current Queen Elizabeth Class aircraft carriers were saved in the recent SDSR from the same fate as the MRA4, because of the unavoidable painful penalty-sensitive clauses hard-wired into the contracts, much of which was put together from the client end. (*Comments by Volker Rühe and George Robertson are taken from the German news agency ddp/ADN.*)

Whatever the money spent in getting the Typhoon into front-line service, it is unlikely to have been used to make right what was wrong about other defence concerns. The simple fact was that a new fighter was required. Despite the original expectation that it would be employed flying against high-performance Russian fighters over the European Central Region, it does not follow that this aircraft has no place in any post Cold-War scenario. All the equipment used by the world's armed forces today is equipment which was expected to be deployed in a war against the Soviet Union, or by the Warsaw Pact against NATO. The anti-Eurofighter lobby are right that the original primary intention was indeed to fly against Soviet super fighters as the most likely foreseeable instance at the time of its early development, but they are utterly wrong to insist that the UK, alone in Europe and NATO, can dispense with any form of realistic air defence capability. As of September 2010, RAF interceptors had been scrambled no fewer than twenty-three times over the preceding sixteen months. This is certainly not on the scale of the 1970s and 1980s, but it represents a measurable increase from the 1990s.

The further argument that a cheaper, indeed lesser, alternative could be far more sensibly sought is an interesting one, but this kind of proposition always depends on the background of who makes it. It may well be the case that an off-the-shelf existing US fighter also intended originally to fight the Soviets would suffice. The critic with the Navy background will argue, and with some sense, that an existing carrier-based American fighter, e.g. the F-18 Hornet/Super Hornet, would meet every requirement, but of course such a proposition reckons without BAE Systems and the desire of Britain's political elite for greater European co-operation. That said, the Typhoon, for all its expense, had already arrived and was comfortably in service with overseas orders by the time of the 2010 election.

The Typhoon has a great deal of potential for its future development, but this still does not stop its detractors. Throughout the summer of 2010, the British press circled over the Eurofighter as a candidate for the chop or severe reductions, for all the world as if it was still at the prototype stage. The pre-coalition Liberal Democrats wanted to cancel the later Tranche 3 order, the most capable version. As it is, the earlier Tranche 1 aircraft will be sold off. With the blunt demand that the RAF would not just lose a number of aircraft but that a whole type was going to disappear completely, some genuinely expected, perhaps even hoped, the most capable and newest airframe would be the one to go, for the sin of soaking up so much in procurement costs during its gestation period. That a whole combat type was to be lost is a further indication of how far from balanced the SDSR was, but a truly radical and unexpected decision that came as a blow to both the RAF and the Royal Navy was the one to end the maritime reconnaissance and anti-submarine role carried out by the RAF.

Since the Second World War, the RAF has maintained an airborne maritime presence, from the Stranraers of Sir Denis Spotswood's† era to the Nimrod MR2. The Nimrod is fitted with a MAD (Magnetic Anomaly Detector) boom which detects variance in the magnetic levels below the water's surface, and is the principal tool

---

† Sir Denis was a pre-war and wartime Coastal Command pilot, who flew many maritime aircraft including Stranraers, Hudsons and Catalinas. He later transferred to commanding Night Fighter Squadrons, was the first Officer to command Strike Command on its formation in 1968, and was appointed Chief of the Air Staff in 1971. He retired from the RAF in 1974 at the rank of Marshal of the Royal Air Force.

in submarine detection. The Maritime Patrol Capability covers a broad spectrum relating to defence against sea-borne threats: Anti-Submarine Warfare, the protection of Fisheries, Search and Rescue and Maritime Reconnaissance. However, the fact that the Nimrod Force made a vital contribution to the protection of the Royal Navy's Strategic Submarine Fleet makes it difficult to reconcile with Cameron and Foxe's decision. This has been the responsibility of the Air Force from 1936 to 1969 through Coastal Command, then No. 18 Maritime Group, then No. 3 and finally No. 2 Group in descending order as the Air Force shrank. Despite controversy and concerns about the Nimrod MR2 and the heavily reduced order for Nimrod MRA4s, not to mention the unresolved technical bugs, no one expected the Prime Minister to cancel the order for the nine remaining aircraft. On 19 October 2010, Cameron announced that the maritime patrol aircraft was among the victims of the SDSR, also making it clear that failure to get a grip of the programme, halt escalating costs and still falling short of operational use were the reasons it was to continue no more. There was no reassurance that the nearly £4 billion so far spent was at the point of fruition, although the claim that the aircraft was not operationally ready is widely challenged, with attempts to clarify just how far from operational readiness it truly was. Some say there was only some additional working on fuel lines to be carried out following a further change in safety specification as a result of the loss of an MR2 over Afghanistan on 2 September 2006. A tenth of the procurement black hole was represented by the amount so far spent on the MRA4. From the fact that there were supposed to be twenty-one rather than nine airframes available, that the MRA4 should have been operational as far back as 2003, and, further, that it was three-quarters of a billion pounds over budget, it is clear that this was another classic case of procurement mismanagement. Having been selected over the widely used P-3 Orion and the later version of the French Atlantic 3 as the RAF's future maritime patrol aircraft in 1996, the first development aircraft was yet to fly in 2003. In subsequent Defence Reviews the number of airframes to be upgraded was trimmed back. Sixteen aircraft was all that was deemed necessary in 2004, and in 2006, when the production contract was signed for twelve aircraft, three were destined to be development air frames, leaving just nine operational ones which were not expected until 2012. While the SDSR was taking place, the forecast for the MRA4 was that none of the aircraft were ready for operational deployment, and it remained uncertain whether they would be ready by 2012.

The Navy, rather than the RAF, has since investigated the possibility of acquiring a replacement, most likely to be the P-8 Poseidon, if accepted, which is based on the Boeing 737 airframe. In the meantime, and as far as can be determined, the role of anti-submarine warfare in respect of territorial waters and approaches has been placed upon the Navy's existing Merlin HM1s. However, their main responsibility is to render anti-submarine warfare in respect of fleet defence, the same as the Sea

The long-serving Nimrod MR2. The decision to cancel its replacement, the MRA4, was particularly radical as it left the UK with no Maritime Patrol Aircraft. (*Mark Kwiatkowski*)

Harrier had been for air defence of the fleet. Although not much has been said, there is continued concern that the inevitable movement of Russian submarines through UK waters has taken place with impunity. It has also been suggested in the wake of cancellation that the UK could rely upon the goodwill of its allies to monitor its surrounding approaches, but this requires a hefty degree of good faith and trust with whoever that might be and could also place the British government in a very difficult position, not necessarily directly related to the role of maritime reconnaissance but should finer political considerations prove difficult to entertain elsewhere.

The real sin is that the current state of affairs has been allowed to develop at all. It is quite unprecedented to be reduced to the point of dismissing a vital operational role entirely. The reasons for doing this, as far as the economic circumstances dictated, were hard to argue against, but why has there not been a more realistic contingency plan announced, or is the role this aircraft was intended to fulfil that easy to discard that no explanation is needed to describe why the country can do without it?

A further, unexpected, victim of the review is the Bombardier Raytheon Sentinel R1. This particular mount, based on an executive jet design, is quite some size, much bigger than the familiar Lear jet often seen in the movies flying the rich and sinister around. It provides a much needed ground targeting and surveillance service

Shackleton MR3 of 201 Squadron, a dedicated Maritime Patrol Aircraft. Anti-submarine warfare was considered a principal requirement and therefore the Shakleton MR3 was a component part of UK defence strategy, until the introduction of the SDSR. (*Peter R. March*)

to the Army and is currently engaged in operations over Afghanistan. It was also needed recently over Libya. Before the Libyan conflict happened, the SDSR process determined that the Sentinel would go as soon as the Afghanistan operations were complete – again, the 'use it or lose it' doctrine of modern-day British political culture regarding defence equipment and personnel – as if to suggest that it has been determined by HM government's superb new crystal ball that, from 2015, the Sentinel R1 will for ever more be surplus to requirements. Certainly, its work is not so unique that there is no other conceivable use for it outside Afghanistan.

As a 'Strategic Defence and Security Review', and while spending was clearly the driving force behind the exercise, the aim was essentially to determine exactly what threats and challenges the country might face in the foreseeable future and, looking beyond the headland of the future, to estimate as best as possible, what it may have to contend with at short notice. The Nimrods, apart from providing the vital anti-submarine air cover for the strategic submarines which the coalition (well, certainly the Conservative rump of it) set so much store by, have also played a vital part in search and rescue, especially co-ordinating some quite high-profile rescue missions over the years. Many ships' crews owe their lives to the presence of the RAF's Nimrods over the previous four decades. Questions were also raised over whether the MRA4 should have been cancelled back in March 2008, when eight MPs on the Commons Select Defence Committee said it might be worth 'cutting its losses'. And while the popular media description 'spy-plane' is rather glib and misleading, ELINT (Electronics Intelligence) operations have been part of the remit of the Nimrods increasingly beyond just the dedicated handful. Recent questions in the Commons regarding the future of UK maritime air surveillance have met with a disconcerting response from Peter Luff, Minister for Defence Equipment, Support and Technology, that an investigation into the long-term requirements for a maritime surveillance capability has been completed, but that details are being withheld as their disclosure 'would, or would be likely to, prejudice the capability, effectiveness or security of the armed forces'. The decision to scrap the MRA4 has been condemned by as many ex-defence chiefs as those there have been who have condemned the decision to retain the Typhoon and Tornado. Very soon following the axing of the MRA4, in a scene yet again, far too reminiscent of the TSR2, the airframes were axed, literally.

Not long after the review findings, the US government offered to base a Wasp Class aircraft carrier in the Thames Estuary during the Olympic Games. If the intention was to highlight the increasingly hapless state of Britain's defence overall, then it certainly was not lost on the Cameron government, which reportedly turned down the offer on the grounds it made the UK look weak. No kidding. One would certainly think so after the standing down of the Invincible Class aircraft carriers. In an interview with Andrew Marr, the outgoing Chief of the Defence Staff, Sir Jock Stirrup, said that the previous Labour government had denied requests by the defence chiefs to remove certain aircraft and ships from service as the defence budget was under pressure. This was another contributor in part to the £38 billion deficit. What strikes an unusual chord is the head of the British armed forces arguing for a reduction in service assets when so often the story is the other way round. To explain this, defence spending had, shall we say, not kept pace with the operational cost as well as procurement costs, which for more than ten years had ballooned ahead of the budget. In addition to the massive equipment programmes which had been ordered, in many cases add-ons were requested to original specifications, which seems invariably to be an unavoidable development. What is hardest to understand about Sir Jock's claim is politicians refusing the opportunity to remove more beastly hardware from the military people. One can only surmise that the cuts up to that point were deemed deep enough, that anymore would be too damaging politically. But it still doesn't seem plausible.

The RAF further attracts criticism in the way it defends its remit and assigns its senior officers. Among the recent glut of anti-light blue criticisms, one which has been made on occasion is just how the RAF sees itself, not to mention how the other two services and the array of pundits see it and what they expect from it. The chief complaint is that the RAF remains committed to its traditional reason for existing at all: to strike from the air against air and ground threats. For this reason, indeed, those RAF officers who get within a whisker of high command tend, other than being heads of specialised roles, to be pilots. They are then further narrowed down nearer the top to pilots who have trained in air-to-air and/or air-to-ground combat flying, the pure military end, or as it is subjectively put, FJ (fast jet) pilots. This term is used in a derogatory fashion, for all the world to conjure up the impression that the senior ranks of the RAF consist of characters who are out to preserve some kind of elitist position at all costs, like a club full of retired racing car drivers. But by the same token, you will not find a First Sea Lord who has not at some stage skippered a frigate or a destroyer, or commanded a submarine. Many former commanders of the latter vessels tend to move on to high rank in the Navy. The Army has, relatively speaking, been the most diverse when appointing General Officers. But again, no one gets to command the Army who has not at some stage commanded a front-line fighting unit, infantry and armour. The current Chief of the General Staff, Sir Peter Wall, has the Royal Engineers as his original unit. But what may not be fully understood is that the Engineers are no support function *per se*; they form an element of the teeth arms in the Army and training is focused on operating at the front line. Furthermore, to underline the point, Wall commanded the quite elite 16th Air Assault Brigade then 1st Armoured Division long before he came to command the Army overall. Indeed, everything about his background from the outset has seen him serving with the airborne forces. Looking further back, the prominence of Chiefs of the General Staff with infantry origins is all but invariable. All certainly have held command from battalion level forward in either infantry or armour. This would be the equivalent of commanding, if you will, any fast-jet front-line squadron for an airman. But this quite specific point only holds as far back as the early 1980s. Any further back from there and among the RAF's senior commanders there was virtually no fast-jet flying experience beyond familiarisation trips – not the same thing. For them it was tail-dragging props, with many of the earlier post-war leaders and before having experience of open cockpits and canvas. The simple point is that all military Chiefs of Staff should logically bring to the top actual experience of the core remit of their respective services.

The loss of the RAF's remaining Harriers as a result of the SDSR will, by default, include those operated by the Royal Navy. If they were retained they would, of course, continue in use by both services, but to lose the carriers and retain the Harrier would have singularly made the least sense of all. However, they are all going because the intransigent view of the government was that one of the three fast-jet types in operation had to go. Each of the three fulfils a particular role, but clearly the Treasury influence over the military in this regard has destroyed any notion that this review yielded any space for military considerations. When the review findings were revealed on 19 October 2010, there was much wailing and gnashing of teeth from all outside of the RAF that not only had the Typhoon survived but the RAF's other equally unpopular fast jet, the Tornado, had also escaped with a loss of two squadrons. The Harrier, much loved and perhaps the only one which the other services saw any point in, was the one to be retired.

It had been suggested in earlier press reports that the Chief of the Air Staff had this time bent someone's ear in order to ensure the survival of the Tornado, and when the announcement was made, the shock had quite an impact. No one was under any illusions about there being unpopular surprises from the SDSR, but this was another particularly unfathomable one from the military viewpoint, if a perfectly rational and agreeable one as far as the ledgers were concerned. The three types in the running essentially rendered three different roles. There is no doubt that the Harrier was the pick of the litter in terms of the media and likely public sympathy, and one could expect not just the Navy but perhaps the Army school of thought to be in favour of the Junior Service hanging on to the Harrier, even at the expense of both the Tornado and Typhoon. If the pro-Harrier lobby had had their way and the Tornado been the candidate chosen for the scrap heap, as the stark SDSR choice was, Cameron would have been placed in a very awkward position come the Arab Spring, very much contrary to the popular perception that the Harrier would have been the ideal solution to the implementation of a no-fly zone over Libya. That it would have been a princely asset is not in dispute, but in no way was it the airframe of choice.

The National Security Council had set its collective heart on ditching one of the three combat types very early on. This position was non-negotiable, and it seemed that anyone and everyone outside the light blue fraternity was eager for the Harrier to survive. To use a modern phrase, it was a 'no-brainer'! Also noticeable was that the lobby outside of the RAF was quite contemptuous of the other two airframes. The position of the Air Staff seemed to tend more towards wanting all the toys in the box, but if pressed into such a dilemma then the airframe to go should be the one least relied upon both now and in the future. The balance of the situation as of 2010 was as follows. The Tornado GR4 was the most numerous type, with 132 of them altogether. This was also the most versatile aircraft in terms of ground attack ordnance, being able to carry Paveway II and IV laser-guided bombs, Brimstone and Storm Shadow. The former is an anti-armour missile, while the latter is on the way to being a more strategic weapon aimed at more critical infrastructure targets including military operations centres, power stations and other installations vital to an enemy power's ability to continue to prosecute military actions. What marks out the Storm Shadow as a particularly vital weapon is the ability to launch it from a significant distance, typically over 150 miles. The Harrier, at the time of the SDSR, could carry all the Paveway types but was yet to get Brimstone, and Storm Shadow was not on the cards at all. Tornado also has the longest unrefuelled range, a crew of two and a twin-engine configuration. The latter point is an important tick in the plus column. Further, and again contrary to popular opinion, the Tornado is the one with the supersonic acceleration at all altitudes, whereas the Harrier remains a subsonic platform. Some of these points can mean little when taken alone and when considering just how useful they are in certain situations, but when added up to reach a decision as to which should live and which should perish, they make for substantial arguments in favour of one over the other.

The Harrier existed in far fewer numbers, nearly half, with about 72 airframes. This point was actually argued by the pro-Jump Jet lobby as an attribute for their favoured jet, an argument on behalf of the Treasury this time, claiming that this meant more money would be saved by axing the more numerous Tornados instead. Further comparisons also gave the Tornado the edge with its superior all-weather performance; indeed, much of what the Tornado had as standard could only be claimed as future expected features for the Harrier. To lose the clear advantages of the Tornado over the Harrier for the sake of either public sentiment, Naval fixed-wing aspirations or the preference of the other two services to retain the one aircraft most closely suited to their more specialised requirements, and with a greater saving to the Exchequer, would have left the Air Force with a far more woefully emasculated front line and one which would actually have been found desperately wanting some months later in Libya. If the intransigent fiscal demand of a fast jet-type to the slaughter had seen the Tornado go, the fewer number of Harriers would have been sorely stretched to meet the demands of the Afghanistan deployment and operate a relatively small number from a carrier at the same time. They would have done well, but would have been restricted by their small number. There is no certainty, of course, that the one available carrier on task would have been within reasonable sailing time of a position from which to begin air operations which would have been more economical than the round trips made initially by the Tornados from Marham. Given the fact that Operation Ellamy began as soon as UN resolution 1973 was passed, it would not do for the Navy's single carrier to be still a day or two away from the theatre of operations. As it was, coalition air attacks on Libyan armed forces reacted just in the nick of time to avoid a likely massacre in Benghazi.

That said, the Sea Lords do have a point about the retention of the Harrier and the carrier. It is undeniable that this combination remains the best option for supporting any need to deploy, say, to retake the Falklands once again. However, the tipping point would appear to lie elsewhere. Perhaps the ideal solution would have been to retain all three fast-jet types but reduce the number of Tornados by a slightly greater degree than two squadrons. But this, again, is simply to address the needs of the Treasury and absolutely nothing else. There is no military sense whatsoever in what has been done. Of course, number three in the FJ running stakes, and undoubtedly far less popular with the other two services than even the Tornado, is the Typhoon. The reason, as covered earlier, is because of the amount of money it has soaked up since its inception, and it is blamed, irrationally, by many as the reason for there not being more money available for other defence procurement projects.

The Typhoon was a long time gestating, but by the time of the SDSR it was fully operational and equipping three out of five planned front-line squadrons. The long-term promise for its development make it the most able of the three airframes. Unquestionably, the Typhoon's performance outstrips that of the competition, with a stratospheric ceiling and an unimaginable rate of climb. Manoeuvrability is effortlessly ahead of the other two. From 2014, it is expected that it will carry the same air-to-ground weapons as the Tornado GR4, including Storm Shadow. One might think that as this is all yet to be realised, this puts the Typhoon behind the Harrier, but this would be to miss a vital point. The Harrier in any event had a far shorter lifespan. It is the Typhoon, still in production (such as can be described), not the already dwindling Harrier airframes, that can be relied upon to still fill any gaps thirty years hence.

When it came to enforcing the no-fly zone over Libya, only the Typhoon answered the strict remit of what a no-fly zone is meant to be: that is, a defined piece of airspace in which military aircraft of one air arm are not allowed to operate; if they attempt to do so, they get shot down by the no-fly zone enforcer. That was the Allied forces on this occasion. If they had tried to do this with just Harriers, as opposed to the Sea Harriers which were deemed surplus to requirement during Geoff Hoon's hastily cobbled together review in 2004, they could very well have found out all about air-to-air combat once again. The Typhoon is first and foremost an air defence fighter, and it is the existence of such an aircraft in the West which has brought about the difficult-to-quantify situation whereby the lack of a direct challenge to modern air defence fighters has put the need for them in question. And this is what the aim is after all – to avoid potential conflict.

Essentially, four countries have become significantly affected by seemingly populist uprisings across North Africa, described as the Arab Spring, from Tunisia to the Gulf States. In Tunisia, the uprising was relatively quick and successful. Egypt, where Hosni Mubarak, one time good friend of the West, believed acquiescence was the most advisable path to take, ended up at the mercy of the courts in a country where clear leadership and democracy seem further away than ever, now that the upper hand resides with President Mohammed Morsi of the Muslim Brotherhood. In Syria, President Bashar al-Assad so far continues to hold his own against an ongoing public revolt, and, of course, Colonel Muammar Gaddafi in Libya recently met a gruesome fate at the hands of rebels.

So far, there has been no western intervention in any but Libya, and the reason why Libya was singled out early on would appear to have something to do with Gaddafi's own forces making rapid headway against the rebels. On the day that the first intervention by French Rafale jets took place, the Libyan army was on the point of routing the uprising and on the edge of the last rebel stronghold, Benghazi. Some weeks earlier, on 28 February, Cameron caught many by surprise by publicly calling for a no-fly zone to be imposed over Libya, the intention seemingly being to protect the civilian population from the bullets and bombs flying in both directions. The idea was initially criticised in a quite candid manner by the US Defense Secretary, Robert Gates, a man not keen on military intervention. The American defence chief dismissed such a call as 'loose talk', believing the no-fly zone would be possible only following military action and citing the need to be able to suppress Libyan early warning, communications and anti-aircraft systems as well as confronting the Libyan air force.

Having brought Gaddafi in from the cold, albeit through the efforts of Blair, the British government jumped ahead of everyone else in calling for action against the regime. However much was made about the impartiality of a no-fly zone, what was surprising was that, on this occasion, the chief backer of such action, after initial misgivings, was the French President, and the instigator was the British Prime Minister rather than the US President. Otherwise, the initial response from other European powers was quite predictable, and the no-fly zone proposition found few backers. The German Chancellor, Angela Merkel, was unsurprisingly far from keen on any kind of military resolution, while appearing to want to do something by reviewing 'all necessary options'. Whether or not this varies from all possible options, I do not know, but the concerns of Gates and the need first to destroy the Libyan command and control element on the ground certainly proved not to be the case, and Cameron was right to intervene. A week later, and with Gaddafi's now increasingly loyal forces making inroads against the rebels, the suggestion of a no-fly zone was aired again, this time with some interest from the White House. Bearing in mind the embarrassing position of the British government arising from a fiasco involving what was reported as an SAS unit sent into Libya with a government representative in order to meet with a British farmer and ending up being taken prisoner by the rebels before being released, Foreign Secretary William Hague stated that any no-fly zone would need a broad consensus. Yes, it would, and to be fair, Cameron had spoken not a moment too soon. Because of his quite public rebuke by Robert Gates, the West's 'great and good' leaders lost an early initiative. This in turn emboldened Gaddafi to unleash the bulk of his loyal forces against the rebels. With increasing support, crucially from the Arab States, the no-fly zone with additional latitude to do everything short of landing ground forces was passed by the UN Security Council on 18 March. The next day, French Rafale aircraft were in action during the early morning, and RAF Tornado GR4s from Marham carried out raids at night, flying a 3,000-mile round trip and refuelling three times during the sortie.

However, that intervention only went so far and led those involved in enforcing the no-fly zone to move swiftly towards providing the Libyan rebel movement with the key to victory, their very own (free of charge) modern air force. Gaddafi's forces were, in time, run to earth and the rebels were victorious on the back of continued air attack and close support sorties. The air defence (no-fly zone enforcement) side of things was carried out serenely, with the far more capable French Rafales and RAF Typhoons operating over Libya not at all unexpectedly without challenge.

It might be observed that the initial success encouraged similar boldness by other Allied countries to commit their fighters too. There was a touch of bitter irony about all this, though. The British government had only just identified which two Tornado squadrons were for the chop, Nos 13 and 14, but the Tornado became the most heavily used RAF aircraft throughout the campaign, carrying out direct long-distance attack sorties. These lengthy missions involved often as many as three or four inflight refuelling rendezvous. Eventually, sorties were being flown from Gioia del Colle air base in Italy. This created a sour grapes attitude among mainly retired Naval officers who were deeply unhappy, quite understandably, about the carrier fiasco, and suggested bias on the part of the RAF Commander of the Joint Services Command, endlessly pointing out the low cost of operating Harriers from a carrier four miles off shore compared with flying Tornados and Typhoons from either East Anglia or an air base in Italy. What they never spoke up about were the realities of a Harrier/carrier-based air combat fleet of very limited size.

The knockers found many negatives in the operation of the Tornado and Typhoon over Libya and the Tornado over Afghanistan, but what really caused offence was that RAF personnel deployed to Gioia del Colle were being billeted in a quite impressive nearby hotel instead of being accommodated under canvas on the edge of the airfield. Once again, former service critics, this time mostly former Naval officers, started taking an interest in cost comparisons. The cost of the hotel bill and the cost of maintaining a constant presence in the air over Libya was extravagant as far as some were concerned, and the latter was designed to impress the politicians. Commander Nigel Ward, who commanded a squadron of Sea Harriers during the Falklands campaign, commented: 'If the RAF cannot have all the comforts of home they tend to complain like Girl Guides … it appears to be one rule for the RAF and different rules for the other two services.' Once again, it is difficult to argue with decorated senior officers over such matters, but they are not necessarily right or unbiased themselves. That hotel bills are being cited as reasons for re-examining the defence budget is part of the overall rage at the loss of the Harrier. As for basing RAF personnel of all ranks in such opulent conditions, I am sure this is out of the ordinary for any of the services and arose more by circumstances. It was certainly not something that anyone who is happy to praise the armed forces at any other time would deny them, even if it is the Junior Service landing on its feet again. It can only be hoped that it was worth it, for the means represent one thing, the aim entirely another.

The Arab Spring is already looking like turning into what some experts are starting to call the Jihadist Winter. With concerns that progressive pro-western thinking is looking less likely to prevail in either Libya or Egypt, a worst-case scenario is being envisaged whereby unity across the Arab States will come through a fundamentalist Islamic hegemony, a new Caliphate, as it has been described. It is not at all absurd to imagine such an alliance would be supported by China, which currently seeks to spread its influence and physical presence far afield, Africa and the Middle East already being regions subject to Chinese expansion. While Syria descends into civil war, UN proposals for sanctions against Assad have been vetoed by Russia and China. Recent developments concerning the exploration for oil near the Falklands have brought the subject of the ownership of the Islands back to the fore internationally, and Cameron has been pressed to make public assurances that their sovereignty is not up for negotiation. Given these geopolitical situations, no end of informed people have pressed the case to revise the decision over the Harriers before it is too late.

It is at times like this, far too often recently, that politicians attempt to justify horrendous cuts to the defence budget as leaving the military complex leaner, fitter and more flexible. The Hoon cuts of 2004 were described in such terms but did not provide any such improvement, and matters have been left to sheer good luck and some reliance upon others, quite specifically the Americans. It was US forces, albeit not as eagerly committed by the White House, that rendered additional military assistance over Libya which the British and French could not provide. Truth be known, with regard to the Falklands and any situation in which British forces would be required to retake them, the ideal aircraft, recently in service, to have to hand would be both the Sea Harrier and the recently withdrawn Harrier GR version. The demand would be for both a carrier-borne fighter and an attack aircraft, as in the first Falklands conflict. But even better would be carriers capable of carrying a longer-range higher-performance type, perhaps even the French Rafale or American Super Hornet. In the meantime, the Typhoon is currently deployed in the Falklands and although highly capable aircraft, they are few in number – only four in total. The Typhoon, upon which so much depends, has been deeply cut in numbers and remains after a considerable period far from fully deployed. This situation goes far back before the collapse of the economy, to (and I make no apology for mentioning it once again) the words 'peace dividend' and the absolute refusal by Parliament to accept that this expectation was compromised as soon as it was mentioned.

Britain now has no clearly formed agenda; the present state of future planning, post-SDSR, is best described as not yet decided. The Harriers have been sold to the US Marine Corps for a price which very much favours the customer. On an interesting note, the US Army faces a reduction of nearly 100,000 personnel, an approximate 12 per cent cut with greater investment in more of the niche elements of the military spectrum: Special Forces and drone technology. All assets for sure, but whether a genuine step forward from, or alternative to, nearly 100,000 combat-ready soldiers is open to debate and is very much dependent on what is needed where and when. Against this, the US Marines still cannot let the opportunity pass to buy up the RAF's Harriers.

Having lost the current carrier capability, the UK government still sees the carrier, and bigger and far more capable ones than those it has just lost, as a vital component of the future. The Navy was prepared to lose a considerable chunk of the rest of the surface fleet in order to ensure the future of the Queen Elizabeth Class carriers but, as mentioned earlier, the cost of dismissing them made their retention the cheaper option. The problem here though is just what to do with these new carriers when built. It is said that only one will eventually be operational, as intended; the other may be converted to a quite elaborate commando assault carrier, or retained as a spare. That the first and foremost carrier will fill its remit at all depends upon the availability of a worthy strike fighter to operate from it.

Originally, when the two carriers were ordered, this was to be the F-35B. One of three variants, this one has VSTOL capability like the Harrier, and the popularity of this function in the British mindset can be the only reason why it was picked. Otherwise it falls far short of the range and payload of the other two. In order to perform the vertical/short take-off-and-land party trick, the F-35B needs a quite heavy lift fan and a swivel nozzle at the rear. These are the means by which it can vector thrust evenly and hover. Because of the accommodation of this apparatus, the aircraft is considerably heavier and of course has far less room for anything else, such as weapons, additional systems and fuel. When the aircraft is airborne in conventional flight, which it will be 99.9 per cent of the time, come what may, the lift fan and associated apparatus will not only take up space but will be dead weight, which can only hamper performance outside range and load. Intended as a cheap alternative to the increasingly prohibitive expense of more elaborate new-generation fighter designs, e.g. the F-22 Raptor, the F-35 was aimed at a wide range of western air arms, mostly F-16 operators, as the economical option, in much the same way as the F-16 and the original F-18 were the economy class alternative to the F-15 back in the 1970s and 1980s. Since its selection against other competitors, this aircraft has become so expensive that not only the UK but other would-be operators are now looking at cheaper alternatives to the cheap alternative. Having made this well-advised decision to opt for the intended carrier version, the F-35C, one of the few sensible decisions to come out of the SDSR, but again influenced by Treasury considerations, the in-service date slipped by some years, to 2020. It has since slipped again, to 2030, largely due to difficulties in addressing some quite fundamental points, such as the actual ability to land and take off from a carrier deck. Meanwhile, of all ironies, BAE Systems offered the Indian Navy a navalised version of the Typhoon, and the French are hoping that the UK will see sense and buy their proven Rafale, which they successfully and quite logically managed to convince India to purchase instead. The Rafale, being a tried and tested modern carrier strike fighter, and a cheaper option, was sure to beat the mooted 'Sea Typhoon' in this instance.

Another and more attractive option to the F-35 is the F-18E/F Super Hornet, which could yet be selected as the UK's cheaper alternative to the cheap alternative. None of these aircraft are VSTOL but they work well and once airborne pack a powerful punch coupled with an abundance of performance. For the time being, and despite escalating costs, the British government continues to publicly pursue the F-35 option, having expended £2 billion in development costs so far. A further problem with the F-35 is that there is no agreed unit cost as yet. Delays keep surfacing, adding to development costs and making firm predictions for the future well-nigh impossible. The Italians, another F-35 customer, seem to have a clearer idea of what they are looking for, a mix of A and B variants, the former being the land-based version. They have recently reduced their intended order from 130 to ninety aircraft. The British government is sufficiently uncertain about how many it will be able to afford that it does not want to predict an order for any more than forty-eight, for the Navy and RAF to share between them – one hell of a drop from 138 of the more expensive B variant. While the eventual number of F-35s remains shrouded in mystery, and will not have much more light cast upon it before the next government Strategic Defence and Security Review, that the Italian air force and navy are looking forward to a revised figure still bigger than the current suggested number for the UK prompts further questions about just how committed the British government is to maintaining any realistic numbers of aircraft on the front-line inventory of the RAF and Fleet Air Arm. If, for the sake of argument, forty-eight is the settled number, at least initially, and if this figure has to provide for an Operational Conversion Unit, even a joint service one, and an Operational Evaluation Unit as well as provide for formed operational squadrons of even a relatively small size, this would be a tiny and inflexible force, no matter how versatile and survivable the F-35 panacea turns out to be. Would such a small number split between two services, each with a different operational agenda, the one to provide a carrier-borne strike and support fighter aimed at reaching hostile targets outside the range of land-based aircraft, such as the Falklands, and the other to provide a home-based rapid deployment force in order to reach sudden crisis areas, such as Libya, or operate on long-term deployments such as Afghanistan, be sufficient?. I use these previous and current operations as simple examples.

In March 2012, the carrier debate surfaced again, with the apparent lobbying of government to change its mind over the decision to convert to catapults and arrester wire (traps) and go back to the F-35B. This is because BAE Systems feel the need to charge an additional £2 billion in order to convert the two new carriers. Given that this equates to two new T45 destroyers, it seems one hell of an involved process, especially considering that neither carrier is that far into construction yet. That the government has decided to review the matter has, of course, brought a reaction from the opposition Defence Spokesman, Jim Murphy, who is demanding that it clarify the issue as soon as possible and has referred to the notion of conventional carrier operations as some kind of facet of American culture and the stuff of romantic images of *Top Gun*, while further describing the Harrier and VSTOL capabilities as something which the British public are more attuned to. And these are the thoughts of a would-be British Defence Secretary! Apparently, he does appreciate that the F-35C might have a slightly longer range and carry a bit more in terms of armaments, but I suppose that is hardly the point so long as the UK has a Jump Jet, a British invention after all. So while the government agonises over its original SDSR decision, and all to keep the runaway costs from running away even further, the sorry modern British political ham-fisted handling of another high-profile defence issue is played out in public again and the date for entry into service slips further away. In the meantime, the US Navy Assistant Secretary, Sean Stackley, has assured government ministers that the cost will, or rather should, be less than half the estimate of £2 billion. But perhaps he is reckoning without BAE Systems and their captive market. As the practical objections now rest on costs alone, it would be fair to say that the original decision to buy the B model, for its vertical landing trick, was where the true disaster occurred.

During the Libyan campaign, C-17A Globemasters and C-130 Hercules were called upon to support the no-fly zone operation as well as continue to support the ground campaign in Afghanistan. What cannot have escaped Britain's defence planners is that, this time, aircraft from every remaining operational air base in the UK were now contributing assets, simultaneously, to a single no-fly zone enforcement. Nimrod R1 (due for the chop), Sentinel (due for the chop post-Afghanistan) and E-3D Sentry aircraft, all from RAF Waddington, were operating out of Akrotiri in Cyprus. That was everything the RAF had. During the previous Gulf Wars and the Falklands, entire aircraft types could be left out of the conflict as simply not required on the occasion. There is no depth, no give; successive British governments are now trying to manage the armed forces rather like a corporate business. If the military chiefs manage to win a victory outright with fewer soldiers and weapons then anything outside what was required quickly attracts awkward questions as to what they actually do.

With the reduction of the remaining Tornado GR4 squadrons from seven to five, which has left the RAF, since April 2011, with a front-line operational combat force of eight squadrons, in addition there are now two squadrons equipped with the MQ-9 Reaper UAVs. The manned element, at the time, included three Typhoon squadrons so far stood up. Here comes a curious twist in the tale since this book went to proof, a fourth squadron has stood up, two years ahead of the expected date. It was also expected that two more of the five remaining GR4 squadrons would stand down in a like for like exchange with the fourth and fifth Typhoon units, maintaining a steady minimum of eight squadrons between both types. As of December 2012, the total is nine. While this book was being finalised, events seemed to be overtaking expectations, the exact reason for which remains unclear. Apart from observations made by former senior officers and experts, we are getting used to hearing from

Along with the Blackburn Beverley, the Argosy was the RAF's other Troop Transport of the 1960s; both were replaced by the Lockheed Hercules and Hawker Siddeley Andover. (*John Wharam*)

serving senior officers as well on the present state of Britain's defence structure as a whole. Air Vice-Marshal Greg Bagwell, AOC No. 1 Group, was in December 2010 quoted in *The Sunday Telegraph* thus: 'Am I happy to be down at that number [eight squadrons] next April? No, it worries the hell out of me.' He continued: 'I can just about do Operation Herrick [Afghanistan] and the QRAs [air defence operations]. Can I do other things? Yes, but at a risk.' When the RAF's Lightning interceptors were reduced to just two squadrons and a Training Flight, it retained no fewer than seventy airworthy airframes concentrated at Binbrook, in order to keep two squadrons with twelve aircraft each and the Training Flight of about eight aircraft ticking over. The Air Vice-Marshal further described the withdrawal of the Harrier force as taking the country below what was regarded as a sensible position, and, most importantly, leaving it with a lack of ability to regenerate such operationally deployable assets quickly, should they be needed in a hurry.

Apart from the cuts which came with the review, the MoD had further announcements to make. A further squadron, not mentioned in the SDSR, was also in the process of standing down: No. 111 Squadron, the last Tornado air defence unit. The public story was that No. 111 was being replaced, like for like, by the third Typhoon squadron, No. 6. This was not strictly the case, but with so many units disbanded piecemeal since the early 1990s, it is difficult to see a formed plan or framework within which there was a noticeable transition from the Tornado ADV and Jaguar to the Typhoon, as had been the plan prior to arriving at the stage where a coalition of American-led forces found themselves tipping Iraq upside down in the hunt for non-existent WMDs. The remaining Tornado attack squadrons now represent the only wholly offensive air capability of the RAF, save for the covertly operated Reaper UAV squadrons. There are two now that No. 13 has been stood up to join No. 39 currently in Nevada. The Typhoon squadrons being deployed are not expected to be able to do all that will be asked of them until before 2018.

The General Atomics MQ-9 Reaper is a remote operated drone aircraft or UAV as the common parlance has it. Indeed, it is a UCAV (Unmanned Combat Air Vehicle) and can be armed with a number of air-to-ground munitions, principal among which is the Hellfire missile which is also carried by the Apache AH-1 attack helicopter operated by the Army. It will be easy to see the Reaper as lasting proof of the application of unmanned aerial technology; it is cheap and it works in its current format. The Reaper, however, is not quite the machine depicted in recent Hollywood movies, like *Skyline*. It is not a high-performance jet-powered agile unstoppable force. It is a large glider with an enormous wing and is powered by a 900 shp (shaft horsepower) Honeywell TPE331-0 turboprop engine. This provides less power than the Rolls-Royce Merlin engine which developed 1070 hp in the earliest model Spitfires and Hurricanes of the Battle of Britain. The Reaper, with a top speed of 260 knots, has been used with some success over Afghanistan and Libya, but these remain what have become known environments for Allied aircraft. Even so, the attrition of UAVs has been high, much of this having been blamed on the weather and technical malfunctions, but there are also claims that some have been shot down by the Taliban. However, this latter point has been little more than hinted at in public reports. Suffice to say, as of June 2007, the UK alone had lost fifty drones of various designs, due to technical problems. While the USAF has lost a number of UAV MQ-1s and MQ-9s, thus far the RAF has lost no MQ-9s. The age of UCAVs with a performance comparable to that of current and future manned fighters, like the F-35, is still a long way off.

The project to find a future replacement for the Tornado GR originally took the title FOAS (Future Offensive Air System), a deliberately less than specific reference as the future type could not be determined as a manned or unmanned design, or indeed a mixed proposition. This endeavour was officially abandoned once the prospects of the F-35 started to firm up. There is one candidate that was seen as a possible successor, even if only in part, to the Tornado in the long run. This beast is called Taranis and may indeed become the first truly front-line remote-piloted combat aircraft with sufficiently high performance to be sent against targets through far more hostile airspace than was encountered over Libya and Iraq or is currently faced over Afghanistan. That said, nothing is clear and recently it has been rumoured that further down the line, a number of A version F35s may be purchased. These have been mooted more as a Typhoon replacement though.

The next Strategic Defence and Security Review is due in 2015, presumably just after the general election. For this reason alone, the picture not just for the RAF but for all three of the UK's armed forces looks about as clear as a plastic beaker full of canal water. One likely significant change on the horizon has been highlighted in a report by the International Institute for Strategic Studies. The report pointed to the shift in the balance of military power from West to East, and in particular to the emergence of China as a global superpower, not necessarily well disposed to the western democracies, and which is allocating significantly more funding to increasing the size of its armed forces and improving its technology.

What may prove particularly worrying for European defence and security arrangements is the reaction of the US government to the changing global picture. Having become a significant feature across North West Europe since the build-up of American forces in Britain during the Second World War, the USAAF European commands are likely to be thinned out as substantial elements are redeployed back to the US and, in all probability, bases around the South China Sea. So, in future, the emphasis of US force deployment is ever more likely to be in the Philippines, South Korea, Australia and New Zealand. It is not just American concern about interests in the Far East that is propelling this change of strategy, but the attitude of European countries in respect of their own security concerns and American perceptions of them. In January 2012, the US sent a carrier strike group to the Strait of Hormuz following a threat from Iran to mount a blockade as a response to threatened oil sanctions. The British and French governments, desperate to be seen to be doing their bit, each sent a single frigate. Britain initially had been overlooked by the Americans as they considered its contribution to be not worthwhile. Even if you factor in the relative difference in provision based on GDP and population between either France or Britain compared with the US, that the US Navy can dispatch a carrier strike group, with a second in the area and a third on the way, highlights the disparity between American military capability and resolve in comparison with that of Britain and the rest of Europe, which is frankly a disgrace as well as acutely embarrassing. It is this kind of absurd behaviour on the UK's part that has contributed to America's growing dismissive attitude towards the countries of Europe. But it does not stop bombastic statements by the British Foreign Office, which a couple of weeks later saw the Foreign Secretary, William Hague, admonishing the Russian and Chinese governments for vetoing a UN resolution calling for President Assad of Syria to order his army to stop attacking, and therefore quelling, armed insurrection.

It may be little more than differences of opinion as to what is and is not justified, but going back to the height of Cold War fears, even before the bolder stance taken by the Reagan administration, Europe was always regarded by the US as never much more than lacklustre in its general approach to maintaining the military balance between NATO and the Warsaw Pact. Now, while nothing has yet been settled, the Americans are poised to take advantage of the situation and leave continental Europe to pick up whatever slack they believe there is to pick up.

The UK has a reputation within Europe for being particularly militaristic, and the British defence budget is often seen as being on the heavy side, with some justification. However, what translates into boots on the ground, to use a popular phrase, has always seen the UK trailing behind the two most closely comparable nations, France and Germany. The Army is to be brought back from its remaining bases in Germany by 2020, and the post-SDSR round-up is said to have come to the conclusion that the RAF could do with losing further air bases. Two of the bases to be closed are in Scotland, Kinloss and Leuchars (the former brought about by the loss of the Nimrod), and both are to receive those units of the Army which return from Germany. The RAF, it is understood, had a preference to retain Leuchars, the hitherto planned second base for the Typhoon. The RAF is actually keen to retain both its remaining fast-jet bases in Scotland.) Indeed, the first of the expected three squadrons had already become operational at Leuchars when the government's post-SDSR round-up declared that Lossiemouth would become the sole remaining operational air base north of the border. There was some scuttlebutt doing the rounds beforehand that the Army had indicated a preference to move into Leuchars, which has since the early days of the Cold War been assigned to the role of providing the QRA force to cover the northern part of the UK and the Atlantic approaches to the north.

Again, whether the Army had been able to use favourable influence in the basing decision is not a confirmed fact, but one story suggested Leuchars was preferred because of the nearby St Andrews golf links, and however flippant that may sound, the new Defence Secretary, Philip Hammond, has since admitted that the cost of moving the Typhoon wing to Lossiemouth and the remainder of the Tornado GR4s from there to Marham is marginally greater than leaving the Typhoons at Leuchars and moving the Army into Lossiemouth, but he believes there will be benefits in the long run.

There is, of course, another problem to contend with here, in the shape of possible Scottish independence. The Scottish National Party, following recent success in Scottish parliamentary elections, are now in a position to pursue this ultimate aim. If Scotland is to become an independent country in every sense, then the question has to be addressed as to how exactly UK defence plans are to be restructured. The SNP and their force of nature of a leader Alex Salmond believe that an independent Scotland will follow the Norwegian model in general economic terms and in defence-related matters too. Whatever the economic concerns for Scotland should independence be brought about, to try and shape a military force on a similar footing to that of Norway would be an order of some magnitude. It would be especially so with regard to the element of the RAF intended to be based at Lossiemouth. The three Typhoon

Despite facing closure as an RAF station, Leuchars has become home to a second operational Typhoon Squadron. Aircraft of the two resident units, Nos 1 and 6 Squadrons, are seen out on the apron. (*Mark McEwan*)

squadrons represent just over half of the full number of 'Tiffies' (the Typhoon has acquired the affectionate wartime nickname given to the Hawker Typhoon of that era) that the RAF, as it now is, hopes against hope to stand up. This in turn, under current planning, including OCUs, will represent at least 25 per cent of the future combat fleet, subject to there being no revision up or down. It has been suggested that a future Scottish air force will inherit this.

The facts are that Scotland accounts for just 8.5 per cent of the overall UK population, but before we start dividing up the assets in a proportionate manner or otherwise, there is plenty for the SNP to think about here in terms of overheads and tax revenue in respect of wider public spending. Without the apparatus in place to ensure a properly functioning army, navy and air force, all of which the SNP give the impression that they believe is manageable, then there is not going to be anything of the kind of new Scottish military force which seems to be envisaged. It has been suggested that the vagueness of SNP policy, as much as is known, would see those people from Scotland serving in the UK armed forces invited to form at least a nucleus force to be built upon, but this is where cost is certainly going to become a problem. Scottish service personnel are not likely to be found serving in the British forces in perfectly formed proportions, to be simply transferred. They will be top heavy in certain disciplines and sparse in others, certainly not sufficiently balanced to form a breakaway force whether air, land or sea. Of the three services, a Scottish army would perhaps pose less of a challenge than the other two, but a challenge just the same, with identifiable line units amounting to six infantry battalions and an armoured regiment. However, the trouble for a future wholly separate Scottish state would be standing up its own training schools and forming other combat arms needed to support the infantry and armour; in other words, engineers, signals and artillery. After that come logistics, medical services and the requisite facilities and infrastructure. When considering just where to start with a new navy and air force, the situation is far from clear-cut with regard to how the SNP define such a future force and how it would be maintained and deployed. This is not a new proposition, the SNP having put forward the very same reply to the question of Scottish defence in 1976, when full independence was last on the agenda. At that time, Scottish Labour MP Tam Dalyell felt the need to give the then SNP proposals the time of day, even though he himself thought the notion 'far-fetched and balmy'. To this end, he approached the RAF and the Navy with a list of questions with which to seek professional opinion. These questions assumed a Scottish force of quite a substantial size, his belief being that the time had come to address such a possibility, but he also felt that serious consideration in public might do something to contain thoughtless and rampant nationalism.

At the time, Scotland would have inherited three ready active and substantial military airfields: Leuchars, Lossiemouth and Kinloss. The SNP also proposed that Scotland would take on about an eighth of the RAF. The assessment then, as now, was that to run/create any air force would be very expensive indeed to the Scottish exchequer. This is not at all meant to sound patronising, but without very deep and far-reaching reliance on the existing RAF structure for example, having to put such a thing together from near enough scratch would place an enormous demand on resources as well as outside expertise. It was further objected in the 1976 assessment that Scotland would continue to play a part within the NATO structure, but the SNP today first claimed they would leave NATO then that they would remain, but with all nuclear weapons removed from Scottish soil and waters, although remaining no less ambitious otherwise. That the RAF is measured on a functional basis rather than a geographical one was noted in the 1976 proposal as well. When the present government was reviewing the future basing strategy of the RAF on the basis of the UK continuing unchanged, Salmond objected that if another RAF station in Scotland closed along with Kinloss, already due to close, two-thirds of the RAF would be wiped out in Scotland. This is quite misleading; what would be lost would be two air bases, no more. As to the units to be based on them or the one remaining, that is another matter. There are four operational combat squadrons in Scotland presently and when one of the two remaining bases closes, there are likely to be at least four squadrons left, perhaps more. The exercise here is to make more economic use of basing capacity. I would consider it a base closure too far, but the loss of an airfield does not represent the loss of the units based there as SNP concerns suggest.

Again, as for the Army, there is the question of the presence of adequate training and maintenance facilities, the provision of deep maintenance for whatever aircraft types are flown, the flying and technical training schools and where they would go. A cheaper but no less money-draining option would be, at least in the initial stages, to arrange for the use of such facilities elsewhere – in England? The only other likely suitable out-of-area training locations would be Canada and the US. This is not something which has yet been publicly discussed or properly challenged, certainly not before the Scottish voters, and seems to have been overlooked by the strategists of the nationalist movement. As with personnel, Britain's armed forces are deployed and structured as a single-nation force, there being no proportionate entities in each home country. The total military elements in Scotland are not on their own a self-contained component but simply specific elements of a much larger one. A further, most awkward problem would be the construction of the aircraft carriers at Rosyth and, most sensitive of all, the SSBN bases at Holy Loch (USN) and Faslane (RN). It has been said that if the facilities did not exist, it would push the US government to some considerable lengths to try and create them somewhere else. As the SNP have an anti-nuclear policy which calls for the removal of such facilities, this too may prove difficult when trying to negotiate assistance in other areas, especially if the US Navy, not to mention the Royal Navy, are compelled to leave these places to seek accommodation elsewhere. When these matters are examined in depth, and I am not claiming that they have not, they raise a list of thought-provoking questions, and it will be interesting to hear a considered response from the Scottish nationalists. Other than the nuclear issue, there is the question of the Joint Strike Fighter project. The current planning is for the base at Lossiemouth to become the primary location. Should Scottish independence come to pass, what would become of this? It is almost certain that the UK government would waste no time in making alternative arrangements, with the F-35 base camp being moved to somewhere in England or Wales, it being unlikely that an independent Scottish government would wish to remain with this programme.

Presumably, the priority demand to justify a Scottish air force and navy would be the protection of oil and gas platforms, and whether Scottish owned, controlled or neither, the responsibility would logically fall upon the Scottish state to protect these installations to a standard acceptable to all interested parties. If not, then it is difficult to see just what kind of sovereign state Scotland would be. And I say this as a Scot. The SNP believe Norway to be the closest comparison to Scotland, but the cost of generating an independent air force and navy on a similar level, however much they are able to gain from the division of assets following divorce from the rest of the

UK, would place a very serious challenge to the level of public spending required in order to put in place the infrastructure and organisation to oversee such a wide and far-reaching programme of development and transition. Of course, this state of affairs would also spell trouble for the government in Westminster. The break-up of the union, however small the chunk that secedes, would affect the UK's status within the European Union and could affect its position as a permanent member of the UN Security Council. The removal of Scotland takes away 5¼ million people, two major population centres, and those facilities such as submarine bases that reside there. If military assets and personnel are not to form the nucleus of a Scottish force, then what is currently based there will need to be redeployed in England just as with the F-35. With a smaller population and reduced tax revenue, for all that is said about the Barnett Formula and English largess toward the Scots, this will still mean a significant reduction to the UK Treasury, and all these problems are going to culminate in one huge headache for everyone concerned. Perhaps the biggest loss, for everyone, if the UK is broken up would be that of international standing and influence, and for all the popular negative comment at home about British prestige today, the country may have to confront a truly substantial loss of the prestige we still have.

Apart from the many retired senior military officers, opposition MPs and historians who have lined up to criticise the SDSR, the Commons Select Defence Committee have also placed their reservations on record, with concerns that the review is destined to leave the country's armed forces unable to cope with any new challenges that may present beyond 2015, and that they are struggling with present commitments. However, the government denies all charges and does not accept that the armed forces can no longer meet the full spectrum of operations. If the truth were known, the mainstream political establishment, as one, sets far greater store by the political impact of prioritising funding for the military establishment. It sees votes melting away with every penny spent on defence and security matters. Every government seeks to do whatever it can to get by with as little as possible in peacetime and, as we have come to learn from the mindset of the modern British politician, when forces are deployed on a war footing overseas, as well. Another recent coalition wheeze, following the debacle of the attempt to privatise SAR, is to try and do so again.

While not quite core to the military remit, this service has been admirably and most reliably found by the RAF and Navy since the Second World War. In November 2011, the then Transport Secretary, Justine Greening, announced another scheme to remove this responsibility from the services which have maintained it for so long at minimum inconvenience to the taxpayer to a new civilian organisation. As always, the government line is that this will free the armed forces to concentrate on more direct military operations. But I beg to differ. Personnel currently employed in this role will to all intents and purposes disappear from the payroll. They will not be added to other operational commitments *per se*. The budgets, assets and personnel will shrink accordingly. In times of war, the SAR element would deploy in all conditions to rescue downed air crew, whatever the circumstances. A civilian unit would not be deploying anywhere far from British shores. That is to say, that should the need arise it will not be sent, as a service unit, to an overseas theatre of operations. But somewhere you can bet someone has calculated this end of the defence budget to be dead money and so something more enterprising has no doubt been found again.

The new Chancellor's objection to the continued maintenance of the hallowed strategic nuclear deterrent through capital expenditure, and the decision to force the Defence Secretary to pay for it directly out of his own budget (let no one accuse the Labour Party exclusively of military ignorance ever again), means that the UK, despite having the fourth largest defence budget on the planet (which I do not doubt) will have the lowest possible return. But there is no way that so few military assets, no aircraft carriers, only eight small operational fighter squadrons, due to shrink further, and an Army of fewer than 100,000 represents the fourth largest and most capable military force in the world. Indeed, so poorly representative of our huge defence budget is the military order of battle that nothing short of a comprehensive investigation by the National Audit Office and Fraud Office would do in order to explain exactly where all the money goes.

Recently, the chair of the Defence Select Committee, Margaret Hodge, accused the MoD of spending £1.1 billion from a defence programme to purchase state-of-the-art armoured vehicles covering the period up to 2021. Apparently, this money was spent without the purchase of a single vehicle. Further, in order to redress the current defence budget deficit, the MoD took a total of £10.8 billion out of the procurement budget to balance the books, leaving £5.45 billion behind but insufficient to cover the remainder of the project. The Treasury then handed back £2.8 billion from reserves to help rescue the situation by buying mine-resistant vehicles instead, leaving a shortfall and meaning that the armoured vehicles sought will remain unavailable until 2025. The Select Committee accused the MoD of ordering cutting-edge equipment without considering the costs in relation to just how much money is likely to be available in the long term. It is the lack of appropriate armoured vehicles that has resulted in the demand for helicopters such as the Chinook and Merlin to move troops around Afghanistan and, of course, brought about the media-driven public enthusiasm for helicopters in force and wanting to know why copious numbers of them were not available.

Despite my own defence of the Eurofighter Typhoon, I have to agree with what is being brought to light now and the criticisms made. This is ultimately leading to a single tank, a single aeroplane, a single submarine, all packed with mind-boggling software but having taken an entire lifetime to get right, having gone ten times over budget, and having been reduced twentyfold from the original order – which one imagines would be the minimum required to meet projected operational requirements – and still not working quite as well as originally specified. We are promised that the current government, once it has finished scaling down the in-place front-line capability in order to put the MoD's financial house in some kind of order, will ensure that procurement in the future will better match funding with expectations and the likely threats to be posed against our sceptred isle. Returning quickly to the Eurofighter, it should be remembered that the story behind this and other projects, and of course the involvement of BAE Systems, goes back to the late 1970s. By the time public bickering erupted between the individual service lobbies as to what was the cause of everyone else's ills, the Typhoon fighter aircraft was operational and its further development as a much needed strike/attack fighter firmly in hand, with no other realistic alternative option available. Now is not the time to be looking for an alternative or, much less, to be considering yet another of these fashionable new capability gaps that have become popular in the last fifteen years or so. How can politicians who were responsible for the farrago of bungled and byzantine procurement processes and, when presented with the choice of avoiding Iraq and Afghanistan, whether for the greater good or not, placed British soldiers in harm's way, get upset because the Army requires certain types of equipment in order to reduce significantly the number of casualties being brought back to Lyneham or Brize Norton courtesy of defence cuts? Perhaps they should admit that the peace dividend is a fleeting wish, stop ransacking other military front-line capabilities, and accept that they cannot do such things yet still look to drive defence expenditure down to 2 per cent or less of GDP.

A more general observation on military service today is that since the second Gulf War a great deal of praise for the armed forces has come from both the media and politicians. Christmas messages from ministers and opposition leaders always include a special mention about the brave men and women of our armed forces. *The Sun* newspaper and ITV have got together for the last four years to produce an annual televised presentation ceremony with the kind of title only the tabloid press could dream up, 'The Millies', which uses the format for the many entertainment awards ceremonies and seems to have become a popular annual event. Elsewhere, with genuine sincerity, people have lined the streets of Royal Wootton Bassett and other rural towns to pay respects to the deceased as they are returned from Afghanistan and the like. Twenty and more years ago, the IRA, fully active, invariably struck with lethal results, but for the soldiers killed in this particular front line there were no streets lined with solemn members of the public. America went through a similar re-examination of the public's relations with their armed forces following the Vietnam War, when entire C-5 Galaxy aircraft were filled with caskets, each containing someone's son killed in a controversial conflict not of their choosing. These returned bodies had no solemn congregations to line the streets and fight back tears. You would not think it was the same country at the time of the first Gulf War.

As for Britain's new-found political mileage in heaping praise on those in uniform, whether in conflicts unavoidable or avoidable, there appears to have been a price to pay for the new regard in which the armed forces are held – conditions of service. I would take service in the pre-New Labour era every time. There was no need then for politicians to insist on their commitment to military covenants; the military covenant just was, and no one in the media or Parliament felt any need to mention it.

If successive Prime Ministers continue, as Blair, Brown and Cameron have, to deploy further dwindling military assets on overseas campaigns it may very well result in a dreadful and bloody debacle, a dreadful chapter to be entered into the history of HM Forces. The simple lesson learned following the two world wars was this old Roman maxim: 'If you desire peace, prepare for war.' A minimum state of readiness was behind the very success of defence policy from 1945 through to 1990. There is another maxim, by Tacitus, which perhaps pertains to today's political establishment: 'They created a desert and called it peace.' The end of the Cold War has instilled an alarming belief that what had gone before was some kind of era of a wartime economy. It was nothing of the sort. Now there is a growing belief that Afghanistan, originally a counter-terrorist operation which morphed into a peace-keeping one and then into a counter-insurgency campaign, is a protracted state-on-state war. If it is, then it is one which the largest coalition contributor, America, has already conceded. When 2014 is reached, the year of the coalition military withdrawal, what will be the response if the Taliban are as active as they were in 2006 and infiltration is rife within the Afghan government forces? At the time of writing, not just Argentina but a number of other South American countries are banding together to impose a blockade in the South Atlantic; America, Israel and Iran seem unable to avoid slipping towards military action and all that could mean. Because Britain has sought to play a significant role on the world stage since 1997, but has failed to make the necessary capital investment in order to make any kind of substantial contribution, it now finds itself virtually impotent when faced with possible situations which were once possible to resolve diplomatically precisely because the UK carried a reasonably big stick and enjoyed a degree of respect from its allies. Those situations are increasingly likely to develop in a direction not necessarily to our advantage, as someone once said. With a growing belief that Britain is already incapable of managing its defence affairs as successfully as those of much smaller countries, without recourse to others who may not always find our interests conveniently in tandem with their own, then the future can only be described, at best, as uncertain. Finally, we fool ourselves if we imagine for one second that we can go it alone or play our part as a significant ally, with any standing at all, if we do not have our own air force.

Index